ASSURING QUALITY IN ONLINE EDUCATION

Practices and Processes at the Teaching, Resource, and Program Levels

Edited by *Kay Shattuck*

Series Foreword by Michael Grahame Moore

STERLING, VIRGINIA

Sty/us

Published by Stylus Publishing, LLC
22883 Quicksilver Drive
Sterling, Virginia 20166-2102

Library of Congress Cataloging-in-Publication Data
Assuring quality in online education : practices and processes at the
teaching, resource, and program levels / edited by Kay Shattuck.
    pages cm. — (Online learning and distance education series)
Includes bibliographical references and index.
ISBN 978-1-57922-871-2 (pbk. : alk. paper)
ISBN 978-1-57922-870-5 (cloth : alk. paper)
ISBN 978-1-57922-872-9 (library networkable e-edition)
ISBN 978-1-57922-873-6 (consumer e-edition)
1. Computer-assisted instruction—Standards. 2. Distance
education—Computer-assisted instruction—Standards.
3. Quality assurance. I. Shattuck, Kay, editor of compilation.
LB1028.5.A745 2014
371.33'4--dc23
                                                            2013030036

13-digit ISBN: 978-1-57922-870-5 (cloth)
13-digit ISBN: 978-1-57922-871-2 (paper)
13-digit ISBN: 978-1-57922-872-9 (library networkable e-edition)
13-digit ISBN: 978-1-57922-873-6 (consumer e-edition)

Printed in the United States of America

All first editions printed on acid-free paper
that meets the American National Standards Institute
Z39-48 Standard.

Bulk Purchases

Quantity discounts are available for use in workshops and for
staff development.
Call 1-800-232-0223

First Edition, 2014

10   9   8   7   6   5   4   3   2

ASSURING QUALITY IN ONLINE EDUCATION

ONLINE LEARNING & DISTANCE EDUCATION
Leadership, Innovation, Policy, & Practice

Additional titles in our
ONLINE LEARNING AND DISTANCE EDUCATION series
edited by Michael Grahame Moore

CULTURE AND ONLINE LEARNING
Global Perspectives and Research
Edited by Insung Jung and Charlotte Nirmalani Gunawardena
Publication date: Spring 2014

WEB 2.0 FOR ACTIVE LEARNERS
By Vanessa Dennen
Publication date: Fall 2014

Also available in this series:

LEADING THE E-LEARNING TRANSFORMATION OF HIGHER EDUCATION
Meeting the Challenges of Technology and Distance Education
Published in association with The Sloan Consortium
By Gary Miller, Meg Benke, Bruce Chaloux, Lawrence C. Ragan,
Raymond Schroeder, Wayne Smutz, and Karen Swan

*This book is dedicated to the memory and work of Bruce Chaloux,
who along with other pioneers of distance education blazed the trails for
building dynamic networks to assure that each learner has the opportunity
to access quality education.*

CONTENTS

PART THREE: PROCESSES FOR ASSURING QUALITY
             AT RESOURCE AND PROGRAM LEVELS

ACKNOWLEDGMENTS

I thank Michael G. Moore for the excitement and energy he continues to provide as I work along with my colleagues to move theory and research into the daily practice of online and blended distance education. When he invited me to do a book on quality assurance, I immediately knew I wanted to call on those colleagues with whom I had worked or, at the very least, scholars whose work I follow. A reading of the contributing authors in the table of contents identifies members of my community of practice. Each is a skilled educator in his or her own right. I thank each author, especially the lead author of each chapter, for being patient with my efforts as editor to keep the chapters focused on specific dimensions of a quality assurance system. I take full responsibility for the presentation and flow of the book. It reflects my attempt to weave together the chapters into a resource that will provide readers with practical understanding of and processes for assuring quality in this growing field of online education. In addition to Michael Moore, acquisitions editor Sarah Burrows and production editor McKinley Gillespie at Stylus provided me with invaluable guidance and support. On a personal level, my work on this book would not have been possible without the continuing support of Duane, Tracey, Gina, and friends.

Kay Shattuck
October 2013

FOREWORD

Michael Grahame Moore, Series Editor

This book is about distance education in its contemporary online form, and it is about quality. It is the second in the Online Learning and Distance Education (OLDE) series to be published by Stylus Publishing. The previous publication focused on the responses of administrators and other leaders to the challenge posed by the explosion of demand for education online. Now, in this new book, we will take readers to the core of that challenge. Summed up succinctly in chapter 2 with the metaphor of the iron triangle, this challenge is addressing the explosion in demand for access to both higher and continuing education, while both constraining the cost that otherwise impedes accessibility and maintaining quality. In future books in this series, we will address both access and cost issues, but here and now we come to grips with the all-important problems posed by that third side of the triangle, establishing and maintaining quality. The book addresses this issue in its many aspects, particularly focusing on the behaviors of instructors and course designers and the management of institutions. Traditionally, as Shattuck notes in the preface, it has been assumed that if an institution has a good reputation, which is dependent primarily on the perceived expertise of its faculty, then it offers a good-quality educational program, and the quality of educational programs has been certified through a process of peer review. But, popular opinion has now turned against trust in "inputs." As the editor comments, "times are changing" owing to growing public concerns about higher education quality and affordability—again, the iron triangle. A revision of concept and practice with regard to quality assessment, with a focus on results—on "outputs"—now ranks high on the agenda in national debates and in policy discussions within every institution. And this new focus is affecting the everyday practices of every instructor and, indeed, every student.

Online learning, the most evolved form of distance education, offers unprecedented opportunities for innovation in teaching and learning and in institutional structure and management. It should be apparent to us all, however, that the explosion of interest and activity in the field has resulted in the development of many programs that fall far short of what is known to be best practice. Understanding this, and understanding what is indeed good quality, is essential if we are to enjoy successful, full capitalization of the potential of modern technology. Pulling together the many strands that constitute a profile of quality programs has been Dr. Shattuck's achievement, and we must be grateful to her for assembling the outstanding authors who have contributed to this volume. They consist of some who are primarily practitioners and others who devote their time to research and teaching (and we recognize the two are not mutually exclusive!). Thus, as is intended for all books in the OLDE series, although this installation references both research and theory, its core is experience—the experiences and insights of teachers as well as accrediting and other quality assurance agencies. Never before has such real-world experience addressing the quality side of the triangle been compiled into one volume as it is here. Consequently, I am delighted to have this opportunity to introduce Dr. Kay Shattuck as editor of *Assuring Quality in Online and Distance Education: Practices and Processes at the Teaching, Resource, and Program Levels* and to thank her and her colleagues for their willingness to share their knowledge with us in this second book in the Stylus OLDE series.

Michael Grahame Moore
Distinguished Professor of Education,
The Pennsylvania State University

This book is about practices and processes for assuring quality in online education. It is a collection of chapters in which contributors share scholarly and practice-based expertise from their experiences in continuously improving the interrelated dimensions and levels of online education. The book is organized into three parts: (a) Overview and Implications of Practices and Processes for Assuring Quality, (b) Quality Assurance and Continuous Improvement at the Course Design and Teaching Levels, and (c) Processes for Assuring Quality at Resource and Program Levels.

Before moving further we will stop to consider the definitions of *quality*, *systems perspective*, *stakeholders*, *accreditation*, *standards*, *practices*, and *processes* as key concepts. Although the word *quality* is touted frequently in relation to education, it is an abstract variable, and this makes it difficult, albeit important, to establish an agreed-upon definition. For our purposes, dimensions adapted from Harvey and Green provide some common language: quality in education is about excellence, consistency, fitness for purpose, value for money, and transformation (as cited in Chalmers & Johnston, 2012). Those dimensions capture outcomes, continuous processes, the many types of consumers of education, financial accountability, and acquisition and application of knowledge.

Traditionally, quality in U.S. education has been determined by the perceived status of the institution and perceived faculty expertise (Rees, 2007) and by a reliance on a system of peer review to provide certification of meeting specific standards of quality. But times are changing. The 2013 *America's Call for Higher Education Redesign* from the Lumina Foundation and Gallup identified growing public concern about higher education quality and affordability. The opening of educational opportunities and resulting growth in online education, along with the swift emergence of for-profit educational enterprises, put online education squarely in the middle of the "quality" discussion (Daniel, 2012).

To really get a grasp on quality in online education, a framework is necessary. Nearly two decades ago, Moore and Kearsley (1996) wrote about the benefits of understanding distance education from a systems perspective. A *systems perspective* takes into consideration the interrelated parts of an educational enterprise that must function in a planned and deliberate way for successful outcomes. Moore and Kearsley (2012) explained,

> Because distance education requires using a range of technical and human resources, it is always best delivered in a system . . . which consists of all the component processes that operate when teaching and learning at a distance occurs. It includes learning, teaching, communication, design, and management. . . . These processes, are impacted by, and have an impact on, certain forces in the environment where they operate—the physical, political, economic, and social environments in particular. So even these frameworks within which the educational system operates can be seen as part of a larger supersystem. (p. 9)

By thinking of online education as part of a larger supersystem that includes human resources and interactions, the question becomes, Who determines quality in distance education, and how? Lampikoski asked that very question in 1995 and wrote, "Any distance education system incorporates many different elements and processes and the actual degree of importance given to these varying components depends upon which interest group is going to interpret quality" (para. 4). Lampikoski suggested that there are (a) exoteric influences, such as government, employers, professional bodies, and quality controllers, and (b) esoteric influences, including management, teachers, and customers or students. These are the major *stakeholders* who value different aspects of education (Thompson & Irele, 2007); who define quality from different perspectives; and who are engaging, monitoring, funding, or benefiting at different levels of online education (Mariasingam & Hanna, 2006).

The historical roots of distance education in the United States are in adult and continuing education; thus, the early stakeholders were primarily participating adult learners and adult educators. These educators had a calling to make learning accessible via technology to nontraditional, lifelong learning adults at the back door of the traditional university (Wedemeyer, 1981). Early academic stakeholders produced a body of research that focused on the quality of teaching-learning interactions and outcomes but rarely focused on quality at broader program and institutional levels, such as management, administration, and policy (Berge & Mrozowski, 2001; Hirner, 2008; Jung & Latchem, 2012; Moore, 2007; Phipps & Merisotis, 1999; Shattuck, 2003; Zawacki-Richter, Bäcker, & Vogt, 2009). Distance-education opportunities were moved quietly among small groups of champions until the increasing visibility of online education attracted the attention of regional and program accreditation bodies.

Unlike other countries, the United States does not have a single governing educational minister (Jung & Latchem, 2012); instead, there is a system

YBP Library Services

ASSURING QUALITY IN ONLINE EDUCATION: PRACTICES
AND PROCESSES AT THE TEACHING, RESOURCE,...; ED.
BY KAY SHATTUCK.   Paper   256 P.
DULLES: STYLUS PUBLISHING, 2014
SER: ONLINE LEARNING AND DISTANCE EDUCATION.

TITLE CONT: AND PROGRAM LEVELS. ED: PENNSYLVANIA
STATE UNIVERSITY. COLLECTION OF NEW ESSAYS.

ISBN 1579228712   Library PO# AP-SLIPS

		List	35.00	USD
9395 NATIONAL UNIVERSITY LIBRAR	Disc	5.0%	
App. Date 4/30/14 SOE 8214-09	Net	33.25	USD

SUBJ: COMPUTER-ASSISTED INSTRUCTION--STANDARDS.

CLASS LB1028.5   DEWEY# 371.334   LEVEL ADV-AC

YBP Library Services

ASSURING QUALITY IN ONLINE EDUCATION: PRACTICES
AND PROCESSES AT THE TEACHING, RESOURCE,...; ED.
BY KAY SHATTUCK.   Paper   256 P.
DULLES: STYLUS PUBLISHING, 2014
SER: ONLINE LEARNING AND DISTANCE EDUCATION.

TITLE CONT: AND PROGRAM LEVELS. ED: PENNSYLVANIA
STATE UNIVERSITY. COLLECTION OF NEW ESSAYS.

ISBN 1579228712   Library PO# AP-SLIPS

		List	35.00	USD
9395 NATIONAL UNIVERSITY LIBRAR	Disc	5.0%	
App. Date 4/30/14 SOE 8214-09	Net	33.25	USD

SUBJ: COMPUTER-ASSISTED INSTRUCTION--STANDARDS.

CLASS LB1028.5   DEWEY# 371.334   LEVEL ADV-AC

of voluntary, peer-review-based *accreditation* organizations that provide certifications of quality for programs and institutions. This self-regulating system has been functioning since the 1880s, but many in academia now fear that accreditation will be federalized (Eaton, 2011). Academe is no longer a cloistered environment. Those working in institutions of higher education have been accustomed to holding operational and outcomes data close to the vest, and the level of public and funder questioning of quality that comes in the wake of increasing costs and debt burdens to students, funding entities, and parents has challenged the academy to provide more transparency.

In the 2000s pressure intensified for accreditation organizations to provide external validation by certifying the quality of online programs. The suitability of regional accrediting commissions, given their purpose and practices, as arbiters of institutional quality has been questioned since the Department of Education began determining an institution's eligibility for federal financial aid on the basis of its accreditation status. Over the years formal and informal inquiries from a variety of sources have challenged the efficacy of accreditation, which is essentially a private process originally designed for institutional self-improvement. One of the most high-profile efforts of recent years to repurpose accreditation resulted from the work of Secretary of Education Margaret Spellings's 2005 Commission on the Future of Higher Education, which focused on access, affordability, quality, and accountability. The commission report, *A Test of Leadership: Charting the Future of U.S. Higher Education*, recommended that accrediting agencies impose accountability measures on institutions and make accreditation reports accessible to the public, with information presented in a framework that enabled comparisons among institutions (U.S. Department of Education, 2006, p. 25).

Pressure on regional accreditation (also known as institutional accreditation) to become more transparent has not let up in the years since the release of the Spellings report. In the summer of 2012, the American Council on Education's Accreditation Task Force released a report including recommendations for "steps colleges, universities and regional accreditors can and should take to ensure accreditation meets its public accountability responsibilities given the enormous diversity of American higher education" (para. 2). Those recommendations include increasing transparency, increasing evidence about student success, promoting cooperation, and expanding participation. But, assurance of quality in online education cannot rest on the regional accreditation process alone.

Why This Book?

This book is an attempt to call attention to dimensions of quality assurance to freshen a dialogue on the continuous improvement of online education in a framework that emphasizes the needs of stakeholders. The professional and scholarly online education literature illustrates that although excellent work is being done, it is not often done using a multifaceted approach. This book provides resources and information about adaptable continuous-improvement processes for those responsible for assuring quality in online education.

Contributors to this book were initially invited to craft a chapter focusing on an identified dimension of quality assurance for online education and to consider it from the perspective of stakeholders of online distance education. Themes emerged from early exchanges with the contributing authors. First, a focus on learners and learning was obvious. It was clear that the authors' priority was ensuring the effectiveness of the learning process even when writing about administrative, resource, and accreditation topics. To avoid redundancy, a discussion of learning theory is not included in most chapters, but I can assure readers that student learning outcomes are at the heart of all chapters in this book.[1]

Second, using inputs (from stakeholders) and outputs (to stakeholders) as a framework for exploring the interdependence of components of a system of online education that includes transparency could be seen in many of the early drafts. An inputs-and-outputs framework is discussed in the first chapter and is threaded throughout the book.

The third theme that emerged as authors prepared their chapters was that assuring quality has two components: (a) established *standards* and *practices* for improving outcomes and (b) *processes* for applying those standards when assessing and engaging in continuous-improvement activities in online education. Best practices are collections of educational techniques that provide guidance for achieving quality (Inglis, Ling, & Joosten, 1999). Ideally, they are succinct statements that are informed by research and established by a community of practice. These statements (standards) need to be applied to the everyday interactions and operations in education. Being aware of standards is not enough. For example, after a review of 50 years of educational research, Chickering and Gamson (1987) established what is now a classic best-practices model of seven principles for good practice in undergraduate education.[2] But, any effort to improve teaching must include individual instructors translating and applying those seven principles (best-practices standards) in their own educational setting. This form of individual interpretive practice in applying established standards can have excellent case-by-case results, but the simple promotion and adoption of standards does not ensure improvement. As a case in point, Winegar (2000) explored the impact of exposure to Chickering and Gamson's principles (standards) on the behavior (practice) of instructors who were teaching online. Despite positive attitudes, when exposed to the standards, instructors did not significantly change their

teaching methods. Having standards, and even excitement about the existence of standards, does not ensure changes in practice.

In summary, best practices and standards are necessary but not sufficient
to assure quality. They can be static, be comfortably self-perpetuating, or
fall to the bottom of to-do lists. Best practices, standards, and even assessment instruments are only the beginning of a system for assuring quality.
Processes—those purposeful, resourceful, and interactive steps that provide
assistance in the translation of standards into action, that allow for tailored
creativity in application by and for various stakeholders, and that guide evaluation efforts—are critical. The real work of quality assurance lies in meaningful processes for the dynamic application of best practices, standards, and
assessment of outcomes.

Outline of Chapters

In the first chapter, "Stakeholders of Quality Assurance in Online Education:
Inputs and Outputs," Adair and Díaz set the stage for a quality assurance
discussion by applying an open systems theory of organizational behavior
(Stroh, Northcraft, & Neale, 2002) to online education.[3] They identify the
input and output dimensions of funding, regulation, and online student profiles and go on to explore the areas in which quality should be addressed in
online education: (a) institutional commitment; (b) courses, curricula, and
instruction; (c) assessment practices; (d) learner support; (e) faculty support;
and (f) program evaluation practices. Adair and Díaz conclude that vetted
processes, tools, and initiatives already being used throughout the United
States can be shared, adapted, and applied in continuous-improvement
efforts and in the dissemination of meaningful information about educational processes and outcomes to stakeholders. They relate these encouraging
processes to other chapters in this book.

In "Cost, Access, and Quality: Breaking the Iron Triangle Through Disruptive Technology-Based Innovations," Porto addresses the iron triangle
faced in education. As she writes on page 18, "Increase in access is imperative
to respond to the growing demand for higher education. . . . Likewise, cost
has to be constrained to maintain accessibility, and quality needs to be maintained notwithstanding the boundaries of cost-effectiveness and scalability."
Porto is encouraged, however, by new applications of social learning theory
and by the access to learning made possible by evolving technologies that
might help transform teaching and learning. The chapter begins with a brief
look at the current landscape of emerging technologies—including mLearning, open educational resources, and massive open online courses. Although
the landscape will continue to change, Porto offers a refreshed version of

Sherry's (2003) quality assurance scheme as a framework that can support discussion and decision making related to disruptive innovations in distance education.

Next, Moore and Shelton present "The Sloan Consortium Pillars and Quality Scorecard." The pillars of quality in asynchronous learning—(a) access, (b) learning effectiveness, (c) scale (cost-effectiveness and commitment), (d) faculty satisfaction, and (e) student satisfaction—are best understood as interdependent quality elements. They are sets of standards for institutions to use in measuring progress in achieving quality. As Moore and Shelton suggest, benchmarking promotes effectiveness, efficiencies, and innovation. The authors also present the Quality Scorecard for the Administration of Online Programs as an instrument for institutions to use in documenting administrative commitment to high-quality online programs. The scorecard can serve as a vehicle to make public the institution's commitment to quality.

In "K–12 Online Learning: Recommendations for Assuring Quality," Patrick, Wicks, and Powell provide a wealth of information and resources for quality in K–12 online learning. After briefly discussing existing standards of quality in K–12 education, they turn to how the current quality standards are used by governments, institutions, programs, and schools. The authors conclude on page 61 that while online and blended learning hold an exciting promise to "transform the education system and enable higher levels of learning through competency-based instruction," there is much to be done "to achieve this promise." Recommendations for federal, state, and district/school policies for improving quality assurance practices in K–12 online and blended learning are provided.

Morrison, Paulson, and Poulin walk us through the "Progress Toward Transparency and Quality Assurance." *Transparency* means providing easily accessible, understandable, and useful information to targeted stakeholders about processes, practices, and results of measurement in education. The authors critique four current transparency projects and make recommendations for a more coordinated and consumer-friendly approach. As they note, accountability in U.S. higher education is not a passing phenomenon.

Adair begins the second part of the book—"Quality Assurance and Continuous Improvement at the Course Design and Teaching Levels"[4]—with the chapter titled "A Process to Improve Course Design: A Key Variable in Course Quality." She notes on page 81 that "the design of the course—the planned components and structure for delivery—may not even be immediately apparent to the student or at least not separable from the other elements contributing to the quality of the course." However, an "input variable to the educational process [high-quality course design] has the potential to mitigate some deficiencies in technology, infrastructure, and student readiness and . . . can guide faculty performance to some extent." Quality Matters is described not only as a set of established standards (a rubric) for assessing and improving the quality of the design of a course but also as a faculty peer-review process for continuous improvement that has demonstrated that a focus on quality in course design can become a lever for broader institutional improvement.

Ragan and McQuiggan submit "A Model for Determining the Effectiveness and Impact of Faculty Professional Development" as a means to provide decision makers with meaningful information about professional development activities for purposes of continuous improvement. They also present information about the significance of faculty development activities. Faculty preparation is emphasized as central to supporting successful learning outcomes for online students. Thus, those programs need to be grounded in theory and education principles if the outcome is to be transformational. Ragan and McQuiggan then integrate Kirkpatrick's (1994) steps of evaluation, Guskey's (2002) critical levels of information, Plank and Kalish's (2010) preassessment planning, and Hines's (2009) dimensions of quality program assessment. They offer a quality transformation faculty development assessment framework that provides a stepped approach to quality assurance with suggested strategies and metrics at each phase.

In the chapter "The Power of a Collaborative, Collegial Approach to Improving Online Teaching and Learning," Bogle, Day, Matthews, and Swan present an application of a backward-design and collaborative/collegial approach to assure course design quality and implementation through a collaborative, peer improvement process. In doing so, they outline the Community of Inquiry (CoI) framework that is the underpinning of their approach to course design and teaching for improved student learning. A course redesign model is described. The chapter concludes with practical recommendations and advice for those programs and institutions desiring to make similar improvements in their online courses and programs.

"Engaging Online Faculty and Administrators in the Assessment Process" is taken up by Stephens-Helm, Powell, and Atwood as they describe the importance of and process for measurement of learning effectiveness. They posit that although faculty and colleges often have negative views of data collection and other accreditation requirements—foisted on them from the outside and not part of their core function—an embedded collaborative approach can inform internal and external stakeholders about student achievement, establish reciprocal relationships, promote accountability, and provide assessment data for decision making.

In the chapter "Disability and Accessibility: Proactive Strategies to Improve Quality," Frey and Kearns emphasize the important role universal design plays in improving access to learning for all students, particularly those students who have a disability. Frey and Kearns caution that students in higher education voluntarily choose to inform instructors and institutions of a disability; it is therefore important for accessibility to be addressed at the beginning of the course-creation cycle, rather than retrofitting add-ons as necessary. The authors make recommendations for institutional policies (including a web address for a generic accessibility policy for online courses), faculty and staff training, and a quality review process. This chapter includes doable applications and is a step toward addressing the concern raised by Crichton and Kinash (2013) that "while legislation continues to mandate inclusive practices for disabled learners, actual practice remains challenging and patchy" (p. 228).

A team of educators collaborated on the next chapter, "Assuring Quality for an Expanding Population of Culturally Diverse Students." Shattuck, Linder-VanBerschot, High, Main, Wang, and Black examine the impact of culture on the design and delivery of online courses. As they note, the cultural implications of the quality of online learning have been studied by a small group of internationally focused researchers and practitioners, but the issue takes on new relevance as online learning expands to include a more diverse learner base. The authors include design strategies to address cultural inclusion and culturally responsive teaching online.

The final part of this book concerns assuring quality at the resource and program levels. Thompson and Kuhne's chapter, "Ethics Matters: Assuring Quality at the Academic Program Level," calls attention to the need of moving beyond the whats and hows of academic programs to the whys—why our program has these goals, why we target this audience, why we choose to use these technologies, why we choose and support faculty in this particular way, why we use these criteria for program evaluation, and why program decisions are made by this particular process. They identify some areas that involve ethical tensions that need to be resolved or negotiated, including issues related to the use of adjunct instructors.

Chakiris addresses "Academic Advising: A Link to a Quality Experience for Students" by sharing practical, firsthand experience in advising students who are engaged at a distance with an educational institution. She carefully points out that the casual use of the term *online learning* to describe any student studying online puts those students who are studying outside of the physical campus of the institution in jeopardy, as reflected in their satisfaction, persistence, and success. Thoughtful and intentional opportunities for interaction—for current and prospective students—need to be built into an institution's structure. Additionally, Chakiris emphasizes the benefits of establishing a partnership between an adviser and a student. This corroborates comments on the topic by Curry (2013), who wrote, "Academic advising provides an opportunity for distance students to connect with a concerned college staff or faculty member who can contribute to their academic success" (p. 201). Chakiris applies the National Academic Advising Association's Standards for Advising Distance Learners as guides for building the online distance learner advising infrastructure.

Providing information for internal decision makers and for external stakeholders is the topic of the next few chapters in the final part of this book. Siemens and Long (2011) clarified that two types or levels of analytics are used in education: First, learner analytics are used at the course level (discourse analysis, social networks), departmental level (predictive modeling, patterns of success/failure), and institutional level (learner profiles, performance, and knowledge flow) (para. 10). Second, academic analytics are used at the institutional, regional, and national/international levels.

Ice, Layne, and Boston present "Learning Analytics: A Tool for Quality Assurance." This chapter outlines data mining and learning analytics and provides a guide for the initial exploration of data collection and for establishing and refining an institutional intelligence system. The authors work on the premise that the ability to harvest information from an institution's data collection pools will yield quick responses and action by decision makers. But, the authors posit, to be an effective tool for quality assurance and improvement, learning analytics is not just working up numbers. Interpreting and applying numbers to outcomes in education can be challenging for many administrators and faculty.

Next, the human dimensions of data collection are considered by Díaz, Boston, Layne, and Ice as they focus on the actionable knowledge available to higher education administration and staff by "Using Principles of Knowledge Management for Educational Quality Assurance." The authors point out that leadership in what Flumerfelt and Banachowski (2011) have called "confronting ambiguity" (p. 224) is a key input in higher education and that increased use of knowledge management as a framework for quality assurance might result in even more discomfort for faculty and staff who likely already feel bombarded by external calls for transparency. On page 216, the authors offer a reality check: "In higher education, many are metaphorically sitting on gold mines of evaluative data that are not being used."

In the chapter "An Adaptive Model for Calculating Contact Hours in Distance-Education Courses," Powell, Stephens-Helm, Layne, and Ice report on a method for calculating contact hours in distance-education courses. They provide an in-class calculation spreadsheet (those activities captured in a learning management system) and an "outside-of-class calculation spreadsheet" (preparation activities) that can be adapted and used by faculty members in determining student contact hours for a course. In providing this practical, how-to guide, the authors mention that contact time is only one of many forms of engagement that impact successful learning outcomes.

U.S. higher education institutions must prepare for official visits by representatives from accreditation bodies and organizations. As Biro, Mullins, and Runyon note in "The Role and Realities of Accreditation: A Practical Guide for Programs and Institutions Preparing for an Accreditation Visit," since the 1880s the voluntary, peer-review system of accreditation has served as the validation process for quality in higher education. In response to the growth of online education, the eight regional accrediting bodies in the United States collaboratively developed and adopted best practices for electronically offered degree and certificate programs. On one hand, distance-education administrators knew that they would have to work harder to demonstrate and document their institution's compliance with these best practice principles. On the other hand, most were grateful to have a common, nationally based set of quality standards they could consult and implement. These interregional best practice guidelines made it easier for institutions to justify the need to establish institution-wide practices—such as offering comprehensive student services that distance learning and face-to-face students could access equally—for the college president and other higher-level administrators and to help persuade them to change their current, well-established processes to accommodate a new type of learner. Finally, the authors discuss how online distance-education program administrators can prepare for a successful accreditation visit and conclude by examining federal and state efforts to address quality in distance-education programs.

Julie Porosky Hamlin and John Sener provide some final thoughts. First, as someone whose dissertation research and subsequent professional engagement focused on quality assurance in higher education, Porosky Hamlin asks, "When questioning the fundamental acceptability of education delivered online, is it 'quality' we mean or 'legitimacy'?" (p. 259). Next, Sener, author of *The Seven Futures of American Education: Improving Learning and Teaching in a Screen-Captured World* (2012), encourages readers to recognize that any work on assuring quality and continuous improvement in online education is really work on assuring quality in education—period. He adds that while working on efforts to ensure successful learning outcomes, we must let stakeholders of online education know that we are aiming higher than sterile comparisons with the generic, traditional campus-based courses.

The overall aim of this book is to promote a culture of quality and transparency for those working in education, especially those involved with online education. The intent is to provide grounding in the dimensions of quality and their interrelated aspects within a system of quality assurance and continuous improvement. Like the other contributors to this book, I hope readers will advance the discussion, actions, and transparency of assuring quality in education that is delivered online.

Notes

1. For those interested in reading some of the exciting discussions from the interdisciplinary field of learning theories and education (learning science as a discipline), I suggest exploring the work of Bransford et al. (2006). They embrace a decade of synergy among (a) implicit learning and brain research, (b) informal learning, and (c) designs for formal learning and beyond.
2. Those principles were later applied to "technology as lever" by Chickering and Ehrmann in 1996.
3. Similar theoretical frameworks have been applied to the educational setting. For example, Rees (2007) applied a logic model approach as the theoretical framework when viewing nontraditional higher education programs as systems with inputs, processes, outputs, and outcomes, and Hirner (2008) defined *inputs* as "factors consciously made by the institution in support of its program" and outputs as "indicators that an organization can point to as signs of success" (p. xii).
4. Readers seeking specific best practices for online teaching in higher education and "how to teach online" information are encouraged to explore the work of Bigatel, Ragan, Kennan, May, and Redmond (2012); Darabi, Sikorski, and Harvey (2006); Smith (2005); Southern Regional Education Board (2006); and Varvel (2007). Although a myriad of how-to books and training is available, I would suggest checking with local colleges and universities, as well as educational consortia. For example, MarylandOnline (http://www.marylandonline.org/coat/) provides an online certification course for online teaching that is suitable for both adjunct and full-time faculty; and Jurgen Hilke at Frederick Community College is leading a MarylandOnline-funded study that will result in the identification of competencies for online teaching.

References

American Council on Education (ACE). (2012, June). *Assuring academic quality in the 21st century: Self-regulation in a new era.* Retrieved from http://www.acenet.edu/news-room/Pages/Assuring-Academic-Quality-in-the-21st-Century.aspx

Berge, Z. L., & Mrozowski, S. (2001). Review of research in distance education, 1990 to 1999. *American Journal of Distance Education, 15*(3), 5–19.

Bigatel, P. M., Ragan, L. C., Kennan, S., May, J., & Redmond, B. F. (2012). The identification of competencies for online teaching success. *Journal of Asynchronous Learning Networks, 16*(1). Retrieved from http://sloanconsortium.org/sites/default/files/jaln_16n1_5_The_Identification_of_Competencies_for_Online_Teaching_Success.pdf

Bransford, J., Vye, N., Stevens, R., Kuhl, P., Schwartz, D., Bell, P., . . . Sabelli, N. (2006). Learning theories and education: Toward a decade of synergy. In P. A. Alexander & P. H. Winne (Eds.), *Handbook of educational psychology* (2nd ed., pp. 209–244). Mahwah, NJ: Lawrence Erlbaum.

Chalmers, D., & Johnston, S. (2012). Quality assurance and accreditation in higher education. In I. Jung & C. Latchem (Eds.), *Quality assurance and accreditation in distance education and e-learning: Models, policies and research* (pp. 1–12). New York: Routledge.

Chickering, A. W., & Ehrmann, S. C. (1996). *Implementing the seven principles: Technology as lever.* Retrieved from the TLT Group website: http://www.tltgroup .org/programs/seven.html

Chickering, A. W., & Gamson, A. F. (1987). Seven principles for good practice in undergraduate education. *Washington Center News.* Retrieved from http:// wwwtemp.lonestar.edu/multimedia/SevenPrinciples.pdf

Crichton, S., & Kinash, S. (2013). Enabling learning for disabled students. In M. G. Moore (Ed.), *Handbook of distance education* (3rd ed., pp. 216–223). New York: Routledge.

Curry, R. F. (2013). Academic advising in degree programs. In M. G. Moore (Ed.), *Handbook of distance education* (3rd ed., pp. 201–215). New York: Routledge.

Daniel, J. (2012). Foreword. In I. Jung & C. Latchem (Eds.), *Quality assurance and accreditation in distance education and e-learning: Models, policies and research* (pp. xiii–xvi). New York: Routledge.

Darabi, A. A., Sikorski, E. G., & Harvey, R. B. (2006). Validated competencies for distance teaching. *Distance Education, 27*(1), 105–122. doi:10.1080/ 01587910600654809

Eaton, J. S. (2011). Federalizing accreditation: A quandary for higher education. *Inside Accreditation with the President of CHEA, 7*(1). Retrieved from http://www .chea.org/ia/IA_2011.01.18.html

Flumerfelt, S., & Banachowski, M. (2011). Understanding leadership paradigms for improvement in higher education. *Quality Assurance in Education, 19*(3), 224–247. doi:10.1108/09684881111158045

Guskey, T. (2002). Does it make a difference? Evaluating professional development. *Educational Leadership, 59*(6), 45–51.

Hines, S. (2009). Investigating faculty development program assessment practices: What's being done and how can it be improved? *Journal of Faculty Development, 23*(3), 5–19.

Hirner, L. J. (2008). *Quality indicators for evaluating distance education programs at community college* (Doctoral dissertation). Retrieved from ProQuest. (Document No. 304518115)

Inglis, A., Ling, P., & Joosten, V. (1999). *Delivering digitally: Managing the transition to the knowledge media.* London: Kogan Page.

Jung, I., & Latchem, C. (Eds.). (2012). *Quality assurance and accreditation in distance education and e-learning: Models, policies and research.* New York: Routledge.

Kirkpatrick, D. L. (1994). *Evaluating training programs*. San Francisco: Berrett-Koehler.

Lampikoski, K. (1995). *Who determines quality in distance education?* Copy in possession of author.

Lumina Foundation and Gallup. (2013, February 5). *America's call for higher education redesign*. Retrieved from http://www.luminafoundation.org/publications/Americas_Call_for_Higher_Education_Redesign.pdf

Mariasingam, M. A., & Hanna, D. E. (2006). Benchmarking quality in online degree programs status and prospects. *Online Journal of Distance Learning Administration, 9*(3). Retrieved from http://www.westga.edu/~distance/ojdla/fall93/mariasingam93.htm

Moore, M. G. (2007). *Handbook of distance education* (2nd ed.). Mahwah, NJ: Lawrence Erlbaum.

Moore, M. G., & Kearsley, G. (1996). *Distance education: A systems view*. Belmont, CA: Wadsworth.

Moore, M. G., & Kearsley, G. (2012). *Distance education: A systems view of online learning* (3rd ed.). Belmont, CA: Wadsworth.

Phipps, R., & Merisotis, J. (1999). *What's the difference? A review of contemporary research on the effectiveness of distance learning in higher education*. Retrieved from Institute for Higher Education Policy website: http://www.ihep.org/assets/files/publications/s-z/WhatDifference.pdf

Plank, K., & Kalish, A. (2010). Program assessment for faculty development. In K. J. Gillespie & D. L. Robertson (Eds.), *A guide to faculty development* (2nd ed., pp. 135–149). San Francisco: Jossey-Bass.

Rees, D. W. (2007). *Evidence-based quality assurance: An alternative paradigm for non-traditional higher education* (Doctoral dissertation). Available from ProQuest Dissertations and Theses database. (Document No. 304720801)

Sener, J. (2012). *The seven futures of American education: Improving learning and teaching in a screen-captured world*. North Charleston, SC: CreateSpace.

Shattuck, K. (2003). [Updating and expanding the Berge and Mrozowski study]. Unpublished raw data.

Sherry, A. C. (2003). Quality and its measurement in distance education. In M. G. Moore & W. G. Anderson (Eds.), *Handbook of distance education* (pp. 435–459). Mahwah, NJ: Lawrence Erlbaum.

Siemens, G., & Long, P. (2011, September). Penetrating the fog: Analytics in learning and education. *Educause Review Online, 46*(5). Retrieved from http://www.educause.edu/ero/article/penetrating-fog-analytics-learning-and-education

Smith, T. C. (2005). Fifty-one competencies for online instruction. *Journal of Educators Online, 2*(2). Retrieved from http://www.thejeo.com/Ted%20Smith%20Final.pdf

Southern Regional Education Board (SREB). (2006). *Standards for quality online teaching*. Retrieved from http://publications.sreb.org/2006/06T02_Standards_Online_Teaching.pdf

Stroh, L. K., Northcraft, G. B., & Neale, M. A. (2002). *Organizational behavior: A management challenge* (3rd ed.). Mahwah, NJ: Lawrence Erlbaum.

Thompson, M. M., & Irele, M. D. (2007). Evaluating distance education programs. M. G. Moore (Ed.), *Handbook of distance education* (2nd ed., pp. 419–436). Mahwah, NJ: Lawrence Erlbaum.

U.S. Department of Education. (2006). *A test of leadership: Charting the future of U.S. higher education.* Retrieved from http://www2.ed.gov/about/bdscomm/list/hiedfuture/reports/final-report.pdf

Varvel, V. E. (2007). Master online teacher competencies. *Online Journal of Distance Learning Administration, 10*(1). Retrieved from http://www.westga.edu/~distance/ojdla/spring101/varvel101.pdf

Wedemeyer, C. A. (1981). *Learning at the back door: Reflections on non-traditional learning in the lifespan.* Madison: University of Wisconsin Press.

Winegar, M. L. (2000). An exploration of seven principles for good practice in Web-based courses. *Dissertation Abstracts International: Section A. Humanities and Social Sciences, 61*(7), 2674.

Zawacki-Richter, O., Bäcker, E. M., & Vogt, S. (2009). Review of distance education research (2000 to 2008): Analysis of research areas, methods, and authorship patterns. *International Review of Research in Open and Distance Learning, 10*(6). Retrieved from http://www.irrodl.org/index.php/irrodl/article/view/741/1433

PART ONE

OVERVIEW AND IMPLICATIONS OF PRACTICES AND PROCESSES FOR ASSURING QUALITY

1

STAKEHOLDERS OF QUALITY ASSURANCE IN ONLINE EDUCATION

Inputs and Outputs

Deborah Adair and Sebastián Díaz

This chapter serves as an introduction to this book primarily by drawing attention to the multidimensional aspects of quality assurance, as well as to the diversity of invested stakeholders, both of which are blooming in scope. Quality serves as a unifying theme that binds the interests of all stakeholders involved in the educational enterprise. Whereas quality concerns were previously confined to experts involved with total quality management (TQM), institutional research (IR), and continuous quality improvement (CQI), these concerns are now everyone's business.

Quality assurance is a dynamic process that must continually respond to changes in education. Pedagogy continues to change as it responds to shifts in theory, technology, learning topics, learner characteristics, social contexts of learning, demography, and sociopolitical influences. A commitment to quality assurance provides the discipline to balance two major types of change: that which is imposed upon the academy and that which is proactively initiated from within as part of strategic planning and data-driven decision making. Both of these types of change are increasingly being demanded of educators.

The late management guru and accidental sociologist Peter Drucker (1993) illuminated the nexus between quality and change when he offered the following warning regarding the emerging Knowledge Society:

> Indeed, no other institution faces challenges as radical as those that will transform the school. The greatest change, and the one we are least prepared

3

for, is that the school will have to commit itself to results. The school will finally become accountable. (p. 209)

Drucker's warning, coincidentally, applies to all sectors of education: K–12, postsecondary, graduate, and postgraduate, as well as traditional campus–based, blended, online, private sector, and not-for-profit sector.

In this context of increasing accountability, the rapid growth in online learning adds complexity as distance education is used to facilitate teaching and learning in areas we may never have anticipated. Online learning continues to serve as a catalyst for innovation in education in ways that extend well beyond technology. Our continued experimentation with distance learning calls into question a variety of foundational issues regarding what constitutes quality in teaching and learning.

Distance education is not new, nor is the concern about quality (Irele, 2013). In fact, it has been an event of record since the 1700s (for a detailed timeline, see International Museum of Distance Education and Technology, n.d.). But the growth of online formats of distance education provides an opportunity for all stakeholders to inform the delivery, measurement, and outcomes of education. In this period of change enabled by digital technologies—the "cyberization" of education—we find, "if not a new Golden Age, then certainly a golden opportunity and we are just starting to learn how to make that happen" (Sener, 2012, p. xii).

This chapter is organized around the systems approach to the relationship among inputs, process, and outcomes and the idea that positive, purposeful change will occur only when we can understand and improve the key components of quality processes. System inputs (should) influence process, and process subsequently influences outcomes, which in turn completes the cycle by affecting the inputs for the next iteration. This circular paradigm embraces the concept of continuous improvement and identifies areas of opportunity in the pursuit of quality assurance.

The Context: Stakeholders' Inputs and Outputs

It becomes challenging to define a high-quality education. Is it about the experience? Is it about the result or benefit of an education? What kind of result indicates quality and for whom? And who decides when we have achieved quality? Quality is a highly relative concept that has meaning only when the standards and level of achievement necessary to meet those standards are understood and shared. To measure *quality*, to improve it, to achieve it, we need to define it so that it becomes explicit and transparent. A quality assurance process is dependent on such a definition.

If education is considered from a systems perspective—as a transformation process with education providers receiving inputs into the system, plying their trade through the institution's processes, and producing outputs of interest to stakeholders—we can define quality standards and levels at various points in the process. These institutional processes, including and especially those occurring in the classroom, are the "black box" in our education system because the activities involved in transforming inputs into outputs are obscured for most education stakeholders. In higher education, it has been difficult to establish explicit definitions of quality that are applicable to processes across institutions because of the great diversity in mission, audience, and educational approaches. This is often even a challenge within institutions. Johnson (2010) warns of the myopic view that results from creating impenetrable silos within an organization. Quality assurance within the black box tends to be relative, self-assessed, and not particularly transparent to the educational consumer, except through the awarding of accreditation. Identifying quality inputs (e.g., incoming student characteristics, state and federal funding levels, and legal requirements) and outcomes (e.g., degree attainment, graduate job placement) is simply easier and therefore more frequently observed and measured by educational stakeholders. Golden opportunities present themselves in what we do with these inputs and how we manage the educational processes to achieve desired outputs.

To this end, the need for clear and well-articulated systems for quality assurance in education has never been greater. The challenge is that inputs have become more impoverished—in some cases because of, or in reaction to, online education—but the level of outputs required is higher than ever. Increased public scrutiny of online and distance education has led to new and reemphasized legislation and the creation and refocusing of governance organizations and policy-making bodies. The new regulatory landscape has created a more restrictive, complex, and in some cases counterproductive operating environment for education providers. With the current economic crisis, public funds for education are at an all-time low. Record levels of student debt, an anemic job market, and pervasive skepticism about online learning have the public questioning the value of a college education or at least its return on investment. And the very success of online learning—achieving its initial mission of access by opening education to all types of learners, not just traditional students filtered by rigidly defined selection processes—has made the input of learner characteristics widely variable and, on the whole, less suited for our traditional system of education.

Measuring Inputs and Outcomes

Outside of endowments and investment revenue, external funding from sources such as student tuition, federal financial aid, and state appropriations is carefully forecasted and seen as a requirement for a quality educational experience. Institutional infrastructure, faculty and staff positions and salaries, academic services, student support resources, and a host of other expenses depend on it. To the extent that the number of applications, acceptances, and enrollments are critical variables in such external funding formulas, institutions have a vested interest in anticipating and managing those numbers. But the quality of the applicants and of the accepted students may matter even more to some institutions. Incoming student quality is often interpreted as a measure of quality for the institution itself. Selectivity, the percentage of applicants an institution accepts, along with test score averages of the accepted students, is a measure of quality used by many college rating services as well as by students and parents (Lumina Foundation, 2012). The better prepared a college's incoming student class, the more elite the institution is perceived to be. This is one reason for the increasing use of tuition discounting—especially among independent colleges and universities, where it has hit an all-time high and actually led to a net tuition decline of 2% between 2007 and 2008 (Hamill & Marea, 2009; Kirshstein & Wellman, 2012). The assumption is that students compete for space at institutions that provide the best education (with selectivity as the proxy measure of a quality education), with the intention of achieving the best life outcomes. But this assumption relies on measurement of inputs and outcomes, not of the educational process itself. Just how much do these desirable outcomes depend on the quality of the inputs and how much on the educational process? Can equivalently good outputs be achieved when the quality of inputs varies? When financial resources are scarcer, the regulatory environment tighter, and learner needs more varied, how do we achieve a universally and equivalently good outcome from higher education? The answers to these questions are at the core of this book's examination of quality assurance practices.

Funding as an Input Variable

Whereas growth in online learning enrollments and programs is still strong, funding for public higher education institutions overall has been on the decline for years and has been significantly affected by the recent recession and recent changes in federal funding. Insights from the Delta Cost Project (Kirshstein & Wellman, 2012) reveal,

> The furor over the cost and effectiveness of a college education has roots in deep socioeconomic challenges that won't be solved with an online app.

Over decades, state support per student at public institutions has dwindled even as enrollments have ballooned, leading to higher prices for parents and students. State funds per student dropped by 20 percent from 1987 to 2011, according to an analysis by the higher-education finance expert Jane Wellman, who directs the National Association of System Heads. (Carlson & Blumenstyk, 2012, para. 12)

Outcome Implications for Funding

The state funding model for higher education has changed and is not expected to return to previous levels even as state revenue rebounds. The implication of this new normal for higher education funding is that states will require improved efficiency with funding tied to positive outcomes (Pattison & Eckl, 2011). Affordability, student completion, and account-ability are now the key issues in education in general and online learning in particular.

Regulation as an Input Variable

Concerns about the increase in the cost of education and the consequent bal-looning of student debt have led to increased public scrutiny and the creation or enforcement of more restrictive regulation and policies. The threat of ever more intrusive legislation, poised to usurp responsibilities traditionally under the purview of accrediting bodies, institutions, and faculty, recently led the Council for Higher Education Accreditation (CHEA) and the American Association of University Professors to draft an advisory statement on the role of accreditation in academic freedom. This statement pointedly addresses the threat of political pressure to institutional autonomy and academic freedom, both seen as central to a quality education, and adds that such threat "shows no promise of abatement" (CHEA, 2012, p. 1).

Online education, in particular, has drawn increased scrutiny over output measures. Legislators have voiced increasing concern over how well online education and, in particular, for-profit providers are serving stu-dents (Field, 2011). The Gainful Employment Rule (U.S. Department of Education, 2011), reauthorized under the 2008 Higher Education Opportunity Act, tied student loan repayment rates and income-to-debt ratios to federal financial aid as a mechanism to improve student gradua-tion rates and loan defaults. In 2010 the U.S. Department of Education issued new regulations aimed at program integrity, including the state-authorization requirement for postsecondary institutions providing edu-cation at a distance to out-of-state students. These institutions must meet state requirements and document approvals in each state where they do business (WCET, 2012).

Outcome Implications for Regulation

At the same time these regulations aim to prevent negative outcomes, a strong public interest in and concern about the effectiveness of our education system could lead to the support necessary to achieve desired positive outcomes. As of this writing, 36 states have enacted specific goals for degree attainment (Lumina Foundation, 2012), and public and private sources of funding are being directed toward particularly promising initiatives in support of degree-attainment goals. The threat of requirements with a singular focus on regulating outputs and institutional practices outside of the educational process (though intended as a way of assuring quality for students) may simply serve to divert an institution's attention toward compliance without a corresponding focus on preparing and educating the learner.

Online Student Profiles as an Input Variable

Reports on the demographic profile of online students reveal the "typical" online student is not the traditional 18- to 22-year-old full-time student living on campus but is female (67%), between the ages of 25 and 44 (58%), enrolled primarily online (87%), and an undergraduate (66%) (Noel-Levitz, 2011). Moreover, these aggregated national statistics for online learners are simply more pronounced versions of demographic trends affecting all of higher education. By 1986 nontraditional students as undergraduates were already the majority (Sener, 2012). Nontraditional learners, especially online learners, have priorities and motivations that are different from those of traditional students. Students enrolled primarily online see convenience, flexible pacing in program completion, work schedule, and program requirements as the most important considerations in enrollment decisions.

Outcome Implications for Online Student Profiles

Learners seeking online education want shorter and more affordable courses, and they want to be able to transfer previously earned credit (Aslanian & Clinefelter, 2012). They perceive that many institutions are not meeting their expectations in at least some of the educational experiences they most value—clearly defined assignments, excellence of instruction, responsiveness of faculty, timely feedback from faculty, and the value-to-cost relationship of tuition (Noel-Levitz, 2011). Soares's (2013) "Manifesto for College Leaders" is offered as a "catalyst" to college learners and points out that although post-traditional learners—"individuals already in the work force who lack postsecondary credentials yet are determined to pursue further knowledge and skills while balancing work, life, and educational responsibilities" (pp. 1–2)—are a diverse group, they can no longer be viewed "as an aberration in the demand for higher education services" (p. 2). Higher education will need to attend to the needs of these students by creating "learning aligned with a knowledge society and innovation economy" (Soares, 2013, p. 16).

Students now have better access to data and information, which provides them with more choice and voice in the educational process. Increasing the transparency of quality in process and output and explicitly acknowledging students' perspectives will be required for institutions seeking a competitive advantage. An increased focus on common standards throughout disciplines, institutions, and educational systems seems certain.

Addressing Quality in Online Education: The Many Dimensions

The call for change in the U.S. educational system has come from a variety of stakeholders and is being driven by economic, social, and regulatory imperatives. It has become loud enough and persistent enough to encourage innovative and exciting experiments in the structure and delivery of education by academic institutions as well as by a rapidly increasing number of policy groups; public and private foundations; and nonacademic, for-profit companies. Yet, strategic attention needs to guide innovation to ensure that quality exists and that we continue to make significant progress in its pursuit. A comprehensive and programmatic review of quality in our online initiatives would include evaluation of institutional commitment; courses, curricula, and instruction; assessment practices; learner support; faculty support; and program evaluation practices (all these criteria are applied in a Quality Matters program audit being field-tested as of this writing).

Institutional Commitment

The level of an institution's commitment to its online programs is a key area for quality assurance. Online programs used to fuel enrollment growth and generate revenue to fund other areas of the organization, or solely for short-term financial returns for stakeholders, do not have the same integrity of purpose as programs supported by institutions with a sustainable, ongoing commitment to education for all students. An assessment of quality would consider online initiatives as an enterprise warranting both financial and strategic investment. Online programs that fully support and integrate with the institution's mission can refine an institution's focus, priorities, internal policies, and external policy compliance by requiring their applicability to all learners—including those outside of the traditional on-site classroom. The extent of institutional commitment to online instruction not only is difficult to observe but is now more likely than ever to vary significantly across the different types of organizations and initiatives offering online education. Program integrity and ethics are a key concern in the rapidly developing landscape of educational innovation (see chapter 12, "Ethics Matters: Assuring Quality at the Academic Program Level"). Now is an opportune time to reevaluate assumptions, perceptions, and judgments about both the purpose and practice of online education.

At the institutional level, assuring quality must include an understanding of how the principles of knowledge management can be used to collect data and information to produce actionable knowledge (see chapter 15, "Using Principles of Knowledge Management for Educational Quality Assurance"). Methodologically, online programs will need to explore new approaches to quantitative and qualitative data analyses that inform these comparisons. The respective infrastructures and data architectures will need to be revamped to allow for the complex exchange of data. As concerns for accountability grow, institutions must move beyond the collection of such data for their own internal use and begin to share data with stakeholders, including prospective and current students. Transparency for stakeholders is becoming increasingly important, and significant initiatives toward this end are being developed in higher education (see chapter 5, "Progress Toward Transparency and Quality Assurance"). However, as the critical indicator of the appropriateness and sustainability of the institutional commitment to online education, accreditation remains the primary quality assurance mechanism for most stakeholders, especially those stakeholders controlling federal financial aid (see chapter 17, "The Role and Realities of Accreditation: A Practical Guide for Programs and Institutions Preparing for an Accreditation Visit").

Courses, Curricula, and Instruction

Because students experience online learning through the courses, the curricula, and the instruction, the quality of these components in the education process is of practical and immediate importance to students, faculty, and administrators. They have a longer-term impact on outcomes of concern to all stakeholders. Quality assurance processes should look to valid standards for quality, and evidence of the achievement of these standards, in the construction of the online learning environment and in the resources and policies that affect it. Such quality assurance practices would consider design practices, such as creating course elements that are coherent and navigable by the students and that are aligned and constructed to engage and support student learning (see chapter 6, "A Process to Improve Course Design: A Key Variable in Course Quality"). These courses and curricula should look to support the time and place limitations of online students, address the different needs of culturally diverse learners (see chapter 11, "Assuring Quality for an Expanding Population of Culturally Diverse Students"), and demonstrate a commitment to accessibility for all learners (see chapter 10, "Disability and Accessibility: Proactive Strategies to Improve Quality"). The delivery of instruction should be no less supportive of these aims; a quality assurance process that acknowledges the importance of instructional delivery that supports the institution's mission, considers instructional expectations and practices, and assesses opportunities for faculty development is central to any attempt to achieve quality in teaching and learning (see chapter 7, "A Model for Determining the Effectiveness and Impact of Faculty Professional Development"). Open-access courses, those relying on open educational resources for content, and those relying on student-generated content represent some of the newest innovations in courses and curricula and therefore may come with the least-developed processes for assuring quality; however, a framework to assure quality in these educational experiences will be required for wider adoption of these innovations (see chapter 2, "Cost, Access, and Quality: Breaking the Iron Triangle Through Disruptive Technology-Based Innovations").

Quality assurance processes that require broad collaboration within and across different institutions and constituencies and that are focused on continuous improvement may have the best chance of creating the kind of shared understanding of quality necessary to evaluate the rapidly developing innovations in distance education (again, see chapter 2). Any discussion regarding what constitutes quality in course content and curriculum involves, at best, difficult, often politically loaded, contentious debates. Discussions of the quality of course content and curriculum often need to be preceded by arguments over what content is needed. Regardless, we are reminded here that work on continuous quality improvement in education is not a purely objective process and that our roles related to consensus building may heighten the multidimensionality of our work. This is especially true as the world of online learning expands and matures. As the public increasingly comes to accept *how* online learning is facilitated, we will be challenged to help evaluate *what* is taught through distance education.

Broadly adopted and applied quality standards provide an opportunity to discriminate in practical ways between the many course and program offerings in distance education. Quality assurance processes that engage stakeholders, including students, at different levels in and across institutions may have the most staying power. They become sustainable because the responsibilities of work and evaluation are shared and powerful because more stakeholders have a voice in the discussion about teaching and learning (see chapter 9, "Engaging Online Faculty and Administrators in the Assessment Process").

Assessment Practices

The kinds of assessment practices that institutions use and ways they use them are also key components, or levers, for quality in the education process. Student performance assessment within courses, the ways in which the individual assessments are aligned with course and program objectives, and the ways in which they provide developmental feedback for students are critically important to both students and faculty. The types of assessments institutions use to evaluate student learning outcomes can help assure quality throughout the curriculum and ensure that program objectives are being met. As we move beyond seat-time measures, we need quality assurance processes that help us understand and evaluate the kinds of contact, interaction, and engagement that are important to student learning (see chapter 16, "An Adaptive Model for Calculating Contact Hours in Distance-Education Courses") and that can help us implement what we are learning about predicting student success from the aggregation of large data sets across institutions (e.g., the Predictive Analytics Reporting Framework Project) and the application of learning analytics (see chapter 14, "Learning Analytics: A Tool for Quality Assurance").

Quality assurance around course and institutional effectiveness requires data that go beyond student performance and student learning outcomes to include the review and comparison of program outcomes across programs, across different delivery modalities, and across different student groups. Engaging faculty and administrators in assessment practices helps to ensure commitment to the process in which quality is continually pursued (see chapter 9, "Engaging Online Faculty and Administrators in the Assessment Process").

Learner Support

Because learner support provides a foundation for student success, a quality educational experience includes processes and resources that are customized to the needs of the online learner. Technical support, online access to resources, orientation to online learning technologies, accommodations for learning disabilities, academic and counseling resources all need to be provided in a format appropriate for online delivery. The kinds of support and resources provided to the online learners should reflect the extent that an institution's online learners differ from its traditional, on-campus learners— in terms of demographics, motivation, or general preparedness for the online educational environment (see chapter 13, "Academic Advising: A Link to a Quality Experience for Students").

As experience with online learning continues to grow and broaden, this student group may soon become the mainstream, and this too should be reflected in the institution's policies and practices for learner support. As of this writing, only 14% of undergraduate students matriculate full-time and live on campus (U.S. Department of Education, 2009). The 86% who do not, whether they are online learners or not, would benefit from many of the same learner support practices necessary for online students. More students are moving online, as evidenced by the continuing robust growth in online learning enrollment—10% between 2010 and 2011 compared to the less than 1% growth in total student enrollments. In higher education, 32% of all higher education students now take at least one online course and more than 6.1 million students took an online course in the fall of 2010 (Allen & Seaman, 2011, 2013).

Students are becoming more likely to enter college with online learning experience and expectations. In K–12, online and blended learning courses exist for at least some students in all 50 states. Currently, 31 states with full-time, multidistrict schools enrolled an estimated total of 275,000 students in online courses in 2011–2012—this is an annual increase of 15% (Watson, Murin, Vashaw, Gemin, & Rapp, 2012). Since 2010 Maine, Indiana, and Tennessee have changed their laws to allow for full-time online schools. Course enrollments (one student taking a one-semester-long online course) have increased by 16% since the 2011–2012 school year to a total of 619,847 enrollments in 28 state virtual schools. It is estimated that two-thirds of districts are offering some type of blended program, making this a fast-growing and high-profile area. As online learning becomes more widespread in K–12 (see chapter 4, "K–12 Online Learning: Recommendations for Assuring Quality"), students who are supported and prepared in their secondary school experience will simultaneously be better prepared and have higher expectations for support in their higher education experiences.

Faculty Support

Online learning is transforming the professorate, as well as other organizational roles in the academy. Quality online teaching requires processes to develop and support faculty skills and abilities to manage the online classroom and provide effective online instruction. Mastering how to teach online allows faculty to focus on the scholarship of teaching and learning and to refine their approach to pedagogy in a manner that can inform and improve their teaching across all delivery modalities—not just in the online classroom. Feedback on performance, policies around online instruction, technical support, and effective tools are all components of quality in faculty support and should support the training and faculty development processes to improve the quality of instruction (see chapter 7, "A Model for Determining the Effectiveness and Impact of Faculty Professional Development").

In support of continuous quality improvement, faculty should be provided opportunities to participate in planning, curriculum development, course evaluation, and program review (see chapter 8, "The Power of a Collaborative, Collegial Approach to Improving Online Teaching and Learning," and chapter 9, "Engaging Online Faculty and Administrators in the Assessment Process").

The increased attention to quality education is calling into question many as of yet unresolved issues related to faculty readiness. This breadth of issues reveals that faculty development efforts continue to be intertwined with measures of quality in education. One way to better envision this breadth is to consider the continuum of faculty autonomy (again, see chapter 8). At one end of the continuum, particularly in a traditional institution where a faculty member delivers instruction on campus, we note that the faculty member plays a central and decisive role in the quality of instruction. By contrast, conscientiously developed online courses require the input of a variety of stakeholders, thus making quality assurance of instruction something that is not the sole domain of the individual faculty member.

Program Evaluation Practices

Ongoing evaluation of online offerings and use of these results for improvement should demonstrate a commitment to quality (see chapter 3, "The Sloan Consortium Pillars and Quality Scorecard," and chapter 6, "A Process to Improve Course Design: A Key Variable in Course Quality"). What matters is not only that the processes for measurement and evaluation are regular and consistent, but also that the processes themselves (including the data collected and the evaluation standards used) are critically reviewed. Appropriate use of institutional data is essential for a meaningful quality assurance process (see chapter 5, "Progress Toward Transparency and Quality Assurance," and chapter 15, "Using Principles of Knowledge Management for Educational Quality Assurance"). Commitment to continuous improvement requires the effective use of data to drive decision making in ways that support the organization's strategic mission and that are transparent to program stakeholders.

Summary

Declines in the quality of inputs and increasing expectations for outputs mean increased scrutiny of the educational activities of academic institutions—long a black box for most education stakeholders. Online education is seen as cause and consequence—affecting inputs and increasing scrutiny of outputs. It also represents a key lever for change in our educational system. For these reasons, assuring the quality of online education is critical. We have long had measures of quality for both inputs (e.g., high school grade point averages and standardized test scores per student spending) and outputs (e.g., job placement and starting salaries for new college graduates); however, the recent concern over the quality of educational outputs is widespread and escalating. Online learning appears to be ushering in this latest wave of discontent as questions about the cost and value of online courses have been turned toward the established system amid calls for "reinvention of education." Students and parents are increasingly finding a college education cost prohibitive, legislators are unhappy with the return (completion rates, student debt, degree attainment) on the expenditure of public dollars, employers are not finding enough students well prepared and with the appropriate skills, students are not finding jobs, and the United States is suffering from a decline in international ranking in test courses and degree attainment.

We do, in fact, have processes, tools, and initiatives under way that can help us systematically and meaningfully acknowledge and improve the quality of both educational processes and outcomes. The chapters in this book present some of these initiatives as they examine the issue of quality assurance in online distance education from the program and administrative levels, at the level of course design and teaching, in the context of academic resources, and from the perspective of accreditation. The evaluation of quality and the processes used to ensure it at different institutional levels and areas of focus, including some interinstitutional processes and practices, can help us better understand the black box in the education process and help us navigate the increasingly complex landscape of quality in online distance education.

References

Allen, I. E., & Seaman, J. (2011). *Going the distance: Online education in the United States, 2011.* Retrieved from Babson Survey Research Group website: http://www.onlinelearningsurvey.com/reports/goingthedistance.pdf

Allen, I. E., & Seaman, J. (2013). *Changing course: Ten years of tracking online education in the United States.* Retrieved from Babson Survey Research Group website: http://www.onlinelearningsurvey.com/reports/changingcourse.pdf

Aslanian, C. B., & Clinefelter, D. L. (2012). *Online college students 2012: Comprehensive data on demands and preferences.* Retrieved from the Learning House website: http://www.learninghouse.com/files/documents/resources/Online%20College%20Students%202012.pdf

Carlson, S., & Blumenstyk, G. (2012, December 17). For whom is college being reinvented? *The Chronicle of Higher Education.* Retrieved from http://chronicle. com/article/The-False-Promise-of-the/136305/

Council for Higher Education Accreditation (CHEA). (2012, October). *Accreditation and academic freedom.* Retrieved from http://www.chea.org/pdf/AAUP-CHEA%20-%20FINAL.pdf

Drucker, P. (1993). *Post-capitalist society.* New York: HarperCollins.

Field, K. (2011, June). Sen. Harkin presses Education Dept. on effectiveness of "gainful employment" rule. *The Chronicle of Higher Education.* Retrieved from http://chronicle.com/article/Sen-Harkin-Presses-Education/127786/

Hamill, M., & Marea, S. (2009). *Tuition discounting study report.* Washington, DC: National Association of College and University Business Officers (NACUBO).

International Museum of Distance Education and Technology. (n.d.). *Distance education timeline.* Retrieved from http://museumofdistanceeducation.com/de/ distance-education-timeline/

Irele, M. E. (2013). Evaluating distance education in an era of internationalization. In M. G. Moore (Ed.), *Handbook of distance education* (3rd ed., pp. 493–506). New York: Routledge.

Johnson, S. (2010). *Where good ideas come from: The natural history of innovation.* New York: Riverhead Books.

Kirshstein, R., & Wellman, J. (2012). Cost model: Insights from the Delta Cost Project. *Educause Review, 47*(5). Retrieved from http://www.educause.edu/ero/ article/technology-and-broken-higher-education-cost-model-insights-delta-cost-project

Lumina Foundation. (2012). *Tracking progress toward an audacious but attainable goal.* Retrieved from http://www.luminafoundation.org/state_work/main_narrative

Noel-Levitz. (2011). *National online learners priorities report.* Retrieved from https:// www.noellevitz.com/upload/Papers_and_Research/2011/PSOL_report%20 2011.pdf

Pattison, S. D., & Eckl, C. (2011). *A new funding paradigm for higher education.* Retrieved from National Association of State Budget Officers (NASBO) website: http://www.nasbo.org/sites/default/files/A%20New%20Funding%20Paradigm %20for%20Higher%20Education.pdf

Sener, J. (2012). *The seven futures of American education: Improving learning and teaching in a screen-captured world.* North Charleston, SC: CreateSpace.

Soares, L. (2013, January). *Post-traditional learners and the transformation of post-secondary education: A manifesto for college leaders.* Retrieved from the American Council on Education website: http://www.acenet.edu/news-room/Documents/ Soares-Post-Traditional-v5-011813.pdf

U.S. Department of Education. (2011, June). *Program integrity: Gainful employment-debt measures* (Rule by the Education Department on 06/13/2011). Retrieved from the Federal Register website: https://www.federalregister.gov/articles/2011/ 06/13/2011-13905/program-integrity-gainful-employment-debt-measures#p-3

U.S. Department of Education, Institute of Education Sciences, National Center for Education Statistics. (2009, October). Undergraduate students. *2003–04 and 2007–08 National Postsecondary Student Aid Study (NPSAS:04 and NPSAS:08).* Retrieved from http://nces.ed.gov/programs/digest/d11/tables/dt11_242.asp

Watson, J., Murin, A., Vashaw, L., Gemin, B., & Rapp, C. (2012). *Keeping pace with K-12 online and blended learning: An annual review of policy and practice.* Retrieved from http://kpk12.com/cms/wp-content/uploads/KeepingPace2012.pdf

WCET. (2012, October 29). State authorization—An introduction [web log post]. *WCET Advance.* Retrieved from http://wcet.wiche.edu/advance/state-approval

2

COST, ACCESS, AND QUALITY

Breaking the Iron Triangle Through Disruptive Technology-Based Innovations

Stella C. S. Porto

In this chapter, I attempt to provide a framework for understanding and assessing a variety of aspects of online education quality within the context of more recent technology-based innovations in the field, many of which have at their core the drive to address the critical relationship among cost, access, and quality.

The relationship among cost, access, and quality has been mentioned frequently in the literature. Because of the tight connections among these three elements and their significance as part of institution and government missions and goals throughout the world, they are often represented by a triangle, the "eternal triangle" or the "iron triangle." Increase in access is imperative to respond to the growing demand for higher education. According to Maslen (2012, para. 1), "The number of students around the globe enrolled in higher education is forecast to more than double to 262 million by 2025." Likewise, cost has to be constrained to maintain accessibility, and quality needs to be maintained notwithstanding the boundaries of cost-effectiveness and scalability. This is an impossible wish list, in which one requirement is potentially incompatible with the other; each of the unyielding sides of the triangle cannot be enhanced without diminishing the other two. Sir John Daniel (2011) explains the evident conflict: "Widen access by packing more students into each class and people will say quality is slipping. Improve quality with better learning resources and costs will go up. Cut costs and we damage both access and quality" (para. 6–8). One consequence of this in postsecondary education is the "unhealthy link between quality and exclusivity" (Daniel, 2011, para. 9), which has played out through the creation of entrance barriers and narrow funnels. Excluding people has become an assurance of quality.

In this scenario, technology has become a potentially powerful answer to the gridlock. Following basic economic principles of scale, technology could have the power to break the triangle and respond efficiently to the demands of greater access, higher quality, and lower cost. Otto Peters (1983, 1998) similarly explained the use of technology in distance education as an "industrialized mode" of education, in which, with a fixed cost, institutions were able to provide access to a larger number of learners by exploring scalability through division of labor and specialized roles. The difference today is that distance education has gained new momentum because of technologies that have eliminated the differences in learning experiences and put to rest the low-quality curse that plagued that mode of learning for decades. However, in many cases, these newer technologies have changed the original principles of scalability, and so to address the issues of cost, quality, and access, emerging technologies need to play the role of disruptive innovation, in terms of not only teaching and learning practices but also key strategic elements in all the service components of a student's life cycle. The principles responsible for the industrial revolution "work even better with the technologies of today's network revolution: the new technologies that let us share, study and socialise simultaneously" (Daniel, 2011, para. 19).

The evolution of online education has shown the strong connection between innovation and the adoption of emerging technologies (New Media Consortium, 2012). According to Veletsianos (2010), "Emerging technologies are tools, concepts, innovations, and advancements utilized in diverse educational settings to serve varied education-related purposes" (p. 3); for the most part, they have demonstrated the potential for being disruptive but are "not yet fully understood, and not yet fully researched" (p. 3). Therefore, the discussion in this chapter is meant to improve our understanding of the impact of such innovations and to help shape strategies for their effective adoption given the contextual constraints of access and cost.

Since the focus of such innovations has been, for the most part, to increase student accessibility to education, it is imperative that I underscore the principles related to openness in education. A definite stance regarding this concept has not been established in the literature. On one hand, David Wiley (n.d.) states that the term *open* "has different meanings in different contexts" (para. 1). Therefore, *open* exists in a continuum; it is a gradient, not a true-false binary concept. George Siemens (2009), on the other hand, considers taking a relative view of the term *open* as an act of "moderation" that is in the end harmful to the effort of actually achieving open education. Graham Atwell (2010) discusses how focusing on open content has perpetuated the idea that the quality of the learning experience is strictly dependent on the availability of content, and the teachers' responsibility is solely to make sure that they gather and provide resources. Within this diverse set of perspectives, I approach openness from Illich's definition of a good educational system:

> A good educational system should have three purposes: it should provide all who want to learn with access to available resources at any time in their lives; empower all who want to share what they know to find those who want to learn it from them; and, finally, furnish all who want to present an issue to the public with the opportunity to make their challenge known. (as cited in Atwell, 2010, para. 25)

As it will become clear throughout this chapter, technology has the potential to help establish a compromise among the frequently confrontational goals of reducing costs, expanding access, and offering quality education. Different stakeholders will prioritize these elements of the triangle in different ways; hence, I will analyze technology from the perspective of faculty, administrators (representing an institutional viewpoint), and students.

First, I will present the current landscape of several of the disruptive innovations inundating the online education field and establish the practical connections between emerging technologies and their interdependencies. Then, I will identify the main quality measures associated with such innovations through a broad framework for quality viewpoints, taking into account the perspectives of the institution, faculty, and students and the tight bonds among quality, cost, and access.

The Landscape

The growth in online education over the last 20 years has been dramatic (Hill, 2012). During most of that time, online education has suffered from skepticism and a general perception of lesser quality. Consequently, it has been dismissed by most prestigious institutions. Institutions have undertaken successive waves of investment in technology to support teaching and learning at a distance. As of mid-2013, the landscape is in great flux, largely because of the emergence of massive open online courses (MOOCs) and the enthusiasm shown for them by many of those same prestigious universities.

During the first decade of the 21st century, a perfect storm of factors has refocused the discussion of online education. Workforce demands have pushed academia to give much more thought to increasing access to education—and to discuss the purpose of higher education more broadly. Concurrently, legislatures, parents, students, and the federal government have pushed for greater accountability regarding the cost of education, which has increased much faster than that of many other services. Finally, faculty, institutions, and employers have tried to maintain quality in the face of these competing pressures. Academic technology, which has been traditionally considered a cost center, now has greatly improved, has become pervasive, and has the potential to help higher education address these pressures. Although all this is true for traditional, face-to-face education, it is much more so for online distance education. The Internet and the development of the World Wide Web as an information delivery vehicle have changed the game. Access to higher education is now enabled by technology, and online learning is seen as a major disruptive innovation in American higher education. Institutions have been forced to reflect on their business models, which include development and delivery of instruction and support services (Aslanian & Clinefelter, 2012).

mLearning

The web has become even more pervasive with the growing availability and diversity of devices providing connectivity. Mobile computing has enabled the surge of an entirely new sector of learning: mLearning. This area has grown exponentially with the use of devices within several categories, including smartphones, netbooks, tablets, e-readers, and laptops. The market for mobile software (apps) is not only a booming industry but also at the fingertips of any user who wants to create new apps and share them with the world in real time, without intermediaries or advanced expertise. In many ways, what once required a computer is now frequently more easily done through a mobile phone. Because smaller devices offer extreme portability and connectivity at a lower cost, mLearning opens new doors for access to education. This type of learning, however, does require rethinking pedagogies. Some of the questions currently being studied by the online education community include, How much and what kind of content can be pushed through mobile devices? What kind of interactive activities are actually effective through such devices? and What models of learning can make best use of this mode of learning (Educause, 2010)?

Open Educational Resources

The open educational resources (OER) wave has been building since the first reference to *open content* by David Wiley in 1998 (Hewlett Foundation, n.d.). The Hewlett Foundation defines *OER* as follows:

> OER are teaching, learning, and research resources that reside in the public domain or have been released under an intellectual property license that

permits their free use or re-purposing by others. Open educational resources include full courses, course materials, modules, textbooks, streaming videos, tests, software, and any other tools, materials, or techniques used to support access to knowledge. (Hewlett Foundation, n.d., para. 2)

This movement has had a significant effect on educational publishing owing to the initiation of several open textbook projects, and together with the technological advancements in user-generated content, it has allowed for "thousands of individual instructors and teachers creating openly licensed learning content" (Reynolds, 2012, para. 4). Olcott (2012) observes that the promise of OER is that of "bridging the digital divide, leveling the educational playing field between developing and developed countries and challenging the restrictive sanctions imposed on open content by proprietary providers and licensing vendors" (p. 283).

As of this writing, OER are focused solely on making content available; they do not provide or suggest ways or scenarios in which they should be used to achieve specific learning outcomes. Therefore, OER are, for the most part, void of specific instructional design information that could potentially associate content with tailored teaching and learning activities and assessment. This is one of the major barriers to the massive adoption of OER.

Massive Open Online Courses

As of the summer of 2013, the hype over the tsunami of MOOC offerings had persisted for a year. Organizations are definitely feeling the pressure to participate in the MOOC movement, and the almost daily headlines announcing the releases of new courses and contracts between start-ups and universities (high profile and not) are impressive (*The Chronicle of Higher Education*, 2012).

Each of the two main models of MOOCs has special traits and is suitable for different audiences, subjects, and learning goals. xMOOCs are mostly organized around presentational materials but also include unstructured discussion forums for participants and quizzes or other standard types of assessment.[1] Some MOOCs have created more authentic learning activities, such as group projects that are assessed via group interaction and peer review. The use of rubrics has helped enhance the feedback process, but contact between instructor and student does not happen at this level given the massive number of participants.

cMOOCs (the *c* stands for "connectivism"), however, are the original form of MOOCs and are completely different. According to Siemens (2004), connectivism synthesizes concepts derived from "chaos, network, and complexity, and self-organization theories" (para. 25). cMOOCs are therefore less structured, and learning is based on the different streams of interaction among participants, who, based on simple guidance from an instructor, communicate with each other through online discussions, Twitter feeds, personal blog posts, and other modes of sharing. Not all participants will take part in each mode of discussion, but instructors will aggregate all these sources into course information streams that are continuously diffused to participants through predefined information channels, such as a common blog, a central Twitter account, and daily newsletters. The learning platform allows users to receive personalized notifications, which help them follow, filter, discuss, reuse, and remix the content created as the course moves forward. This web of connections and exchanges is at the core of the connectivist approach to learning. Thus, cMOOCs are closely related to the learning that happens within communities of practice.

As of mid-2013, acceptance of academic credit for MOOCs was small in scale and clearly controversial, but the potential, and in many cases, the actual, value of MOOCs is not doubtful. There is, however, an inherent dichotomy between the best practices related to well-designed interaction, incorporation of authentic assessment activities, and rich feedback coming from direct contact with the instructor and the need to provide access to a massive number of students (J. Moore, 2005). Technologies are still promising "automated personalized feedback to learners on the basis of their actions" (Laurillard cited in Farmer, 2012, para. 5), but like past attempts to substitute artificial intelligence for human labor, this has yet to be achieved. Therefore, the forces of cost, quality, and access are very much still at odds in this form of online education.

Nonetheless, MOOCs are the best effort seen to date involving multiple players using technology to address the burning educational needs of our time. Such efforts should not be dismissed, but they should also not be overemphasized as the holy grail for solving the problem of access to education. Many moving parts are necessary to make the equation work. After the splashes, there will be a period of maturation and consolidation, during which the loose ends will be tied up. There will also be a moment when we will see MOOCs as a common part of a larger spectrum of options that is "closer to being a form of education that requires less faculty effort and reduces costs" (Farmer, 2012, para. 7).

Cloud Computing and Analytics

The growth in cloud computing has enabled the sharing of data and applications alike. Computing power has shifted to the web. The almost infinite capacity of cloud storage and the advances in data mining have together enabled the collection, management, and maintenance of massive data sets.

Complex algorithms that manipulate large sets of data through a myriad of statistical operations have enabled the creation of new knowledge, going far beyond the learning possible from the original raw data. These algorithms unveil patterns and relationships and help develop predictions and diagnoses of intricate systems or problems. They are now used widely by social media companies to determine the behavioral patterns of consumers by capturing their activities on the web (e.g., navigation and transactions). Learning about consumers allows organizations to target specific groups with products or services of particular interest in a personalized fashion.

Higher education is starting to adopt such practices as well for different purposes, including marketing, retention, intervention, and enhancement of learning outcomes. By collecting data from learning management systems and institutional portals and services, organizations may now employ similar techniques to determine students' learning patterns, identify at-risk students, and find out what kinds of services and resources have greater impact in retention and student success. This brings enormous potential to a more personalized delivery and support system in online education (Wagner & Ice, 2012).

These various online learning trends are operating synergistically to push organizations to change their business models; improve learning effectiveness; and, at the same time, facilitate access to education in a scalable and cost-effective manner. Such changes have a direct impact on the meaning of quality and on the measurement of quality. With the variety and expansion of possible educational paths involving different sets of technologies and appropriate pedagogies, quality benchmarks need to be revisited and reevaluated. What might emerge is a plurality of scales that will be deployed differently according to the context and target student population.

Toward a New Framework for Quality

In this section, I attempt to establish a framework for quality that will support discussion and possibly decision making surrounding disruptive innovations in distance education. At the same time, I consider the iron-triangle relationship among quality, cost, and access previously described. Given that new educational technologies are continually emerging and their effects are not yet clearly determined, the framework postulates several key viewpoints and expectations to help establish directives regarding desired and feasible combinations of quality, access, and cost that account for the perspectives of all stakeholders.

Existing Standards of Quality

The feasibility and appropriateness of changes to existing standards will depend directly on context and formal systems that have evolved over time.

Because accreditation in American higher education is a decentralized process and a unique and collective system of standards does not exist, the number of models, benchmarks, frameworks, and checklists intended to promote and guarantee quality in distance education has proliferated. Most accrediting agencies have expanded their existing standards to include distance learning, in recognition of the existing differences between distance- and traditional-learning models. Examples of such standards are offered by the Council for Higher Education Accreditation (2002), the Higher Learning Commission (2009), and the Southern Regional Education Board (2006). Several other associations and recognized organizations have developed their own sets of principles: the Sloan Consortium's quality framework and scorecard for quality administration (see chapter 3, "The Sloan Consortium Pillars and Quality Scorecard"), the International Association for K–12 Online Learning (see chapter 4, "K–12 Online Learning: Recommendations for Assuring Quality"), and Quality Matters (see chapter 6, "A Process to Improve Course Design: A Key Variable in Course Quality").

Given the extensive literature offering several proposals for frameworks, the task of developing a new framework that will focus on emerging technologies and disruptive innovations within the constraints of quality, cost, and access is accomplished by first considering an extension of Daniel's triangle proposed by Power and Morven-Gould (2011). In the revised triangle, the vectors are named "priorities" and the terms *cost* and *access* are replaced by *cost-effectiveness* and *accessibility*, respectively, to capture their nature as priorities. These revised terms better describe what is to be achieved. Moreover, the new triangle includes references to specific stakeholders: faculty, students, and administrators. These stakeholders are associated with their main priorities: "students are naturally most concerned about accessibility," "faculty will typically be defenders of quality" (Power & Morven-Gould, 2011, para. 20), and administrators are focused on ensuring the cost-effectiveness of the overall system (see Figure 2.1). This is exactly the approach taken herein, where the analysis of the impact of technologies and innovations depends on the stakeholders' roles.

Power and Morven-Gould (2011) argue that "each stakeholder group is naturally inclined to promote its own priority, thereby bringing the parties into conflict" (para. 20) and that for open distance learning to succeed, all groups will have to meet their own needs above a certain predetermined minimum threshold. Power and Morven-Gould describe the push-pull relationship among these three distinct groups. However, for the purposes of the quality framework envisioned herein, the push-pull argument is less meaningful and is not included here.

In 2003 Sherry recognized the intricate and close relationship among these same stakeholders (students, faculty, and administrators) when it comes to quality. She suggested that "learners are at the core of the distance

Figure 2.1. Revised iron triangle.

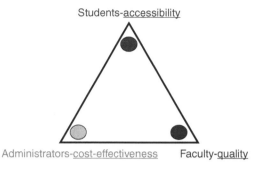

From "Head of Gold, Feet of Clay: The Online Learning Paradox," by T. Power and A. Morven-Gould, 2011, *International Review of Research in Open and Distance Learning, 12*(2), 19–39. Copyright 2011 by T. Power and A. Morven-Gould. Reprinted with permission.

learning picture" (p. 435) and that there are four main types of learner outcomes involved—attitudes, competencies, applications, and impacts. These outcomes require quality responses that are the responsibility of faculty and the institution. Therefore, Sherry's framework clearly underlines that quality should be analyzed with respect to these three different perspectives, even though there are interdependencies among them.

A Revised and Expanded Framework

The approach in this chapter is to combine Power and Morven-Gould's revised triangle with Sherry's quality assurance scheme, producing a revised and expanded framework for the adoption of disruptive innovations in online learning that addresses the fundamental elements and issues associated with quality assurance, while staying within the requirements of expanding access and reducing costs. The goal is to create a framework that considers different models of quality and questions how the adoption of emerging technologies and subsequent disruptive innovations modify or influence the quality expectations of the different stakeholders and how changes will affect decision making when attempting to balance quality, access, and cost.

The table created by Sherry (2003) offers a starting point, and I recommend that readers review the detailed table available in the *Handbook of Distance Education* (Moore & Anderson, 2003). Basically, Sherry's framework of quality outlines viewpoints to consider on topics important to learners, instructors, and institutions.

The new expanded table keeps the same distinct viewpoints but provides additional details relevant to the focus on emerging technologies and disruptive innovations (see Table 2.1). Table 2.1 takes into consideration the

TABLE 2.1
Revised and Expanded Viewpoints on Quality

	Institutional viewpoint	*Instructor's viewpoint*	*Learner's viewpoint*
Interaction	Provides at all levels (course, program, and university-wide) for timely, technology-supported faculty-student, student-student, and student-content interactions, through both synchronous and asynchronous means, as well as through diverse media.	Encourages student and faculty contact, providing clear guidelines and modeling appropriate behavior and protocol. Allows for teaching, cognitive, and social presence. Encourages and stimulates reciprocity and cooperation among students through appropriately designed discussions and assignments. Interaction is at the core of learning effectiveness. Technology is seamless and allows the instructor to focus on the subject matter and best use his or her expertise.	Connects learning activities to his or her own personal and professional experiences, enhancing the value of prior learning, both formal and informal. Interaction is cognitively relevant and provides a sense of belonging through social exchange. Participates in a highly interactive peer-learning community that provides tools for personalization to enhance interest and easiness of access. Facilitates collaboration among peers in an any where/any time environment.

(Continues)

TABLE 2.1 (Cont.)

	Institutional viewpoint	Instructor's viewpoint	Learner's viewpoint
e-Resources	Ensures students effective access and use of a wide variety of high-quality digital resources (e-resources) of diverse media types, including e-journals, digital databases, e-textbooks, e-books, videos, podcasts, and web-based tools for search and bookmarking. Provides incentives and appropriate means for faculty and students to engage in creating new content and shares resources with the wider community. Content becomes part of larger universe of accessible resources, expanding the opportunities for reuse, remixing, and repurposing. Provides appropriate virtual environments for conducting investigative, scientific, and other scholarly activities appropriate for and required by specific subjects.	Uses active learning techniques to promote creation of shareable content and use of existing open content and adds value to such resources when possible. Technology is accessible and requires acceptable effort to be embedded into the learning process. Creates possibilities for students to enhance their technology fluency and information literacy, developing strategies to assess the value and authenticity of e-resources.	Balances active and reflective modes of learning. Has easy access to a variety of resources that are well connected to the prescribed learning activities. E-resources are diverse enough to respond to the needs of different learning styles. More often than not, learner is responsible for engaging in collaborative learning activities and understands these activities' value and the expectations of peers and faculty.

	Institutional viewpoint	*Instructor's viewpoint*	*Learner's viewpoint*
Program evaluation and assessment	Ensures comparability of learning effectiveness between traditional, face-to-face programs when evaluating distance-education programs. Defines and employs quality measures that are based on accepted standards defined by appropriate outside groups/associations/agencies. Uses a diverse set of measures throughout its quality assurance process, including student satisfaction, learning outcomes, retention, and accepted rubrics for best practices in online education. Technology supports collection and analysis of data, which allows for an efficient full-quality assurance process that enables enhancements as well as needed innovations.	Gives prompt, rich, and personalized feedback to students and acknowledges students' effort and commitment. Sees the institution as supportive of teaching and assessment practices that take place within the learning environment through efficient and transparent use of technology. Understands that grading and marking are integral parts of assessment and uses technology for greater efficiency as well as to support integrity and ethical behaviors.	Foresees the possibility of feeling uncertain about learning online but understands the need for self-motivation and initiative in getting the necessary support. Understands the demands of the learning process and what is necessary to become an autonomous learner. Identifies elements that require change in direction and changes in behavior and thought process. Identifies the challenges to overcome and reaches out to the existing resources and support in order to be successful.

(Continues)

TABLE 2.1 (Cont.)

	Institutional viewpoint	Instructor's viewpoint	Learner's viewpoint
Monitoring and progress	Represents programs, requirements, and services accurately online. Monitors whether students make appropriate use of learning resources through appropriate and efficient technology. Uses technology to provide services that support students in a timely fashion, in a personalized online environment, using accurate data and through scalable means.	Uses technology to collect feedback from students to allow for a change of gears as well as summative feedback for enhancement of learning experiences and teaching practices. Emphasizes time on task through an appropriate course and curriculum structure, in which deadlines and due dates receive the appropriate emphasis.	Anticipates fluctuating patterns of learning in which more intense activity will be necessary at times. Uses the tools for self-diagnostics for improvement. Acquires better time-management skills and slowly becomes more autonomous. Develops technology fluency as a way to increase productivity and efficiency.
Planning and oversight	Provides 24/7 technical support to students in the use of technology for learning as well as other support services within the learners' life cycle. Provides the means for students, faculty, and staff to safely communicate complaints and to follow through processes with transparency. Technology supports operational processes, and data is collected and analyzed to help improvement.	Does not have to deal with administrative or tech support issues from students. Perceives students as connected to and supported by the institution. Has the opportunity and the means to provide feedback to the institution and receives acknowledgment and recognition for contributions.	Feels that his or her feedback is valued by faculty and the institution. Knows the mechanisms for providing feedback, which are easily accessible. Understands that his or her behavior online during instruction and use of services will help personalize his or her learning process.

	Institutional viewpoint	Instructor's viewpoint	Learner's viewpoint
	Ensures currency of e-resources, materials, programs, and courses. Values students' prior learning achievements, both formal and informal, and offers appropriate provisions for recognition of such achievements through credit points and other means.	Communicates high expectations. Offers challenging tasks, sample cases, and praise for quality work. Expects integrity and uses existing technology to ensure such behavior within courses.	Understands that the rhythm of learning fluctuates, which also affects the amount of time needed for course work. Understands clearly what is expected and perceives personal and professional growth through the learning experience. Learning experiences are relevant to personal and professional life.
	Assumes (at faculty level) oversight/ responsibility for rigor of programs and quality of instruction in distance education.	Offers engaging learning activities that explore diverse, easily accessible resources with appropriate and rich media.	
Curriculum design and development	Ensures integrity of student work, credits, and degrees, and uses appropriate technology as support. Makes distance education a viable part in all long-range planning, budgeting, and policy development. Provides clear distance-education policies on materials ownership, copyright, compensation packages, and revenue distribution.		

(Continues)

TABLE 2.1 (Cont.)

	Institutional viewpoint	Instructor's viewpoint	Learner's viewpoint
Support	Provides appropriate faculty support services for distance delivery. Provides adequate access to a range of academic and student support services through adequate and efficient technology, such as remedial instruction, community building, internships, and career advisement. Provides appropriate training and continuous professional development for distance-education faculty through the use of technology. Possesses appropriate equipment, technologies, and technical expertise for distance learning, providing possibilities for personalization and customization through the use of technology. Ensures technology used is appropriate to the nature and objectives of programs.	Respects diverse talents and ways of learning, by allowing students to choose project topics, and share diverse/diverging viewpoints. Seeks professional development in areas of study and in online pedagogical issues (teaching practice). Keeps abreast with newer technologies and seeks support from the teaching community. Uses technology to motivate students and to expand the horizons of the subject matter.	Perceives instruction as authentic and current. Perceives clear connections with work experience, promoting enhancement of knowledge as well as skills that can be used on the job. Perceives learning experience and support services as personalized and tailored to his or her needs.

Note. Adapted from "Quality and Its Measurement in Distance Education," by A. C. Sherry, 2003, in *Handbook of Distance Education*, edited by M. G. Moore and W. G. Anderson, pp. 435–459, Mahwah, NJ: Lawrence Erlbaum.

position expressed by Garrison and Anderson (2003) that "e-learning does not represent more of the same" (p. 7) and that we are witnessing a wave of new transformations as a result of technological advances and ubiquity. These changes are cumulative, and despite a few hypes and fads, the effects of such experiences are permanent and change the landscape of education. In that sense, quality and quality assurance have to be revisited and reexamined. Stakeholders take on distinct roles in the face of technological changes and will expect new behaviors from others accordingly. Institutions need to be aware that the support to students and faculty should encompass contextual variables as well. Students, as they become autonomous in their learning process, will slowly, through appropriate guidance, develop the necessary fluency to master the new medium, while navigating through the vast information stream. Interaction is seen as an essential piece of the learning process.

The distinct kinds of interaction—student-instructor, student-student, and student-content (M. G. Moore, 1989)—are all integral parts of learning, each playing a different role and displaying distinct challenges when considered through the lenses of quality, access, and cost. The importance of interaction is well understood through the Community of Inquiry (CoI) model (Garrison & Anderson, 2003). Interaction includes cognitive presence, social presence, and teaching presence. Cognitive presence "speaks to intent and actual learning outcomes" (Garrison & Anderson, 2003, p. 28). Social presence is related to the participants' projecting themselves socially and emotionally. Finally, teaching presence "is defined as the design, facilitation and direction of cognitive and social processes" toward the expected learning outcomes (Garrison & Anderson, 2003, p. 29). The teaching presence is the force that brings together the other two in a structured, meaningful, and purposeful form.

Learning Theories, Assessment, and Newer Technologies

Harasim (2012) discussed the connections between learning theories and newer technologies. She introduced online collaborative learning theory to describe the potential of teaching and learning within the knowledge society, building upon a constructivist approach and exploring further the wide spectrum of possibilities that have emerged with the Internet. This approach focuses on knowledge building through interaction. It encompasses formal and informal learning and connects the two as part of a lifelong continuum.

Although newer technologies have increased the potential and the reach of communication between learners and instructor, they have also altered the economies of scale of distance education, once based on distribution of materials. The easiness with which instructors can now communicate with students has an immediate impact on the costs of online education. Models that count on direct interaction as a main pillar of the learning experience can be crippling to scalability and sustainability. Many of the new emerging technologies tackle this limitation, and newer models of learning are based on social interaction, crowdsourcing, automated feedback generated from analytics, and peer-based learning.

One outcome of maturing technologies and the ability to self-publish and distribute via social networks is to free content creators from the constraints, and costs, of traditional publication and distribution. The definition of OER is broad, sometimes vague, and certainly increasingly promising. Downes (2011) offers a succinct, objective, but all-encompassing definition of OER: "Open educational resources are materials used to support education that may be freely accessed, reused, modified and shared by anyone." The deployment of OER raises the immediate question, How does one assess the quality of self-published or collaboratively published materials, which will depend on the reliability of their sources? As the OER movement matures, it is increasingly apparent that the appropriate use of these resources is not a natural consequence of their availability or even accessibility (Ehlers & Conole, 2010). For e-resources to be employed efficiently as part of the learning process, institutions must support faculty members, students, and staff in sifting through existing resources; have clear benchmarks for quality; and have adequate tools to choose and embed e-resources into effective course structures. This requires investment in technology and personnel. Establishing open educational practices will require different concerted strategies, as well as clear policies and procedures (Conole, 2010). It might require that institutions deploy more structure in management, teaching, and learning to fully use OER in a flexible but sustainable form.

Assessment and Accountability

Assessment of the newer, more widely used online distance-education formats has resulted in attention to assessment of quality. Hrabowski, Suess, and Fritz (2011) pointed out, "National standards of excellence are also emphasizing a culture of assessment" (p. 16). Accountability has come to the forefront of higher education and distance learning. To maintain comparability, learning objectives and program goals need to be independent from the mode of delivery, whereas learning activities should explore technologies and web-based resources to enforce authentic assessment and shared quality standards for course work, such as common rubrics and opportunities for feedback.

When it comes to assessment of online programs, quality assurance models should include several dimensions with clear mechanisms for capturing and analyzing feedback from different stakeholders, including faculty and students. Student satisfaction surveys when automated and used with other measurements can provide information concerning students' learning experiences. Quality assurance processes will need to focus on closing the loop, using data and analyses to improve service and instruction. This is usually when processes break down because the diagnostics of the causes for under-performance are not always conclusive and there is not enough time or staff to explore and test the possibilities. In the existing educational system, more often than not, quality assurance mechanisms are in place for the purpose of generating reports to send to agencies outside the institution. As a result, institutional decision makers are not given the opportunity to intervene in response to the needs of faculty and learners.

Newer technologies need to support the creation of valid automated and adaptive assessment tools, both formative and summative, at lower cost. These technologies should also support and facilitate the process of grading/marking and the inclusion of relevant feedback. Current trends in online education point toward competency-based assessment and performance-based assessment, and several of the current innovations will create different pathways for learning, which will be validated only if credible assessments are in place. Meanwhile, authentic assessment has been proven to produce richer and more meaningful learning experiences, and the use of rubrics supports the assessment process and consistency in evaluations.

Technology has propelled the use of data throughout all organizational processes, for analysis, for decision making, for improvement, and for better understanding stakeholders and variables that affect outcomes. This wave has also reached educational institutions, which have come to understand the power of capturing and analyzing large amounts of data from students. These data include how students behave inside the learning management system, how they access resources, how much time they spend in certain activities, and how they use other support services. Seizing data from all stakeholders—staff, faculty, and students—has the potential to allow for the understanding of individual patterns at a detailed level never available before (Hrabowski et al., 2011).

Analytics should be integrated with assessment. Capturing and correlating data from separate systems have the potential to shed light on students' performance and behavior, which will then help improve learning effectiveness. This kind of data mining can enable adaptive learning, in which students complete personalized activities with authentic and individualized feedback targeting their own instructional needs and learning styles. For some time, the new developments in technology targeting more personalized learning have meant more customization and therefore a higher cost per student, reduced scalability, and less access. Much of the current disruption in higher education coming from online education is a result of the new possibility of achieving customized "massification"—individualized instruction that reaches huge numbers of students.

Given the widening of possibilities for academic development through distinct educational paths, institutions will need to consider creative ways to absorb students with distinct achievements in their learning and working experience. Increasingly students have experienced a mix of formal and informal learning. Institutions must have processes and procedures to accommodate students from different walks of life and recognize and value what these students have already achieved through prior learning, as well as tools to assist in individualized learning paths. Education products can now be tailored to ever-smaller segments of the population that share specific interests. As educational technologies continue to develop, there will be more to choose from and more individualized learning paths available.

Final Remarks

Siemens and Tittenberger (2009) summarize well the two facets of the revolution dramatically affecting higher education: "Today, the duality of conceptual (new models of education, advancement of social learning theory) and technological (elearning, mobile devices, learning networks) revolutions offers the prospect of transformative change in teaching and learning" (p. 1). Despite the inspiring potential, there is a dichotomy in the possible results of technology in learning: On one hand, technology can create an expanded and richer learning experience; and on the other, when we look at the qualities of technological advances within the context of cost and access, it is clear that newer technologies are not all necessarily fit to respond to the growing demands of education. For example, in the various conceptions of openness, quality is seen through different lenses, and thus each conception mandates a distinct approach. These approaches will need to generate disruption at higher levels in order to make a difference for masses of people and allow for continuous improvement and reuse.

We are starting to see technologies accompanied by indispensable, scalable infrastructure that can respond effectively and efficiently to cost and access requirements without negatively affecting learning experiences. These new technologies have the potential to create significant disruptions because they directly affect underlying business models. They alter the tenets that once held quality dependent on high cost per learner and therefore on exclusivity. The reasons that once supported the need for exclusion are now being shaken by technology that has the potential to provide effective learning and wide access at tolerable cost—hence, the recent rediscovery of online educa-tion. A synergy of factors is in play: world economics, social demand for education, and advances in technology that have reduced cost and expanded access to information. Fulfilling the educational potential of these techno-logical advances will require new, unknown strategies; forward thinking from educational leaders; and solid research to help pave the way.

Note

1. The origin of the *x* in xMOOC is somewhat in question, but Stephen Downes (2013) suggests it stands for *extension*; that is, an xMOOC is an extension of, not part of the core, institutional offerings.

References

Aslanian, C. B., & Clinefelter, D. L. (2012). *Online college students 2012: Comprehen-sive data on demands and preferences*. Retrieved from the Learning House website: http://www.learninghouse.com/files/documents/resources/Online%20College%20Students%202012.pdf

Atwell, G. (2010). A radical definition of open education [web log post]. *Pontydysgu Bridge to Learning*. Retrieved from http://www.pontydysgu.org/2010/01/a-radical-definition-of-open-education/

The Chronicle of Higher Education. (2012). What you need to know about MOOC. Retrieved from http://chronicle.com/article/What-You-Need-to-Know-About/133475/

Conole, G. (2010). Defining open educational practices (OEP) [web log post]. *e4innovation*. Retrieved from http://e4innovation.com/?p=373

Council for Higher Education Accreditation (CHEA). (2002). *Accreditation and assuring quality in distance learning*. Retrieved from http://www.chea.org/Research/Accred-Distance-5-9-02.pdf

Daniel, J. (2011, December 15). *The technology revolution: Coming soon to postsec-ondary education*. Retrieved from the Commonwealth of Learning website: http://www.col.org/resources/speeches/2011presentation/Pages/2011-12-15a.aspx

Downes, S. (2011). Open educational resources: A definition [web log post]. *Half an Hour*. Retrieved from http://halfanhour.blogspot.com/2011/07/open-educational-resources-definition.html

Downes, S. (2013, April 9). What the 'x' in 'xMOOC' stands for. Retrieved from https://plus.google.com/109526159908242471749/posts/LEwaKxL2MaM

Educause. (2010). *7 things you should know about mobile apps for learning*. Retrieved from http://net.educause.edu/ir/library/pdf/ELI7060.pdf

Ehlers, U., & Conole, G. (2010). *Open educational practices: Unleashing the power of OER*. Retrieved from European Foundation for Quality in E-learning website: http://efquel.org/wp-content/uploads/2012/03/OEP_Unleashing-the-power-of-OER.pdf

Farmer, J. (2012). MOOCS: The new higher education? *e-Literate* [web log post]. Retrieved from http://mfeldstein.com/moocs-the-new-higher-education/

Garrison, D. R., & Anderson, T. (2003). *E-learning in the 21st century: A framework for research and practice.* London: Routledge/Falmer.

Harasim, L. (2012). *Learning theory and online technologies.* New York: Routledge.

Hewlett Foundation. (n.d.). *Open educational resources.* Retrieved from http://www. hewlett.org/programs/education-program/open-educational-resources

Higher Learning Commission. (2009). *Guidelines for the evaluation of distance education (On-line learning).* Retrieved from http://www.ncahlc.org/Document-Libraries/alpha-document-list.html

Hill, P. (2012, November 1). Online educational delivery models: A descriptive view. *Educause Review.* Retrieved from http://www.educause.edu/ero/article/online-educational-delivery-models-descriptive-view

Hrabowski, F. A., Suess, J., & Fritz, J. (2011, September–October). Assessment and analytics in institutional transformation. *Educause Review.* Retrieved from http://www. educause.edu/ero/article/assessment-and-analytics-institutional-transformation

Maslen, G. (2012, February 19). Worldwide student numbers forecast to double by 2025. *University World News.* Retrieved from http://www.universityworldnews. com/article.php?story=20120216105739999

Moore, J. (2005). *The Sloan Consortium quality framework and the five pillars.* Retrieved from the Sloan Consortium website: http://sloanconsortium.org/ publications/books/qualityframework.pdf

Moore, M. G. (1989). Three types of interaction. *American Journal of Distance Education, 3*(2), 1–6.

Moore, M. G., & Anderson, W. G. (Eds.). (2003). *Handbook of distance education.* Mahwah, NJ: Lawrence Erlbaum.

New Media Consortium. (2012). *Horizon report 2012 higher education edition.* Retrieved from http://www.nmc.org/publications/horizon-report-2012-higher-ed-edition

Olcott, D. (2012). OER perspectives: Emerging issues for universities. *Distance Education, 33*(2), 283–290.

Peters, O. (1983). Distance teaching and industrial production: A comparative interpretation in outline. In D. Sewart, D. Keegan, & B. Holmberg (Eds.), *Distance education: International perspectives* (pp. 95–103). London: Croom Helm.

Peters, O. (1998). *Learning and teaching in distance education: Analyses and interpretations from an international perspective.* Sterling, VA: Stylus.

Power, T., & Morven-Gould, A. (2011). Head of gold, feet of clay: The online learning paradox. *International Review of Research in Open and Distance Learning, 12*(2), 19–39. Retrieved from http://www.irrodl.org/index.php/irrodl/article/view/916

Reynolds, R. (2012). The future of open learning content hinges on ease of use [web log post]. *E-literate.* Retrieved from http://mfeldstein.com/the-future-of-open-learning-content-hinges-on-ease-of-use/

Sherry, A. C. (2003). Quality and its measurement in distance education. In M. G. Moore & W. G. Anderson (Eds.), *Handbook of distance education* (pp. 435–459). Mahwah, NJ: Lawrence Erlbaum.

Siemens, G. (2004). *Connectivism: A learning theory for the digital age.* Retrieved from http://www.elearnspace.org/Articles/connectivism.htm

Siemens, G. (2009). Open isn't so open anymore [web log post]. *Connectivism.* Retrieved from http://www.connectivism.ca/?p=198

Siemens, G., & Tittenberger, P. (2009). *Handbook on emerging technologies for learning.* Retrieved from http://elearnspace.org/Articles/HETL.pdf

Southern Regional Education Board (SREB). (2006). *Standards for quality online courses.* Retrieved from http://publications.sreb.org/2006/06T05_Standards_quality _online_courses.pdf

Veletsianos, G. (2010). A definition of emerging technologies. In G. Veletsianos (Ed.), *Emerging technologies.* Retrieved from http://www.aupress.ca/index.php/ books/120177

Wagner, E., & Ice, P. (2012, July 18). Data changes everything: Delivering on the promise of learning analytics in higher education. *Educause Review.* http://www. educause.edu/ero/article/data-changes-everything-delivering-promise-learning- analytics-higher-education

Wiley, D. (n.d.) *Defining the open in open content.* Retrieved from http://opencontent .org/definition/

3

THE SLOAN CONSORTIUM PILLARS AND QUALITY SCORECARD

Janet C. Moore and Kaye Shelton

In 2001, in the context of increasing accessibility for highly mobile military men and women, the Sloan Consortium designed a quality framework for measuring progress toward goals in each of five quality elements (Moore, 2001). The overlapping circles in Figure 3.1 intend to convey that the pillars are interdependent bases of quality education.

Because institutions have diverse missions, visions, and populations, the framework is purposely flexible so that institutions can gauge relative values and progress toward goals that are important in their contexts. The framework begins by articulating goals in the pillar areas and then selects metrics for measuring progress toward those goals (see Table 3.1).

The Pillars and the Quality Scorecard for the Administration of Online Education Programs

The Quality Scorecard for the Administration of Online Education Programs provides a way for institutions to evaluate administrative practices (Shelton, 2010). Developed through a Delphi study that surveyed experienced online administrators, the Quality Scorecard achieved consensus on the quality indicators that had been published a decade earlier by the Institute for Higher Education Policy (IHEP) (Merisotis & Phipps, 2000). The administrators agreed to keep or revise some of the original IHEP indicators, and they added new indicators. (For more information about the scorecard, visit http://sloanconsortium.org/quality_scorecard_online_program.)

In 2011 the Quality Scorecard for the Administration of Online Programs was introduced as an interactive benchmarking instrument that

Figure 3.1. The quality pillars.

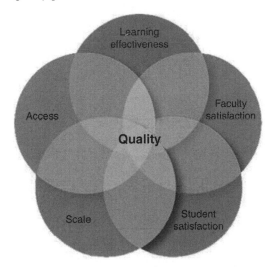

Note: Used with permission. Copyright 2001, Sloan Consortium.

institutions could use to compare their own scores with an aggregated score of all institutions that completed the scorecard or with specific institutions that agreed to share data (Sloan Consortium, 2011).

Quality Scorecard Indicators for Access

The overarching goal of access is that all learners who wish to learn online have the opportunity and can achieve success. In particular, online education is a primary means for expanding access to new populations of learners. Therefore, the scorecard assesses these administrative factors for access:

- Before starting an online program, students are advised about the program to determine if they possess the self-motivation and commitment to learn at a distance.*
- Before starting an online program, students are advised about the program to determine if they have access to the minimal technology required by the course design.*
- Students receive (or have access to) information about programs, including admission requirements, tuition and fees, books and supplies, technical and proctoring requirements, and student support services prior to admission and course registration.*
- Students are provided relevant information: ISBN numbers, suppliers, and delivery modes for all supplies required and instructional materials in easily accessible formats, whether digital, e-pack, or print.

TABLE 3.1
The Sloan-C Quality Framework

Goal	Process/practice	Sample metric	Progress indexes
Access			
All learners who wish to learn online can access learning in a wide array of programs and courses.	Program entry processes inform learners of opportunities and ensure that qualified, motivated learners have reliable access. Integrated support services are available online to learners.	Administrative and technical infrastructure provides access to all prospective and enrolled learners. Quality metrics are used for information dissemination, learning resources delivery, and tutoring services.	Qualitative indicators show continuous improvement in growth and effectiveness rates.
Learning effectiveness			
The provider demonstrates that online learning outcomes meet or exceed institutional, industry, or community standards.	Academic integrity and control reside with faculty in the same way as in traditional programs at the provider institution or organization.	Faculty perception surveys or sampled interviews compare learning effectiveness in delivery modes. Learner/graduate/employer focus groups or interviews measure learning gains.	Faculty report online learning is equivalent or better. Direct assessment of student learning is equivalent or better.
Scale (cost-effectiveness and commitment)			
The provider continuously improves services while reducing costs.	The provider demonstrates financial and technical commitment to its online programs. Tuition rates provide a fair return to the provider and best value to learners at the same time. Tuition rates are equivalent to or less than place-based tuition.	Institutional and organizational stakeholders show support for participation in online education. Effective practices are identified and implemented.	The provider sustains the program, expands and scales upward as desired, and strengthens and disseminates its mission and core values through online education.

Goal	Process/practice	Sample metric	Progress indexes
Faculty satisfaction			
Faculty are pleased with teaching online, citing appreciation and happiness.	Processes ensure faculty participation in matters particular to online education (e.g., governance, intellectual property, and royalty sharing). Processes ensure adequate support for faculty in course preparation and course delivery.	Repeat teaching of online courses by individual faculty indicates approval. Addition of new faculty shows growing endorsement.	Data from postcourse surveys show continuous improvement: At least 90% of faculty believe the overall online teaching/learning experience is positive. At least 80% of faculty are willing or want to teach additional courses in the program.
Student satisfaction			
Students are pleased with their experiences in learning online, including interaction with instructors and peers, learning outcomes that match expectations, and quality services including orientation.	Faculty/learner interaction is timely and substantive. Adequate and fair systems assess course learning objectives; results are used for improving learning.	Metrics show growing satisfaction, per the following: • surveys or interviews • alumni surveys, referrals, or testimonials • outcomes measured • focus group feedback • faculty/mentor/adviser perceptions	Satisfaction measures show continuously increasing improvement. Provider surveys, interviews, or other metrics show satisfaction levels are equivalent to or better than those of other delivery modes for the provider.

- Instructional materials are easily accessible and usable for the student.
- Documents attached to modules are in a format that is easily accessed with multiple operating systems and productivity software (e.g., PDF).
- The institution ensures that all distance-education students, regardless of where they are located, have access to library/learning resources adequate to support the courses they are taking.*
- The course adequately addresses the special needs of disabled students via alternative instructional strategies or referral to special institutional resources.
- Policy and process is in place to support Americans with Disabilities Act (ADA) requirements.
- Technology is used as a tool to achieve learning outcomes in delivering course content.*
- Links or explanations of technical support are available in the course.
- The technology delivery systems are highly reliable and operable, and measurable standards, such as system downtime tracking or task benchmarking, are used.*
- A documented technology plan that includes electronic security measures (e.g., password protection, encryption, and secure online or proctored exams) is in place and operational to ensure quality standards, adherence to the Family Educational Rights and Privacy Act (FERPA), and the integrity and validity of information.*

An asterisk (*) denotes that the indicator was one of the original IHEP indicators.

Quality Scorecard Indicators for Learning Effectiveness

The goal for the learning effectiveness pillar is that the provider demonstrates that online learning outcomes meet or exceed institutional, industry, or community standards. It is widely accepted that there is no significant difference for learning outcomes based solely on delivery mode (Russell, 2001; WCET, 2010). The scorecard assesses these administrative factors for learning effectiveness:

- Instructors use specific strategies to create a presence in the course.
- Course design promotes both faculty and student engagement.
- Student-to-student interaction and faculty-to-student interaction are essential characteristics and are facilitated through a variety of ways.*
- Student-centered instruction is considered during the course-development process.
- Opportunities/tools are provided to encourage student-student collaboration (e.g., web conferencing, instant messaging).

- Guidelines regarding minimum standards are used for course development, design, and delivery of online instruction.*
- Instructional materials, course syllabi, and learning outcomes are reviewed periodically to ensure they meet program standards.*
- Learning objectives describe outcomes that are measurable.
- Feedback on student assignments and questions is constructive and provided in a timely manner.*
- The online course site includes a syllabus outlining course objectives, learning outcomes, evaluation methods, textbook information, and other related course information, making course requirements transparent at time of registration.*
- Expectations for student assignment completion, grade policy, and faculty response are clearly provided in the course syllabus.*
- Selected assessments measure the course learning objectives and are appropriate for an online learning environment.
- Intended learning outcomes at the course and program level are reviewed regularly to ensure clarity, utility, and appropriateness.*
- Alignment of learning outcomes from course to course exists.
- Course evaluations collect student feedback on quality of content and effectiveness of instruction.
- There is consistency in course development for student retention and quality.
- Current and emerging technologies are evaluated and recommended for online teaching and learning.
- Instructional design is provided for the creation of effective pedagogy for both synchronous and asynchronous class sessions.

An asterisk (*) denotes that the indicator was one of the original IHEP indicators.

Quality Scorecard Indicators for Scale

The goal of the scale pillar (formerly, institutional commitment and cost-effectiveness) is that providers continuously improve services while reducing cost to achieve capacity enrollment. The proliferation of business and delivery models (Hill, 2012) has given rise to the use of the term *postmodal* to describe the evolution of learning organizations that enable learners to mix and match delivery modes (Cavanaugh, 2012). In any combination of business and delivery model, a core value of scale is sustaining growth by avoiding, reducing, or sharing time and effort to lower the cost of education to learners and to organizations (Bishop, 2007).

Innovations and competition thrive in today's industry. Thus, when the provider recognizes the value of online education and communicates its strategic value to its shareholders, it must also create a governance structure for mission-based decision making that defines the desired "capacity enrollment" and takes advantage of affordances as they emerge. The scorecard assesses these administrative factors for scale:

- The institution has defined the strategic value of distance learning to its enterprise and to its relevant parts.
- The institution has put in place a governance structure to enable effective and comprehensive decision making related to distance learning.
- A centralized system provides support for building and maintaining the distance-education infrastructure.*
- The course delivery technology is considered a mission-critical enterprise system and supported as such.
- The institution maintains system backup for data availability.
- Faculty, staff, and students are supported in the development and use of new technologies and skills.
- The program is assessed through an evaluation process that applies specific established standards.*
- A variety of data (academic and administrative information) are used to regularly and frequently evaluate program effectiveness and to guide changes toward continual improvement.*
- A process is in place for the assessment of faculty and student support services.
- Course and program retention is assessed.
- Course evaluations are examined in relation to faculty performance evaluations.
- The program demonstrates compliance and review of accessibility standards (e.g., Section 508).
- Recruitment and retention are examined and reviewed.

  An asterisk (*) denotes that the indicator was one of the original IHEP indicators.

Quality Scorecard Indicators for Faculty Satisfaction

The goal for this pillar is that faculty members are pleased with teaching online, citing appreciation and happiness. As expert learners themselves, faculty members are the heart of the learning organization. Yet less than one-third of chief academic officers believe that their faculty accept the value and legitimacy of online education; moreover, "academic leaders that believe it takes more faculty time and effort to teach online has increased from 41.4 percent in 2006 to 44.6 percent this year" (Allen & Seaman, 2013).

From the administrative perspective, the Quality Scorecard indicators intend to ensure that faculty members have training and access to ongoing professional development, have continuous academic assistance, have technical support and information about emerging technologies, are aware of policies, participate in curriculum development, and have regular performance assessments. The scorecard assesses these administrative factors for faculty satisfaction:

- Instructors are prepared to teach distance-education courses, and the institution ensures that faculty members receive training, assistance, and support at all times during the development and delivery of courses.*
- Technical assistance in course development and assistance with the transition to teaching online is provided for faculty.*
- Faculty members receive training and materials related to fair use, plagiarism, and other relevant legal and ethical concepts.*
- Faculty members are provided ongoing professional development related to online teaching and learning.
- Clear standards are established for faculty engagement and expectations around online teaching.
- Faculty workshops are provided to make instructors aware of emerging technologies and the selection and use of these tools.
- Policy for copyright ownerships of course materials exists.
- Faculty performance is regularly assessed.
- Curriculum development is a core responsibility for faculty.

    An asterisk (*) denotes that the indicator was one of the original IHEP indicators.

Quality Scorecard Indicators for Student Satisfaction

The goal of the student satisfaction pillar is that students are pleased with their experiences in learning online, including interaction with instructors and peers, learning outcomes that match expectations, and quality services including orientation. As a consequence of their good experiences, students will become lifelong learners. The scorecard assesses these administrative factors for ensuring student satisfaction:

- Program demonstrates a student-centered focus rather than trying to fit service to the distance-education student in on-campus student services.
- Students should be provided a way to interact with other students in an online community.
- Efforts are made to engage students with the program and institution.
- Students are provided access to library professionals and resources that help them to deal with the overwhelming number of online resources.

- Tutoring is available as a learning resource.
- Throughout the duration of the course/program, students have access to appropriate technical assistance and technical support staff.*
- The institution provides guidance to both students and faculty in the use of all forms of technologies used for course delivery.
- Students have access to effective academic, personal, and career counseling.
- Students are provided with access to training and information they will need to secure required materials through electronic databases, interlibrary loans, government archives, new services, and other sources.*
- Students are instructed in the appropriate ways to enlist help from the program.
- Students are instructed in the appropriate ways of communicating with faculty and students.
- Student support services, such as academic advising, financial assistance, and peer support, are provided outside the classroom.
- Student support personnel are available to address student questions, problems, bug reports, and complaints.*
- Policies are in place to authenticate that students enrolled in online courses and receiving college credit are indeed those completing the course work.
- Minimum technology standards are established and made available to students.
- Courses are designed so that students develop the necessary knowledge and skills to meet learning objectives at the course and program level. These skills may include engagement via analysis, synthesis, and evaluation.*

An asterisk (*) denotes that the indicator was one of the original IHEP indicators.

Conclusion

The foundations of a learning organization—access, learning effectiveness, faculty and student satisfaction, and scale—are also the foundations of a learning society, in which the university's role is to understand and advance its society's capability to scale learning: "The more [the university] widens access to all members of society to benefit from the fruits of the research, the more it supports a genuine 'learning society'" (Laurillard, 1999, p. 120). Benchmarking learning systems promotes more effective practices, greater efficiencies, and innovations. The quality framework and quality scorecard—particularly when the results of using them are made publicly available

(San Jose State University, 2012)—provide opportunity to advance toward the goal of making education accessible to anyone who is qualified and motivated to learn.

References

Allen, I. E., & Seaman, J. (2013). *Changing course: Ten years of tracking online education in the United States.* Retrieved from Babson Survey Research Group website: http://www.onlinelearningsurvey.com/reports/changingcourse.pdf

Bishop, T. (2007). *Research highlights: Cost effectiveness of online education.* Retrieved from the Sloan Consortium website: http://sloanconsortium.org/publications/freedownloads

Cavanaugh, T. B. (2012). The postmodality era: How "online learning" is becoming "learning." In *Game changers: Education and information technologies.* Washington, DC: Educause. Retrieved from http://www.educause.edu/research-publications/books/game-changers-education-and-information-technologies

Hill, P. (2012, November–December). Online educational delivery models: A descriptive view. *Educause Review.* Retrieved from http://www.educause.edu/ero/article/online-educational-delivery-models-descriptive-view

Laurillard, D. (1999). A conversational framework for individual learning applied to the "learning organisation" and the "learning society." *Systems Research & Behavioural Science, 16*(2), 113–122.

Merisotis, J. P., & Phipps, R. A. (2000). *Quality on the line: Benchmarks for success in Internet-based distance education.* Retrieved from the Institute for Higher Education Policy website: http://www.ihep.org/Publications/publications-detail.cfm?id=69

Moore, J. C. (2001). *Elements of quality: The Sloan-C framework.* Nashville, TN: Sloan Center for Online Education.

Russell, T. B. (2001). *The no significant difference phenomenon* (5th ed.). Chicago: International Distance Education Certification Center.

San Jose State University. (2012, January 21). *Sloan-C Quality Scorecard.* Retrieved from https://slisweb.sjsu.edu/about-slis/scorecard

Shelton, K. (2010, December). A Quality Scorecard for the Administration of Online Education Programs: A Delphi study. *Journal of Asynchronous Learning Networks, 14*(4), 36–62.

Sloan Consortium. (2011). *A Quality Scorecard for the Administration of Online Education Programs.* Retrieved from http://sloanconsortium.org/quality_scorecard_online_program

WCET. (2010). *The no significant difference phenomenon.* Retrieved from http://www.nosignificantdifference.org

4

K–12 ONLINE LEARNING

Recommendations for Assuring Quality

Susan Patrick, Matthew Wicks, and Allison Powell

Online learning in K–12 public education is a rapidly expanding field. In 2001 it was estimated that there were between 40,000 and 50,000 total online learning enrollments in the United States (Clark, 2001), and by 2011 the number of K–12 distance-learning enrollments was pegged at more than 1.8 million (Queen & Lewis, 2011), an estimate that most likely did not include most of the more than 200,000 full-time online learning students (Watson, Murin, Vashaw, Gemin, & Rapp, 2011).

In the early days of K–12 online learning, from the mid-1990s to early 2000s, institutions focused on how to start, grow, and sustain online programs. Research studies found that there was no significant difference in students' achievement in traditional classrooms compared with their achievement in online classrooms. As the field of online learning expanded, practitioners became interested in best practices related to course development and online instruction.

From 2001 to 2006, groups such as the Texas Education Agency (TEA), North Central Regional Educational Laboratory (NCREL), National Education Association (NEA), Monterey Institute for Technology and Education (MITE), and Southern Regional Education Board (SREB) began to develop rubrics, guidelines, and criteria for selecting online content. In 2001 TEA developed the *Quality of Service Guidelines for Online Courses* to begin to improve the quality of Internet-based courses for Texas students. In 2002 NCREL released the *Evaluating Course-Equivalent Online Learning Products* rubric to assist districts in their attempts to choose online course materials for students. NEA released the *Guide to Online High School Courses* to provide criteria for a number of important issues for policy makers, administrators, teachers, parents, and students to consider when contemplating creating, adopting, administering, or participating in online courses (NEA, 2006a). Next, MITE released the *Online Course Evaluation Project* in 2006 to provide a criteria-based evaluation tool for assessing and comparing the quality of online courses while focusing on content presentation and pedagogy. SREB released the *Standards for Quality Online Courses* in October 2006 (SREB, 2006a). These standards examined the essential components of high-quality online courses for learners and the increased emphasis on accountability. They also addressed the need for state-level policies regarding online course quality. The standards released by SREB proved to be comprehensive and in line with what the field believed to be true of high-quality online courses, but only a small region in the southeast corner of the country was aware of them at the time.

In the area of online teaching, NEA and SREB had also published guidelines and criteria for high-quality online teachers. So had the Ohio Department of Education and the Electronic Classroom of Tomorrow (ECOT), located in Ohio. NEA published the *Guide to Teaching Online Courses*, which focused on teaching skills, professional development, and the overall improvement to online teaching (NEA, 2006b). In 2004 Ohio Senate Bill 2, which included many of the recommendations made by the Governor's Commission on Teaching Success in the areas of standards, teacher preparation, recruitment and retention, and professional development, passed into law. The law required the authoring of *Standards for the Teaching Profession* (Ohio Department of Education, 2005), which addressed both online and face-to-face teaching. At the same time, ECOT developed the *Teacher Evaluation Rubric*, a collaborative evaluation tool to assess the quality of online teaching (ECOT, 2005). However, a comprehensive set of standards for high-quality online teaching was not developed until 2006, when SREB released *Standards for Quality Online Teaching*, which examined the qualifications needed to be a high-quality online teacher and outlined specific standards for academic preparation, content knowledge, online skills and delivery, and more (SREB, 2006b). This publication was made available in the southeastern region of the United States.

In 2006 the members of the International Association for K–12 Online Learning (iNACOL), which includes a wide cross section of educators in the field of K–12 online learning, requested that the organization develop a set of quality standards that would be recognized at a national level and could be voluntarily adopted and adapted by states, universities, districts, and schools around the world in a variety of ways. Thus, from 2006 to 2007, iNACOL conducted a literature review of the existing course-quality standards across the United States, developed a research survey of the existing criteria, and published the first industry-wide *National Standards of Quality for Online*

Courses (iNACOL, 2007) aimed at K–12 online learning. Later, iNACOL conducted similar literature reviews and research surveys leading to the publication of the iNACOL *National Standards for Quality Online Teaching* in 2008 and the iNACOL *National Standards for Quality Online Programs* in 2009. Most recently, iNACOL revised and published a second edition of the existing *National Standards for Quality Online Courses* (iNACOL, 2011a) and *National Standards for Quality Online Teaching* (iNACOL, 2011b).

Development of Quality Standards and Literature Review

In 2007 iNACOL developed its first set of quality standards, *National Standards for Quality Online Courses*. iNACOL formed expert committees to review all the current literature, research, and standards that had been published regarding online courses. The organization then developed a survey using the criteria for quality listed throughout the literature. Using leading experts' institutional online learning programs, iNACOL sent out a survey to validate the most significant criteria for quality standards. The iNACOL national quality standards were thus developed based on the experience and knowledge of expert practitioners and researchers in K–12 online learning. The result of iNACOL's survey was a robust set of standards that endorsed SREB's regional work in online course quality standards and included a few additional standards.

In 2008 iNACOL followed the same process to develop quality standards for K–12 online teaching. For the teaching standards, committees conducted a literature review, developed a list of overarching criteria for online instruction quality elements, and conducted a survey of experts in the field. iNACOL's survey results similarly examined and endorsed 11 of SREB's (2006b) *Standards for Quality Online Teaching*. Some of the SREB indicators were deleted, and other quality criteria, including two additional standards from the Ohio Department of Education (2005) and ECOT (2005), were added based on the results of the review and survey.

In 2008–2009 iNACOL began to develop quality standards for online learning programs. Although there were rubrics from accreditation of online programs, some work in higher education, and individual program evaluations, no set of published or existing quality standards addressed all the necessary areas of quality at the program level. As a result, the quality standards for online programs relied heavily on expert practitioners to develop criteria for quality standards from a number of existing sources, which are listed as references within those published standards. Once program-level quality standards were developed, a survey instrument was compiled for experts in the field, and the highest-ranked criteria were included in the *National Standards for Quality Online Programs* (iNACOL, 2009).

In 2011 iNACOL began to update and publish a new version of the quality standards for both online courses and online teaching. To refresh the standards, iNACOL again reviewed literature across the field, conducted an analysis of additional existing standards such as Quality Matters (2010), Blackboard's (2007) *Greenhouse Exemplary Course Evaluation Rubric*, and the Illinois Online Network's (1996) *Quality Online Course Initiative Rubric*.[1] After reviewing these criteria, new studies, and other documents, iNACOL conducted new professional reviews of the criteria and developed surveys to update the quality standards. Although the updated criteria included the majority of the standards from the original documents, iNACOL bolstered the standards with the addition of rubrics, course reviewer considerations, and teacher abilities checklists to make the documents more applicable for practitioners. In addition, for course standards, information related to the dimension of blended learning models is included as an indication that the course standards may apply to both blended and online courses.

Existing Practices

Background on Existing Practices Using Quality Standards

iNACOL's (2011a, b) updated course and teaching standards were designed to assist K–12 online programs in selecting and developing high-quality online content and in preparing and evaluating online teachers. The original iNACOL standards were developed in 2007 and 2008 based on the need of practitioners from the field of K–12 online learning to evaluate quality online courses, teachers, and programs. In the early 2000s, schools, districts, and states were looking for resources to assist with selecting high-quality courses. They wanted to know which attributes defined a high-quality course. Standards were developed and adopted voluntarily by school districts and states as they created programs or their own content resources.

Like evaluating digital content, the practice of preparing teachers to teach in the online environment was new. The knowledge, skills, and understanding of using online learning pedagogy, methods, and technology—as well as evaluating these—were new to K–12 teachers. iNACOL (2011b) informed the professional development providers who created online teacher preparation programs. Online programs, districts, and schools began using these teaching standards when hiring and evaluating online instructors. States such as Georgia created online teaching licensure endorsements using these standards.

Use of the Current Quality Standards by Governments, Institutions, Programs, and Schools

Oversight and Quality Assurance

Oversight and quality assurance for K–12 online learning is currently conducted by regional accreditation groups, state governments, and districts. iNACOL worked with the Northwest Accreditation Commission, Middle States Association of Colleges and Schools, and Western Association of Schools and Colleges to develop iNACOL (2009). These standards were developed to assist the regional accreditation organizations in the process of accrediting online programs because their quality criteria for brick-and-mortar schools did not always translate to the online environment.

Since the original course standards were created in 2007, many state departments of education have started to evaluate and authorize online content providers and individual courses. Many of these departments have adapted iNACOL (2007, 2011a) to develop their processes. The standards have been used to create rubrics to determine whether specific courses meet each of the quality standards. The states also evaluate content to determine whether it is aligned with their individual state academic standards and the Common Core State Standards.

Policies and Examples

A few states have adopted policies to assure quality within their online learning programs. For example, in the state of Washington, Watson et al. (2011) reported that the Digital Learning Department

> created a process and set of criteria for approving multidistrict online providers (RCW 28A.250.020). All grandfathered-approved providers are exempt from the initial approval process until August 31, 2012, but must comply with the process for renewal of approvals and approval requirements. ESHB2065 [Engrossed Substitute House Bill 2065] changes the process by requiring that with the 2013–14 school year all programs seeking ALE [Alternative Learning Experience] funding, not just those serving students from multiple districts, be approved. (p. 162)

The state of Texas, through the Texas Virtual School Network (TxVSN), adopted both the course and teaching standards for review and approval of online courses and professional development programs. Watson et al. (2011) reported that "the online courses were reviewed to determine whether they met the Texas Essential Knowledge and Skills (TEKS) standards, as well as iNACOL [2011a] standards. It was determined that all courses offered through TxVSN statewide courses catalog are reviewed prior to inclusion in the catalog"

(p. 154). In addition, each teacher teaching an online course for TxVSN must be certified in the state of Texas in addition to meeting "the professional development requirements of the network for effective online instruction," which are based on mastery of iNACOL (2011a) (Watson et al., 2011, p. 154).

The California Learning Resource Network (CLRN) is a state-funded project that reviews a variety of digital tools and content used for learning against the Common Core State Standards and California's original state standards. Leaders from CLRN and TxVSN cochaired iNACOL's committee to refresh the course standards in 2011. The criteria and considerations of iNACOL (2011a) are the main criteria used for CLRN's online course reviews (CLRN, 2011).

The Indiana Department of Education created requirements for a virtual instruction teaching license under Indiana Senate Bill 179 (2012). The Department of Education contracted with a private consultant to develop a set of educator standards to support this new license. The standards, which were approved in July 2012, are heavily based on iNACOL (2011b). From this set of standards, a state licensure exam is being created.

Other policies in states such as Florida, Massachusetts, Nevada, South Carolina, and South Dakota have also stated that all programs and courses must meet iNACOL's or similar quality standards before being offered in the state (Watson et al., 2011).

Several universities and nonprofit organizations have contacted iNACOL since the release of the standards seeking permission to create professional development programs for online teachers based on iNACOL (2011b). Course content, assignments, and assessments for these programs were developed from the standards. In addition, several online programs around the world have adapted iNACOL (2011b) to develop online teacher evaluation tools.

Quality Standards and Improvement of Practice at the Content, Teaching, and Program Levels

Content Reviews

One role of iNACOL (2011a) is to serve as a basis for course reviews either for a self-evaluation or for an external review or evaluation. Review of online courses for compliance with the iNACOL standards by a knowledgeable independent party provides valuable information about the strengths and weaknesses of specific online courses. The organization that developed the courses can use this information to improve the specific courses reviewed and can also apply the lessons learned from the reviews in future course development activities, thus improving the course quality of those courses as well.

Hiring of Teachers, Professional Development, and Evaluation

iNACOL (2011b) provides criteria to ensure that teachers are able to effectively work with students in online learning environments. These standards focus on communication, pedagogy, assessment, safety, accessibility, and instructional design.

In the 2011 edition of the online teaching standards (iNACOL, 2011b), the indicators for a teacher's knowledge and understanding were published along with a complete set of indicators for abilities a teacher must have in order to demonstrate the standard. These indicators were added in the new version for evaluators and professional developers who wanted to better understand the best and most promising practices for each of the standards. The standards are now easier to adapt when creating training and evaluation tools to prepare and evaluate online teachers.

Program Evaluation

As iNACOL (2009) stated, "A quality online program recognizes the value of program evaluation" (p. 17). Both internal and external evaluations are critical components for ongoing program improvement. Internal evaluations provide an opportunity for immediate feedback on the efficacy of specific aspects of the program, allowing for an iterative approach in program design.

External evaluations provide a fresh set of eyes and allow program administrators to better understand their program's strengths and weaknesses. They also provide the opportunity to design and implement the processes for ongoing data gathering, which will assist the program in understanding the most effective ways to monitor program performance.

What the Existing Standards Do and Don't Do

iNACOL (2011b) provides teachers, administrators, and professional developers with a set of criteria for effective online learning and aims to prepare teachers to better understand technology, new teaching methods, and digital course content so that they can foster a personalized online learning environment for every student. iNACOL (2011a) offers an important measuring tool to help policy leaders, schools, and parents across the nation evaluate course quality and implement best practices. These tools are a valuable resource for practitioners in the field of K–12 online learning who need to select, create, and implement high-quality learning and teaching opportunities for all students using the online environment.

Today, the criteria help K–12 educators understand the standards that are important for course, teaching, and program quality. Ultimately, a set of performance metrics that examines quality assurance for online learning with a focus on student outcomes and individual student growth on learning trajectories must be developed. Such a set of metrics would ensure that online learning could capitalize on its power to offer student-centered and personalized learning environments and that the field would progress toward higher-quality learning experiences for all students.

Status of K-12 Education Quality Assurance Versus K-12 Online Learning Quality Assurance

One of the issues with quality assurance in K–12 education is that most traditional school environments are measured using only inputs. Focusing solely on inputs, such as attendance based on seat time, curriculum inputs, and certifications in the field, means starting from a flawed set of measures. Some of these inputs, in fact, do not assure quality in traditional educational programs, but they are used because they are easy to measure. For example, student-teacher ratios are a common and important quality input criterion for traditional classroom instruction. This factor is relevant for online instruction, but depending on the instructional model and level of learning objectives, skills, and knowledge development, it doesn't necessarily have the same impact. One must be concerned with the number of students in a traditional physical classroom, but what exactly is the online equivalent of such a physical classroom? In addition, some models of online learning change the interaction between teacher and student and may even create entirely new instructional roles. In some cases, these new roles allow teachers to effectively teach a larger number of students by providing students more one-on-one time with teachers than a traditional classroom could provide.

Seat time is an example of an even more problematic input-based quality metric. Even in a traditional classroom, using seat time as a quality metric does not take into account the reality that students learn at different rates. However, when applied to online learning, the issue of seat time raises the question, What learning activities constitute seat time?

The iNACOL national quality standards were developed based on the experience and opinions of expert practitioners and were also largely input-based, focusing on the essential elements, critical success factors, and conditions that are necessary for high-quality online learning implementations. The existing quality standards for courses, teaching, and programs are useful in moving the field forward toward evaluating courses, teaching, and programs. However, ultimately, the measurement of input-based standards alone does not ensure quality in the growth of student learning outcomes. Thus, the next stage in quality assurance for K–12 online learning is the development of outcome-based quality standards and performance metrics for student learning.

In the past 10 years, full-time public online schools have been held to the same standards as traditional public schools, using end-of-the-year state assessments and the accountability system mandated by No Child Left Behind. Although there are a variety of problems with the current system, one of the most significant is that the state assessments do not measure individual student growth trajectories from the time a student has entered a particular course or program to the time he or she exits. Thus, an eighth-grade student who began the year at a fifth-grade reading level and ended the year at a seventh-grade reading level would still likely be measured as a student not meeting standards, despite having made two years of academic progress in a one-year period. Measuring levels of proficiency upon entry and exit is critical to determining proficiency, student academic achievement, and growth related to program effectiveness and quality.

Online schools receive a diverse array of students. The common thread among these students is that they are looking for increased flexibility and student-centered learning. Some online students are advanced; however, many students who have not been successful in traditional education seek a flexible environment that allows learning any time, any place. A large number of online students enrolling in later high school grade levels are behind in grade level, overage, and undercredited. Outcome-based measures need to be developed to go beyond once-a-year accountability data and account for this type of student population. Without an assessment system that focuses on student growth at multiple points throughout the year—measured with multiple assessments, even in the 12th grade—these schools will struggle with the students who transfer in later grades with severe credit deficiencies. On top of the flawed assessment system and these challenges for full-time online schools, the current accountability system does not even include supplemental online courses and programs.

We will avoid going into a full review of assessment and accountability systems. Suffice it to say that unless an accountability system is measuring unique, individual student growth along a student's individual trajectory, it will not provide the transparent growth data needed to determine quality based on student learning outcomes. Using performance metrics based on student learning growth to examine effectiveness is needed at the course level and the program level.

The Need for Outcome-Based Quality Assurance

The online education field today does not differentiate among learning models based on how well they support student learning. Course providers do not systematically collect and share student outcome data, and buyers (typically school districts or state authorizing agencies) generally do not evaluate options based on student achievement. Often, the marketplace emphasizes cost (building or buying cheaper courses and content and minimizing teacher time) rather than the effective use of technology. This is driving what we might describe as a "race to the bottom" that affects students, schools, and providers seeking to provide high-quality options.

If this situation persists, the field of online and blended learning could ultimately contribute little to improving student outcomes (see Figure 4.1). If access expands without assurance that the models available to students are effective, the field may grow, but it is unlikely that it will achieve the educational outcomes we seek. Once it has expanded, the field will also be difficult to reshape. Once low-quality models are in place, it will be difficult to improve their effectiveness or replace them with more effective courses, content, and assessments.

To avoid this scenario, it is essential that the online education field differentiate between high- and low-quality options for students. High-quality, effective courses and content must be recognized as such, become more available to students, and receive the funding they need to thrive. Similarly, lower-quality, less effective courses and content must be identified and made less available to students and less able to receive the funding necessary to continue. Only then will the field of online and blended learning achieve its full potential.

Figure 4.1. iNACOL Strategic plan, June, 2011.

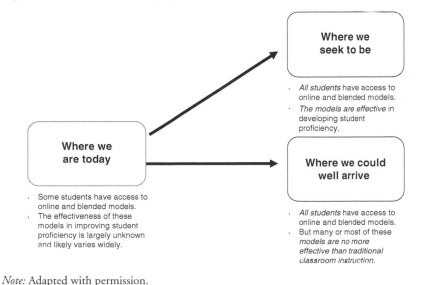

Note: Adapted with permission.

Recommendations

Although recommendations for improving quality assurance practices in K–12 online and blended learning are embedded throughout the chapter, this section summarizes policy recommendations that will help to improve quality at the federal, state, and district/school level.

Federal Policy Recommendations

- Provide incentives for states to use multiple measures of success and include accountability models that measure individual student learning growth on a trajectory.
- Provide incentives for states to establish multiple testing windows for summative assessments throughout the year so that true student progress and growth can be measured in real-time intervals.

State Policy Recommendations

- Move from input-based quality assurance to outcome-based quality assurance using multiple performance metrics. Individual student learning growth and performance is a key metric and should be based on trajectories comparing entry proficiency levels to exit proficiency levels and measuring growth at multiple points throughout the year. Other metrics to consider include proficiency levels, increase in graduation rates longitudinally, closing the achievement gap, increases in student learning productivity (more learning within a given unit of time), college and career readiness, alignment with student-centered goals, and production of the most growth in the most challenged youth.
- Understand and recognize the role quality standards (course quality standards, teaching standards, program standards) based on inputs may play in creating critical success factors, while focusing on outcomes as a measure of the success and effectiveness of innovative K–12 online learning programs.
- Pilot outcome-based performance metrics in programs to conduct research on effectiveness; consider wider adoption with the evaluation of successful metrics.
- Consider a state clearinghouse of multiple, approved online learning providers and online courses with evidence of accreditation and transparent program effectiveness data.
- Create a level playing field for quality assurance in all environments (online learning, blended learning, and traditional learning). If the metrics are correct for measuring student learning goals, then use those across all programs.

District/School Policy Recommendations

- Collect performance metrics focused on individual student growth.
- Include requirements for data collection on effectiveness in requests for proposals for online learning programs and online courses.
- Conduct assessments that are adaptive, showing student levels of proficiency (across the K–12 spectrum) upon entry, formative data on learning throughout a program, and student proficiency upon exit, in order to measure growth at multiple points throughout the year, and report on student proficiency levels.
- Understand and support students in their specific learning goals. Some students use online learning to get caught up on a part of a course or for a short-term period to get caught up or accelerate. Their goal may not be retention but rather successful reentry into another educational setting.
- To aid state accountability for quality assurance, focus data collection on metrics that will support program effectiveness on mastery, the increase in graduation rates longitudinally, closing the achievement gap, increases in student learning productivity, college and career readiness, and production of the most growth in the most challenged youth.
- Consider moving to graduation rates from four to six years for overage, undercredited youth, consistent with best practices for underserved youth who need more time to catch up and successfully complete graduation requirements. Many online learning programs are measured on a four-year rate, even though there are significant new enrollments in the 12th grade of undercredited youth who would benefit from having a six-year graduation rate.

Conclusion

The ultimate power of online and blended learning lies in its ability to transform the education system and enable higher levels of learning through competency-based instruction. Technology-based models allow for rapid capture of student performance data and personalized instruction tailored to the specific needs of individual students. By adapting instruction to reflect the skills and knowledge students have mastered, online and blended models have the potential to keep students engaged and supported as they learn and to help them to progress at their own pace, leading to dramatically higher levels of learning and attainment.

There is much to be done to achieve this promise. Although enrollment in online and blended learning programs is growing rapidly, the field is still nascent and there is great diversity in the effectiveness of courses and content available today. Increasing access alone will not lead to better outcomes for students. For online and blended learning to transform the education system, it is essential that the models available are high in quality and successfully increase achievement. Fulfilling the potential of a student-centric, competency-based system will require that the field of online and blended learning and the policy environment in which it operates evolve to demand models that are not only different but more effective than traditional schooling.

The development of quality assurance in K–12 online learning will be an ongoing effort as the field evolves. Moving to recognize inputs as success factors and enabling online learning innovations to be measured on student learning outcomes instead is an important transition to make to ensure high-quality learning experiences any time, everywhere for our students.

Note

1. A complete list of the literature reviewed for each set of standards can be requested from iNACOL.

References

Blackboard. (2007). *Greenhouse exemplary course evaluation rubric.* Washington, DC: Author.

California Learning Resource Network (CLRN). (2011). *Online course review standards, version 2.8.* Retrieved from http://www.clrn.org/search/courseCriteria.cfm

Clark, T. (2001). *Virtual schools: Trends and issues.* San Francisco, CA: WestEd.

Electronic Classroom of Tomorrow (ECOT). (2005). *Teacher evaluation rubric.* Columbus, OH: Author.

Illinois Online Network. (1996). *Quality online course initiative rubric.* Champaign, IL: University of Illinois.

Indiana Senate Bill 179. (2012). Retrieved from http://www.in.gov/legislative/bills/2012/IN/IN0179.1.html

International Association for K–12 Online Learning (iNACOL). (2007). *National standards of quality for online courses.* Vienna, VA: Author.

International Association for K–12 Online Learning (iNACOL). (2008). *National standards for quality online teaching.* Vienna, VA: Author.

International Association for K–12 Online Learning (iNACOL). (2009). *National standards for quality online programs.* Vienna, VA: Author.

International Association for K–12 Online Learning (iNACOL). (2011a). *National standards for quality online courses.* Vienna, VA: Author.

International Association for K–12 Online Learning (iNACOL). (2011b). *National standards for quality online teaching.* Vienna, VA: Author.

Monterey Institute for Technology and Education (MITE). (2006). *The Online Course Evaluation Project*. Monterey, CA: Author.

National Education Association (NEA). (2006a). *Guide to online high school courses*. Retrieved from http://www.nea.org/assets/docs/onlinecourses.pdf

National Education Association (NEA). (2006b). *Guide to teaching online courses*. Retrieved from http://www.nea.org/assets/docs/onlineteachguide.pdf

North Central Regional Educational Laboratory (NCREL). (2002). *Evaluating course-equivalent online learning products*. Retrieved from http://www.projectsocrates.org/elearning/downloads/eval_online_products.pdf

Ohio Department of Education. (2005). *Standards for the teaching profession*. Retrieved from http://www.ode.state.oh.us/GD/Templates/Pages/ODE/ODEDetail.aspx?page=3&TopicRelationID=521&ContentID=8561

Quality Matters. (2010). *Design standards for online and blended courses*. Retrieved from http://www.qmprogram.org/files/G6-12%20Rubric%20Brochure%202011.pdf

Queen, B., & Lewis, L. (2011). *Distance education courses for public elementary and secondary school students: 2009–10*. Washington, DC: U.S. Department of Education.

Southern Regional Education Board (SREB). (2006a). *Standards for quality online courses*. Retrieved from http://publications.sreb.org/2006/06T05_Standards_quality_online_courses.pdf

Southern Regional Education Board (SREB). (2006b). *Standards for quality online teaching*. Retrieved from http://publications.sreb.org/2006/06T02_Standards_Online_Teaching.pdf

Texas Education Agency (TEA). (2001). *Quality of service guidelines for online courses*. Austin: Author.

Watson, J., Murin, A., Vashaw, L., Gemin, B., & Rapp, C. (2011). *Keeping pace with K–12 online learning: An annual review of policy and practice*. Durango, CO: Evergreen Education Group.

5

PROGRESS TOWARD TRANSPARENCY AND QUALITY ASSURANCE

Cali Morrison, Karen Paulson, and Russell Poulin

Merriam-Webster's online dictionary lists several meanings of the word *transparent*, including "free from pretense or deceit," "readily understood," and "characterized by visibility or accessibility of information especially concerning business practices" (Transparency, n.d.). All these meanings underlie our conceptualization of transparency. Specifically, for the purposes of this chapter, we identify transparency as the open sharing of the processes, practices, and results of measurement in higher education. Quality can be assured through the independent review of transparently provided data or its presence can be implied by the mere act of sharing information.

For decades, the standard method of assuring quality in U.S. higher education has been accreditation—a peer-review process. Institutions of higher education internally review their programmatic qualities, which are in turn reviewed by individuals from similar institutions (see chapter 17, "The Role and Realities of Accreditation: A Practical Guide for Programs and Institutions Preparing for an Accreditation Visit"). Little attention has been paid to the resulting products of accreditation, except for that paid directly to the institution being reviewed. Until recently, accrediting information was usually kept veiled from the public (Western Association of Schools and Colleges, 2012). Although transparency is in part about making data and information available, it is also about ease of use, ease of understandability, and ease of comparability.

Accountability is not a new game in higher education. For decades the higher education community has been discussing how to be more accountable to constituencies (Ewell, 2009, p. 5). The pieces of the equation, however, are continually shifting: Who is accountable to whom, for what are they accountable, who benefits, and what are the consequences for failing the accountability challenge (Burke, 2005, p. 2)?

The 2006 report produced by the Commission on the Future of Higher Education convened by Secretary of Education Margaret Spellings shone a bright light on two primary areas: accountability and quality. The report went further by calling for a federal database to collect student-level information in order to provide greater detail and comparability of institutional data. Most institutions and organizations opposed this type of data management system, citing "worry it would infringe on privacy" (Romano, 2006, para. 9).

During the most recent process to reauthorize the Higher Education Act of 1965, Senator Lamar Alexander put the matter bluntly: "If colleges and universities do not accept more responsibility for assessment and accountability, the federal government will do it for them" (Paris, 2009, para. 19). Out of this threat came the birth of the voluntary accountability movement in which several groups of institutions banded together to create systems for reporting on similar sets of data collected by like institutions.

An underlying assumption of the Spellings Commission's call for greater accountability is that by transparently sharing data and information, the best-performing institutions will be rewarded by a student market that "votes with its feet." Institutions that are not performing well would feel the pinch to improve by a shift in market share to those institutions demonstrating and displaying results. The assumption is that providing students with more information, via publicly shared data on the web, will make them better-informed consumers of higher education. Armed with this information, students will make institutional choices that better fit their needs, and these improved student-institutional matches will result in students being retained longer within their chosen institutions (McCormick, 2010).

Institutions that fear being judged by inappropriate measures, losing enrollments, and facing scrutiny from legislators, policy makers, and investors counterbalance this hope. These fears have proven to be a barrier to many institutions' full participation in any of the voluntary accountability projects. This reluctance to participate has also contributed to what some cite as the biggest fault of the voluntary accountability movement—the appearance of higher education accountability without the substance to make it reality (Kelly & Aldeman, 2010).

Many find that the voluntary accountability systems result in a watering down of data because they share only those pieces of information that have been carefully sifted through and presented in a way to portray institutions as successful (McCormick, 2010). As Peter Ewell stated in his 2009 occasional paper for the National Institute for Learning Outcomes Assessment, "Accountability requires the entity held accountable to demonstrate, with evidence, conformity with an established standard of process or outcome. The associated incentive for that entity is to look as good as possible, regardless of underlying performance" (p. 7).

Transparency and Quality Assurance Systems

Other educational shareholders—taxpayers and tuition payers—attempting to learn exactly what they were getting for their money joined the federal call for transparency. To address these demands, several voluntary initiatives arose, each with a slightly different constituency of institutions. Four voluntary systems will be described. All were formed organically by collections of institutions as vehicles to provide data. Some were formed with the ideal of providing data primarily for student consumption, whereas others had a primary focus on policy makers.

The *Voluntary System of Accountability (VSA)*, founded in 2006 with funding provided by Lumina Foundation for Education, focuses on public four-year institutions and is supported by the American Association of State Colleges and Universities (AASCU) and Association of Public and Land-Grant Universities (APLU). VSA's primary information dissemination tool is the College Portrait (www.collegeportraits.org). The first version of the College Portrait was published in 2007. The College Portrait is a template that colleges and universities can use to display institutional data. It has three sections: (a) student and family information, (b) student experiences and perceptions, and (c) student learning outcomes. Each of the three sections contains information on (a) student and institutional characteristics, (b) student progress and success within postsecondary education, (c) costs of attendance, (d) admissions requirements, (e) postgraduation plans, (f) student experiences on campus, and (g) student learning outcomes (Keller & Shulenburger, 2009).

University and College Accountability Network (U-CAN) was also conceptualized in mid-2006 and is supported, and funded, by the National Association of Independent Colleges and Universities (NAICU). It is open to all private not-for-profit colleges and universities, not just member institutions. The types of information that consumers request and need to make informed college decisions were identified by nationwide focus groups composed of diverse populations. The resulting U-CAN website (www.ucan-network.org) displays institutional data such as admissions, enrollment, academics, student demographics, graduation rates, most common fields of study, transfer of credit policy, accreditation, faculty information, class size, tuition and fee trends, price of attendance, financial aid, campus housing, student life, and campus safety. U-CAN also gives consumers easy access to institution-specific information on average loans at graduation, undergraduate class-size break-down, and net tuition. As noted on the U-CAN website, this information, which comes from the U.S. Department of Education's Integrated Postsecondary Education Data System (IPEDS) survey and the Common Data Set, is often difficult for consumers to find and decipher.

Noticeably missing from U-CAN's efforts are any learning outcomes measures. None are reported at either the institution or program levels. According to the commonly asked questions on the U-CAN website (U-CAN, 2009, section 13), this is because focus groups indicated consumers do not demand outcomes measures, and therefore, the presence of outcomes measures would detract from the user-friendly nature of the website. Additionally, it was thought that it would be impossible to provide outcomes data in comparable ways because no single measure or set of measures encompasses all academia.

The strength of U-CAN lies in its numbers. As of June 30, 2012, 827 colleges and universities had signed up to participate, yet only 632 (76%) have data profiles available on the site, some of which are not fully populated with data. The website has received more than 2 million visitors since its 2007 launch (U-CAN, 2013). This number indicates that consumers are hoping to get information from the website.

Transparency by Design (TbD) was founded in 2007 by the Presidents' Forum of Excelsior College and the following year engaged the Western Interstate Commission for Higher Education (WICHE) Cooperative for Educational Technologies (WCET) to serve as the project manager and third-party data quality assurance reviewer of the institutional and program data. The website, College Choices for Adults (www.collegechoicesforadults.org), was built with funding from Lumina Foundation for Education. At the beginning of 2013, the College Choices for Adults website was shut down after a unanimous decision of the TbD Executive Committee. TbD members, unlike those from the VSA and U-CAN, included a wide variety of institutional types from public to private, from non- to for-profit, from community colleges to primarily graduate institutions. All participating institutions have a focus on serving adult students at a distance.

The distinguishing factors of the data set produced by the TbD initiative include (a) the ability to compare all data side by side, (b) a focus on program-level learning outcomes and assessments, (c) results of those assessments, (d) learner progress metrics to demonstrate student retention and completion rates, and (e) third-party review of data submitted by participating institutions. The College Choices website featured institutional and student demographics, links to cost information as well as measures of student engagement (National Survey of Student Engagement/Community College

Survey of Student Engagement), student satisfaction (Priorities Survey for Online Learners), undergraduate general education learning outcomes (ETS Proficiency Profile), and alumni satisfaction outcomes.

The institutions that participated in TbD tend to enroll a large proportion of nontraditional students who are typically not included in the traditional IPEDS graduation rate survey, which comprises only first-time, full-time degree-seeking freshmen in its initial measurement cohorts. In 2011 College Choices published data on its Learner Progress Methodology, which extends the IPEDS graduation rate survey by including part-time and transfer-in students in addition to first-time, full-time freshmen. It also provided data on students at 150% and 200% of "normal" time (e.g., three years and four years for an associate degree). The TbD initiative chose to adapt the IPEDS graduation rate survey to build on face validity because it is the most widely known measure of student completion. Learner Progress also contained an element of learner retention, which reported, at one year, the percentage of students in the cohort who remained enrolled or had completed study one year later. Like learner completion, the learner retention measure expanded the initial measurement cohort to include learners who are part-time and transfers.

Of the current accountability and transparency efforts, TbD with its College Choices site was the only initiative to report program-level data. Each institution was required to report program-level data for at least two programs, including program demographics such as the number of hours required to graduate, any face-to-face requirements, residency requirements, professional accreditation, specializations, and mission statements. In addition, each program profile provided answers to the following questions:

- What will [a student] learn? [Program learning outcomes.]
- How will the program measure what [a student has] learned? [Evidence of student learning.]
  o How are the outcomes measured?
  o How well did recent students perform on those measures?

Each data item allowed for, and in some cases required, institutions to provide contextual information regarding the methodology for reporting the data and how the institution differs from others (if at all), as well as any other information that would enhance a shareholder's understanding of the data.

TbD focused heavily on providing program-level outcomes data. In conducting market research of potential users, as U-CAN found, respondents did not readily identify that outcomes measures were worth reporting, yet those in the test group were eager to see examples. TbD faced criticism for not mandating a standard, highly comparable set of program outcomes measures. However, as the chair of the project's executive committee, Michael Offerman, stated in 2009 at the launch of the College Choices website, "We probably would have spent the next 30 years getting to an agreement about common outcomes measures. We opted instead to lay things out that have been hidden or secret" (Lederman, 2009, para. 6).

In contrast to the VSA and U-CAN transparency initiatives, TbD implemented a third-party quality assurance review. WCET reviewed all data prior to publication on the College Choices website. Although the WCET review was not an audit, it did ensure that data follow established methodologies, that institutions provided all required information, and that those data were in a format and language accessible to potential adult students.

The American Association of Community Colleges (AACC), in partnership with the Association of Community College Trustees (ACCT) and the College Board, founded *Voluntary Framework of Accountability (VFA)* in 2008. The guiding missive for VFA is "the first national accountability frameworks design *for* community colleges, *by* community colleges" (Phillippe & Farrelly, 2011, slide 3). Development of VFA was supported by Lumina Foundation for Education and the Bill and Melinda Gates Foundation.

VFA serves a unique market sector in terms of both the institutions participating and the students those institutions serve. Many of the commonly used metrics, even those developed by the other accountability efforts, do not accurately reflect the strengths of community colleges. Access and affordability are the foundations of community college missions and may be the best measures of their effectiveness. More recently, community colleges have taken center stage in the national conversation on completion. Thus, as noted in VFA (n.d.), the framework developed by community college leaders is composed of measures in three broad areas:

1. Student progress and outcomes measures evaluate the short-term progress and long-term outcomes of all students who begin their studies at a college in a given period, disaggregated by age, gender, race/ethnicity, and financial aid status.
2. Workforce, economic, and community-development outcomes measures enable community colleges to better gauge their efficacy in meeting their communities' workforce needs.
3. Student learning outcomes measures will initially bring more transparency to how colleges assess and report student learning

outcomes by providing a reporting format based on the National Institute for Learning Outcomes Assessment (NILOA) Transparency Framework and will continue to evaluate other methods for assessing and reporting student learning outcomes in a manner that is useful to the sector.

In 2012 VFA leaders and AACC encouraged participation from community colleges across the country while concurrently building the VFA Data Tool to collect, display, and benchmark. The web-based interface ultimately will enable colleges to display their metrics in a uniform way—with the goal of collecting the first round of data in 2013 (American Association of Community Colleges, 2013).

Common Data Items

As each of these four initiatives progressed toward the same goal of providing quality information for students, parents, policy makers, and institutional decision makers, it was inevitable that they would have some overlap in data reported. Morrison (2012) examined each initiative's reporting metrics as displayed publicly on their websites. Of all the varied data items each group reported at the time, only four were common across all initiatives. Table 5.1 summarizes those findings.

The first two data items that are commonly reported—enrollment numbers (total enrollment or full-time equivalent enrollment) and enrollment status (full- or part-time)—can be found easily using the Internet and are figures that institutions are required to report to the federal Department of Education via IPEDS each year. The other two—completion/graduation rate and success/progress rate—are measures that have not been widely shared previously with the public. In particular, sharing those measures in formats that allow them to be compared and contrasted side by side challenges the comfort zone of many higher education institutions. Openly sharing data, as in the initiatives mentioned previously, is the primary way that the collective accountability and transparency movement has created change. Although their names suggest they are the same, these last two measures are in fact quite different owing to how each metric is calculated by each group: (a) the criterion being measured is common, but the resulting data are not comparable across accountability systems; (b) data should be internally consistent within a particular system of accountability, but often the data are self-reported and not externally reviewed. This leaves the measures open to honest errors, differences in interpretation, and possibly intentional distortion.

TABLE 5.1

Higher Education Accountability and Transparency Efforts Data Set Comparison—Like Data Items

| Institutional Characteristics | College Choices for Adults (TbD) | Accountability Effort | | |
		College Portrait (VSA)	U-CAN	VFA (AACC) Based on V1 Reporting Framework
Enrollment Numbers	Optional reporting (FTE and head count)	Total enrollment	Total enrollment	Total enrollment
Enrollment Status (Full/Part-Time)	Optional reporting	Reported on total enrollment	Reported on total enrollment	Reported
Completion/Graduation Rate	Optional reporting ("Learner Completion"—150% and 200% normal time completion rate for first-time, full-time, part-time, and transfer-in students)	Reported as "Success and Progress Rate"	Uses first-time, full-time freshmen enrolled in degree programs; reported at 4, 5, 6 years for bachelor's	Reported as "Outcomes Measures"—Percentages of students who • completed an associate's degree and did not transfer; • completed an associate's and subsequently transferred; • completed a certificate and did not transfer; • completed a certificate and did not transfer; • completed a certificate and transferred; • transferred but have not received a formal award; • are still enrolled; • left institution with no award and without transfer having earned 30+ credits; • left institution with no award and without transfer having earned less than 30 credits.

(Continues)

TABLE 5.1 (Cont.)

		Accountability Effort		
Institutional Char-acteristics	*College Choices for Adults (TbD)*	*College Portrait (VSA)*	*U-CAN*	*VFA (AACC) Based on V1 Reporting Framework*
Success/Progress Rate	Reported as "Learner Progress" (learner retention and completion)	4-year "Success and Progress Rate" reported for first-time, full-time, and full-time transfer students (i.e., have earned a credential or are still enrolled after 4 years)	Reported as percentage of students who graduate	Reported as "Achieve Year Two Outcomes" (percentage of students who have completed a formal award and percentage of students who transferred to a 2-year or 4-year institution but did not earn a formal award) and "Two-Year Credit Hour Success Rate" (percentage of credit hours attempted [not students] during the first two academic years by the cohort that were successfully completed) Reported by age, gender, race/ethnicity, Pell status, enrollment status (first-term), developmental status (first-term)

Note. All data were gathered from publicly available websites for each accountability effort in December 2011. Adapted from *Higher Education Accountability Initiatives*, by C. Morrison, May 2012, paper presented at the meeting of Lumina Foundation accountability projects, Indianapolis, IN.

Ripples of Change

The various transparency and quality assurance initiatives have contributed to ripples of change that are making accountability better understood and useful within the higher education community. Where the drops fall together, more collective forward progress is made. These four initiatives have pushed the envelope by including measures of graduation/completion and student progress. Each of these measures has been tailored to match and account for student populations better than the current common measure, the IPEDS graduation-rate survey (GRS). The IPEDS GRS currently includes only first-time, full-time freshmen, which excludes on average 38% of the student population (National Student Clearinghouse, 2012). There are varying percentages of adult learners and transfer students at reporting institutions. To gain more clarity into the performance of these nontraditional students, institutions participating in the voluntary accountability initiatives crafted new measurements to account for the diversity among their student populations. The federal government has taken notice, is listening to institutional calls for adaptations or additions to the IPEDS metrics, and has begun the process to create measures to better reflect all students participating in higher education including part-time and transfer students.

Challenges for Accountability Systems

The desire to provide data to current and prospective students is a complicated process. For example, the metrics used from one institutional site to the next are often incomparable. Even seemingly common data elements are not comparable, except internally within the specific accountability system, and then only if those elements have been populated by participating institutions and with strict adherence to the calculation process.

If one were to point to a deficiency in any of these accountability systems, it is one that is shared jointly by all of them. The greatest disservice these initiatives do is constructing their own silos in terms of methodologies, data collection, and reporting systems. Although the specialization of certain data items and prevention of comparisons of apples and zebras are positive adaptations, they are overshadowed by market confusion over which data to find where and what to do with information once it is in the student's or parent's or even policy maker's hands. Without a single access point, many potential learners could be lured into sites that are fronts for lead-generation sites, which provide only enough actual information to convince students to supply their e-mail addresses and telephone numbers. Giving contact information to a lead-generation site results in the student receiving a cascade of contacts from multiple institutions and vendors.

Are We Talking to Ourselves?

Questions arise often from those institutions involved in promoting transparency programs: Who is being provided data and information? For what purpose? Who is actually using the data collected and published to the web? What value are they finding at the various accountability systems? In many ways institutions are talking to themselves: Institutions participating in various initiatives often use data for institutional improvement practices. However, it is much less clear who the actual audience is for these sites. This stumbling block exists for many initiatives that try to serve too many audiences. The divergent needs of policy makers and students make creating comparable data sets quite difficult. Students are interested in answers to the following questions:

- How long will it take to earn a credential?
- How much will it cost?
- What will students learn?
- What can students do with the credential once they have completed the program?

Policy makers in contrast tend to focus on the following:

- What are the retention and graduation rates?
- What are the program budgets?
- Have graduates gotten better jobs? An increase in salary?

The transparency initiatives become entangled when trying to address both sets of questions with a single data set. If students cannot find information they want in a format that makes sense to them, they quickly bounce to the next site. If policy makers misinterpret the information provided at these accountability websites, it could potentially lead to increased reporting burdens, decreased funding, or other policy changes based on incorrect conclusions. Thus, it is imperative for institutions and accountability projects to share, in addition to data, the context and reasons why a student, or a policy maker, should know about these data. It is a delicate balance to provide just enough data and context to satisfy audiences without overwhelming them and causing additional long-term issues for institutions.

Addressing the Future: Next Steps for Transparency, Quality Assurance, and Online Education

Those currently involved in the administration of higher education feel pressure from all sides—the federal government, accreditors, students— to produce more meaningful data that can improve practice and thereby theoretically improve graduation and success rates. To remain relevant, the accountability systems reviewed previously, which, outside of College Choices, are primarily geared at traditional higher education, must broaden their perspectives. Online education is becoming ubiquitous in all higher education institutions; therefore, metrics developed must reflect the shifting student body that comes with this change. Data collection and transparent dissemination must also reflect the change in online education, as the number of blended (i.e., both face-to-face and online) instructional modes is growing. Suggested adaptations include the following:

- Expanding methodologies to include a wider variety of students in such measures as enrollment status (part-time/full-time)
- Enhancing current or creating new standardized measures to include the experiences of the growing variety of students, such as online, blended, and nontraditional students
- Developing metrics with greater comparability across institutions
- Focusing reporting on a single audience, or at least segregating the information by audience
- Providing the information in ways that are more visually appealing and resonate with intended audiences

It is imperative that accountability efforts avoid focusing only on easily quantifiable metrics and ignoring the context and qualitative overlay that gives each institution its distinct identity. The higher education community must continue to be proactive and vigilantly monitor the federal landscape. In 2012 the president of the United States called for, and the Department of Education began producing, a new College Scorecard. According to the College Scorecard website (White House, n.d.), the purpose of the tool is to make it easier for students and their families to identify and choose high-quality, affordable colleges that provide good value. The scorecard will report on costs, graduation rates, student-loan repayment rates and debts, and a metric named "earnings potential"; however, no mention has been made of any efforts to contextualize these numbers. The president's call for this type of dashboard indicates a perceived hole in the market, which accountability/ transparency projects would be wise to fill.

Conclusion

Accountability in U.S. higher education is not a passing phenomenon. As demonstrated, it has been discussed for decades, with many starts and stops. Four of those starts—VSA, U-CAN, TbD (College Choices for Adults), and VFA—have collectively made progress toward the ultimate goal of a more informed college-going population, be they first-time freshmen or their parents returning to finish a credential. Unfortunately, by working independently, these initiatives may have added to consumer confusion. There is still much work to be done to create a culture of accountability and quality assurance as a primary and useful practice, not a mandated directive.

References

American Association of Community Colleges. (2013). *Voluntary Framework of Accountability: Current status*. Retrieved from http://www.aacc.nche.edu/Resources/aaccprograms/VFAWeb/Pages/VFAStatus.aspx

Burke, J. C. (2005). The many faces of accountability. In J. Burke (Ed.), *Achieving accountability in higher education: Balancing public, academic, and market demands* (pp. 1–24). San Francisco: Jossey-Bass.

Ewell, P. (2009). *Assessment, accountability, and improvement: Revisiting the tension*. Retrieved from National Institute for Learning Outcomes Assessment website: http://www.learningoutcomeassessment.org/documents/PeterEwell_005.pdf

Keller, C., & Shulenburger, D. (2009). *VSA 2009 learning outcomes workshops about VSA and the College Portrait*. Washington, DC: Association of Public and Land-Grant Universities.

Kelly, A., & Aldeman, C. (2010, March 2). *False fronts: Behind higher education's Voluntary Accountability Systems*. Washington, DC: American Enterprise Institute and Education Sector.

Lederman, D. (2009, August 4). The challenge of comparability. *Inside Higher Ed*. Retrieved from http://www.insidehighered.com/news/2009/08/04/transparency

McCormick, A. C. (2010). Here's looking at you: Transparency, institutional self-presentation, and the public interest. *Change: The Magazine of Higher Learning, 42*(6), 35–42.

Morrison, C. (2012, May). *Higher education accountability initiatives*. Paper presented at the meeting of Lumina Foundation accountability projects, Indianapolis, IN.

National Student Clearinghouse. (2012, Spring). *Snapshot report adult learners*. Herndon, VA: Author.

Paris, D. (2009, November 6). The clock is ticking. *Inside Higher Ed*. Retrieved from http://www.insidehighered.com/views/2009/11/06/paris

Phillippe, K., & Farrelly, B. (2011). *The Voluntary Framework of Accountability for community colleges, by community colleges*. Retrieved from the American Association of Community Colleges website: http://www.aacc.nche.edu/Resources/aaccprograms/vfa_archive/Pages/default.aspx

Romano, L. (2006, September 27). Spellings calls for tracking of students' performance. *Washington Post*. Retrieved from http://www.washingtonpost.com/wp-dyn/content/article/2006/09/26/AR2006092601460.html

Transparency. (n.d.). In *Merriam-Webster's online dictionary* (11th ed.). Retrieved from http://www.merriam-webster.com/dictionary/transparent

U-CAN. (2009). *Commonly asked questions about U-CAN.* Retrieved from http://www.ucan-network.org/about/page/commonly-asked-questions-about-u-can-2

U-CAN. (2013). *By the numbers.* Retrieved from http://www.ucan-network.org/publications/page/by-the-numbers

Voluntary Framework of Accountability (VFA). (n.d.). *Community college measures of effectiveness.* Retrieved from American Association of Community Colleges website: http://www.aacc.nche.edu/Resources/aaccprograms/VFAWeb/Documents/VFABrochure%20LowResolution.pdf

Western Association of Schools and Colleges (WASC). (2012). *WASC sets example of accountability, transparency in higher education.* Retrieved from http://www.wascsenior.org/redesign/wasc-sets-example-accountability-transparency-higher-education

White House. (n.d.). *College Scorecard.* Retrieved from http://www.whitehouse.gov/issues/education/higher-education/college-score-card

PART TWO

QUALITY ASSURANCE AND CONTINUOUS IMPROVEMENT AT THE COURSE DESIGN AND TEACHING LEVELS

6

A PROCESS TO IMPROVE COURSE DESIGN

A Key Variable in Course Quality

Deborah Adair

Students tend to interact with an online course in a holistic way. The design of the course—the planned components and structure for delivery—may not even be immediately apparent to the student or at least not separable from the other elements contributing to the quality of the course. The way students experience the course is influenced by a variety of factors, including content, faculty readiness (attitude, training, and behavior), student readiness, course technology, institutional infrastructure and policies, and student support. Although students clearly care about outcomes (grades and learning), their actual experience in taking an online course also matters to them (Ralston-Berg, 2010). For them, the assessment of course quality lies as much in the transactional and ideally transformational experience within the course as it does in outcomes beyond the course. In a survey of more than 2,300 students from 31 institutions in 21 states, students indicated that except for instructor-related variables, the way the course was designed was more important than all other factors, including the learning materials. Students agreed that the Quality Matters (QM) course design standards were important to their success in an online course and that these effective course design practices add value and contribute to quality (Ralston-Berg, 2011a, b).

Course design plays a number of important roles in the student experience of an online course; it is an input variable to the educational process that has the potential to mitigate some deficiencies in technology, infrastructure, and student readiness and that can guide faculty performance to some extent. High-quality course design will orient students to the course and provide guidance to ensure that they get off to a good start, that they are aware of institutional policies that impact them, and that they can access student support services essential to their success. A high-quality design ensures the pedagogical approach informing the course is reflected by learning objectives that form the course foundation. It can also guide the implementation of student assessment to allow instructors a broad perspective on students' mastery of content and allow students to measure their own learning. A well-designed course supports the alignment of materials and activities with the learning objectives and structures interaction to engage students to become active learners. It can provide a check to ensure that the technology enabling the various course components facilitates the student's learning experience and is easy to use rather than an impediment to the student's progress and that the course demonstrates a commitment to accessibility for all students.

Although this chapter is focused on assuring quality for online course design, the quality assurance practices we consider are applicable to any courses using technology to deliver instruction and promote student learning. Whether a course is online or blended, synchronous or asynchronous, instructor-led or self-paced, small or large, the design represents the forethought and planning that goes into a course. When the design is articulated and enacted, it can be reviewed for quality.

Assessing Quality of Course Design

Course design is a meaningful focus when evaluating quality because it is an input variable in the educational process that can significantly affect the student experience in a course. Plus, course design quality can be evaluated and improved prior to enrollment rather than during a post hoc review of outcomes that can be influenced by any number of variables. Courses can be designed to quality standards from the start, thereby improving the experience for all students and making the quality assurance process more effective and efficient going forward.

The purpose of quality measurement may be purely evaluative—to identify exemplary courses, to discriminate between acceptable and unacceptable courses, and to perform inter- and intrainstitutional benchmarking. Alternatively, the purpose may be more developmental or diagnostic—for course development and improvement as well as assessment. In either case, the measurement of quality requires standards that are well defined and consistently and appropriately applied. Rubrics are a useful tool to this end, and a number of well-known rubrics have been specifically developed for use in assessing quality in online courses. These include the following:

- Quality Standards Inventory (http://learn.gwnursing.org/Education/ QSI/QSI.html), designed to assess the quality of online courses based on the tenets of active learning and effective teaching principles

- Michigan Community College Association Virtual Learning Collaborative's Online Course Development Guidelines and Rubric (www.mccvlc.org/~staff/content.cfm?ID=108), which evaluates courses on a scale from 1 (beginning) to 4 (exemplary)
- Rubric for Online Instruction (ROI) from Chico State (www.csuchico.edu/celt/roi), which is designed as a self-evaluation tool with six categories of evaluation and three levels (basic to exemplary), with self-nomination for exemplary course recognition
- Online Course Evaluation Project (OCEP) (http://www.monterey institute.org/pdf/OCEP%20Evaluation%20Categories.pdf), developed as a scoring tool with a focus on content and pedagogy developed by a team of professionals to identify and evaluate existing online courses
- Blackboard Exemplary Course Rubric (www.blackboard.com/getdoc/7deaf501-4674-41b9-b2f2-554441ba099b/2012-Blackboard-Exemplary-Course-Rubric.aspx), designed to recognize course creators whose courses demonstrate best practices in four areas
- Quality Matters Rubric (www.qmprogram.org/rubric)

Quality Assurance: Standards and Processes

Although all these tools define quality through the use of explicit standards, the QM Rubric represents a broadly shared understanding of quality because of its widespread adoption. As of late 2012, more than 700 institutions had adopted this rubric because it is current, solidly anchored in research and best practices, collaboratively developed by a community of practice, continually updated and improved, inclusive in scope, and diagnostic rather than prescriptive. The 2011–2013 edition of the QM Rubric for Higher Education consists of 41 standards organized into eight general categories based on research-supported best practices for course design.[1] Although a scoring system and a set of online tools facilitate the evaluation of a course by a team of peer reviewers, the rubric is intended to be a diagnostic tool and comes complete with detailed annotations that explain the application of the standards, the relationships between them, and examples of good and poor practice.

In the QM Rubric, as in other rubrics, quality is defined through the articulation of standards and its meaning becomes apparent because it can be seen and shared. Once a course is reviewed using the QM Rubric and is found to meet the standards to the point that it is recognized for quality, the measurement tool (the rubric) can be referenced as a means of defining the quality of the course. With the application of the rubric, quality can be evaluated and recognized as an attribute of a course. However, it is important to note that such evaluation is only a snapshot of the course at a single point in time. The assurance of quality, in contrast, requires an ongoing process to ensure improvement is continuously pursued beyond the periods of measurement and evaluation. Although episodic evaluation is necessarily a part of a quality assurance process, it is not the sum total. Quality assurance is much less about evaluation and much more about process.

Quality Assurance, Scalability, and the Professoriate

Knowledge grows, information changes, priorities fluctuate. What is high-quality educational content today may not be what we need to teach tomorrow—at least not in its existing form. The scale, scope, and pace of such change, especially in the 21st century, make it impossible to capture, curate, and disseminate knowledge in real time in any centralized way. In higher education, curriculum determination, development, and delivery are highly decentralized, with the responsibility for execution lying largely with the professoriate. The discipline, expertise, and commitment to scholarship that defines the profession drives the content of academic programs and how those programs are offered to students. The responsibility for controlling and improving the quality of education, then, must also reside with the faculty. The faculty, not the various technologies through which we can deliver education, is the key to real and meaningful scalability in quality assurance initiatives. Scalability of the faculty role, rather than scalability of technology or the learning platform, needs to be the focus when we discuss scalability as a solution for quality assurance or for the improvement of education in general. Technology has enabled systems of education to move online and increase; however, education itself is not programmable, and teachers provide the means through which education is adapted and improved.

To be both scalable and efficient, then, a quality assurance process for online courses must ultimately be executed by the faculty. The effectiveness of the process will be determined by the validity of the standards, the consistency of their application, and the presence of a structure that enables continuous improvement. If the need for quality assurance is considered both within institutions and across different institutions, definitions of quality must be shared and a rigorous and consistent assurance process that allows for adaptability to different contexts and course types employed. Quality in this framework is not about meeting a single, narrow, and prescriptive definition but about using inclusive standards with appropriate benchmarks in a process that ensures performance is continually evaluated and improved.

Processes for Quality Assurance

It does not happen all at once. There is no instant pudding. —W. Edwards Deming
(Swiss Deming Institute, n.d.)

Inasmuch as quality is not a onetime state of being but an ongoing pursuit, a continuous-improvement process is essential in assuring quality. Many quality assurance models from business and industry are applicable to education. Perhaps one of the most well-known models with direct applicability to quality assurance in course design is the Deming Cycle—plan, do, act, check (Tague, 1995; also see American Society for Quality, n.d., for an application to an educational institution). The model proposes a process of designing to improve results, implementing the design and measuring performance, evaluating the measurement and reporting to those who can make changes, and acting on the recommendations to improve performance.

The QM program provides an example of this type of quality assurance process applied to course design (see Figure 6.1). The process is centered on the principles of evidence (research and data), collaboration, collegiality, and continuous improvement, and it provides a valid, replicable, and effective way to define and apply standards of quality, to evaluate and analyze performance to those standards, to improve performance based on the analysis, and to evaluate again. Institutions that are engaged in implementing QM as a quality assurance process first develop their institutional capacity— the "plan" in the Deming Cycle—through professional development and other efforts to ensure course development is guided by the QM Rubric

Figure 6.1. The Quality Matters continuous-improvement process.

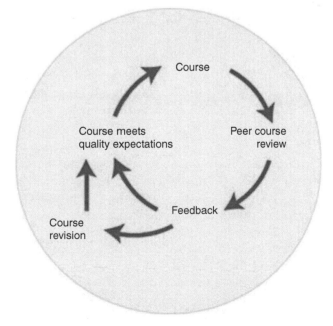

(Ward, 2011). Courses designed and redesigned to meet the rubric standards can have a positive impact on student outcomes (Aman, 2009; Hall, 2010; Harkness, Soodjinda, Hamilton, & Bolig, 2011; Swan, Matthews, & Bogle, 2010; Swan, Matthews, Bogle, Boles, & Day, 2011).

As discussed previously, the QM Rubric is the set of standards, or measurement tools, used by many different types of institutions (two-year, four-year, master and doctoral level, private, public, nonprofit, and for-profit) to review and evaluate the design of their online courses. The resources and process used to develop the tool, as well as the rubric's widespread voluntary adoption, contribute to the validity of these standards as used in the initial development and subsequent evaluation of the quality of online courses. Consistency in the application of the standards is achieved through rigorous training of reviewers. Reviewers must successfully complete a two-course curriculum that includes training about the standards and their interpretation, use of the detailed annotations that are part of the rubric, and the art of providing constructive feedback specifically designed to improve the course. As of late 2012, more than 3,000 reviewers from academic institutions across the United States and abroad have achieved and maintained QM peer reviewer status and are available to serve on local, national, and international review teams. Reviewers must keep their eligibility current through update training on each new edition of the rubric.

The QM review process, the "check" in the quality assurance cycle, is conducted by a three-person team of trained QM peer reviewers. A review conducted by peers is critical to the collegiality of the process and for acceptance and adoption by faculty across the breadth of institutions. Peer review is a familiar and valued process in the academy. QM's definition of *peer* is someone who has current online teaching experience. This definition is not only important to the faculty's acceptance of the quality-review process but is also instrumental in the dissemination and application of quality standards beyond those courses undergoing review. A consequence of training faculty in quality standards in course design and giving them experience applying those standards is the diffusion of quality to those other courses that faculty design and teach and that are not necessarily part of the formal quality assurance process. Evidence to this effect can be found in part in anecdotal reports from institutions implementing QM as well as in data collected in exit surveys conducted for every official QM course review (Sener, 2011). From 2007 to 2012, more than 2,500 online courses were officially reviewed using the QM Rubric and more than 2,100 of those received QM's quality recognition. Under the 2008–2010 edition of the QM Rubric, 2,182 participants involved in the review of 834 courses completed the exit survey. Of the 1,997 reviewers responding to one question, 44% (871 respondents) reported that they made changes to their own online courses as a result of their peer-review service. These data suggest that for every QM course review, there is at least one additional course (and likely more) undergoing some level of quality improvement. This also demonstrates the value of having instructors who are responsible for developing and delivering online courses directly involved in the quality-review process.

A QM review, then, has the potential to improve course quality not only for the institution hosting the review but also for the home institutions of the instructors serving as reviewers (Shattuck, 2012). Reviewers on QM teams serve specific roles, or requirements, with the aim of ensuring rigor and consistency in the application of the standards. A QM review team must be composed of at least one subject matter expert as well as a master reviewer with additional review experience and advanced training to help ensure consistency in the interpretation of standards, clarity and usefulness in the recommendations, and rigor in the review. At least one reviewer must be external to the institution hosting the review.

In a QM review, continuous improvement is the goal. Courses undergoing review are evaluated and scored using the rubric, but the focus is on the constructive and actionable feedback provided by the reviewers who are tasked with taking the student perspective in reviewing the course. Reviewers look at every standard, including those requiring coherence and alignment between course elements, and indicate whether the standard is met or not met. Every standard has a point value: "3" is considered *essential*, "2" is *very important*, and "1" is *important*. Each reviewer makes his or her own determination and is encouraged to provide detailed recommendations (feedback is required for any standard marked "not met"). After the three reviewers complete their review of a course, their scoring and feedback is aggregated into a final report. Majority rule dictates which standards are met, which are not, and the total points awarded. Courses that meet QM standards at this point will have met every essential standard and achieved at least 85% of the total possible points.

In the Deming Cycle, this initial review is the "check" against the QM design standards. But as this is a continuous-improvement process, the "act" stage is demonstrated in the amendment period provided to all course developers whose courses do not yet meet standards. In a QM review, course developers are provided time (typically 14–16 weeks) to make the changes recommended in the final review report. This is an "open" review process that encourages communication and contact between the course developer and the review team throughout the review. (This communication will actually begin before the start of a review, with a pre-review conference call, during which the course developer provides the review team with a proper context for the course and review.) Quick improvement might be made even as the review is being conducted because the team may communicate development opportunities as they work through the review, which may take anywhere from three to six weeks. Once the review period is completed and the final report is provided to the course developer, the recommendations in the report will guide the developer to make changes in the course. Design improvements are often even made in courses that initially meet the QM standards, though QM's continuous-improvement process is intended to ensure that all courses eventually meet QM standards. At the end of the amendment period, the master reviewer serving as the team chair will review the amendments and provide feedback or recognize the course for successfully meeting the QM standards.

The quality-certification mark that QM provides for courses that have successfully completed a QM review is time-limited—up to five years. With the course developer's participation in the review process and the detailed feedback provided to him or her in the final report, the expectation is that the developer will be able to make regular and incremental course updates in a manner consistent with the rubric standards. At some point, however, the course will require another review. The QM Rubric will have undergone substantial change during the five-year life of the quality certification,[2] and it is expected that the course itself will have (or should have) also undergone substantial change, based on enhancements to technology, newer instructional materials, and so on. If a certified course undergoes major change before the end of the five years, the host school is responsible for ascertaining whether the course still meets QM standards or requires a new review.

Support for and commitment to the process is essential to the QM continuous-improvement program, or any other quality assurance process. Institutions looking to implement such a quality assurance system have to identify and commit the necessary resources or develop the internal capacity to support an iterative, ongoing process. Maintaining such a system in education is more likely for schools that embrace a culture of teaching and learning such that quality assurance is internalized and participation in the quality assurance system is required across all levels of the institution.

Implications of Quality Assurance in Course Design

A systematic, institutionalized quality assurance process to improve the design of an online course can focus attention on the distance-learning policies that support or detract from efforts to improve the quality of design. In an online environment, course design will affect the way the student experiences the institution as well as the specific course. The design of the online course structures the learning environment and provides the primary pathway for interaction with institutional resources and rules. Because course design standards and institutional policies will intersect in the online classroom, it is important that these policies do not conflict.

Standards for high-quality design that address learning objectives, prerequisites, and grading policies all have implications for an institution's curriculum policies. For example, the QM Rubric standards require learning objectives that describe measurable outcomes. In some institutions, course learning objectives are determined by program or schoolwide curriculum committees, independent of delivery modality, and these objectives cannot be altered for improvement by individual faculty for their online courses. The inability to meet a particular design standard because of curriculum policies would be identified in a quality assurance processes that was institutionalized and could be a lever for an institution-wide discussion of such policies. In this way, the pursuit of quality in online course design could inform and improve related policies across the institution.

In a similar manner, course design standards relating to the way student policies are communicated can focus attention on the appropriateness of institutional policies relating to student communication behavior and conduct codes, academic integrity policies, penalties for late assignments, withdrawal procedures and deadlines, incomplete grades, and grievance procedures for the online learner. Faculty policies related to work expectations (e.g., response times), online teaching and design skills, course ownership policies, and intellectual property can also be addressed through a quality assessment of course design. An institution's entire student-support infrastructure—technical support, student advising, online registration, counseling services, library services, tutoring services, disability services, financial aid counseling—is likely to have implications for the online learner that come under scrutiny when an institution has committed to a comprehensive quality assurance process for course design.

Quality assurance processes focused on course design, then, become a lever for more widespread institution improvement. Institutionalizing a process for continuous improvement involving faculty, staff, and administration at all institutional levels and in all departments responsible for student support and success is an effective and efficient way to assure quality in online course design. It also has broad impact on the educational enterprise as a whole. For academic institutions, quality starts in the classroom—online or on-site.

Notes

1. While the QM Rubric for Higher Education is featured in this chapter, it is important to note that QM also has a Grade 6–12 Rubric, a Publisher's Rubric, and a Continuing and Professional Education Rubric. In all cases, continuous-improvement processes for using the rubrics are based on a peer-review system.

2. The QM Rubric undergoes an intense review and is refreshed biennially by practitioners and scholars. See overview of QM standards in most recent editions of
   the QM rubrics at www.qmprogram.org.

References

Aman, P. R. (2009). *Improving student satisfaction and retention with online instruction
through systematic faculty peer review of courses* (Doctoral dissertation). Retrieved
from http://ir.library.oregonstate.edu/xmlui/bitstream/handle/1957/11945/Aman
_Dissertation.pdf

American Society for Quality. (n.d.). *Plan-do-check-act (PDCA) cycle.* Retrieved from
http://asq.org/learn-about-quality/project-planning-tools/overview/pdca-cycle
.html

Hall, A. (2010, June). *Quality Matters Rubric as "teaching presence": Application of CoI
framework to analysis of the QM Rubric's effects on student learning.* Presentation at
the 2nd Annual Quality Matters Conference, Oak Brook, IL.

Harkness, S., Soodjinda, D., Hamilton, M., & Bolig, R. (2011, November). *Assessment of a pilot online writing program using the QM Rubric.* Paper presented at the
3rd Annual Quality Matters Conference, Baltimore, MD.

Ralston-Berg, P. (2010, June). *Do quality standards matter to students?* Keynote presentation at the 2nd Annual Quality Matters Conference, Chicago, IL.

Ralston-Berg, P. (2011a). [Online course quality: The student perspective.] Unpublished survey results.

Ralston-Berg, P. (2011b, November). *What makes a quality online course? The student perspective.* Presentation at the 3rd Annual Quality Matters Conference,
Baltimore, MD.

Sener, J. (2011, July). [Quality Matters data mining project: Preliminary research
findings.] Unpublished final report.

Shattuck, K. (2012). *What we're learning from Quality Matters–focused research:
Research, practice, continuous improvement.* Retrieved from the Quality Matters
Program website: http://www.qmprogram.org/research-grants-fy13

Swan, K., Matthews, D., & Bogle, L. R. (2010, June). *The relationship between course
design and learning processes.* Presentation at the 2nd Annual Quality Matters
Conference, Oak Brook, IL.

Swan, K., Matthews, D., Bogle, L. R., Boles, E., & Day, S. (2011). [Linking online
course design to learning processes using the Quality Matters and Community of
Inquiry frameworks.] Unpublished report on continuing study.

Swiss Deming Institute. (n.d.). *The one hundred best Deming quotations.* Retrieved
from http://www.deming.ch/E_quotations.html

Tague, N. (1995). *The quality toolbox.* Milwaukee, WI: ASQ Quality Press.

Ward, C. (2011, November). *The development of technological pedagogical content
knowledge (TPACK) in instructors using Quality Matters training, rubric, and peer
collaboration.* [2010 QM Research Grant]. Presentation at the 3rd Annual Quality
Matters Conference, Baltimore, MD.

7

A MODEL FOR DETERMINING THE EFFECTIVENESS AND IMPACT OF FACULTY PROFESSIONAL DEVELOPMENT

Lawrence C. Ragan and Carol A. McQuiggan

In these uncertain economic times, there is an increased need to provide evidence of the worth and impact of faculty development programming (Hines, 2009; Plank & Kalish, 2010). The assessment and analysis of outcomes of faculty professional development activities could provide meaningful information for use in making decisions about future professional development events. The resulting feedback loop could inform new programming; provide guidance for continuing or changing current programs; determine whether programming is achieving its purpose (Brancato, 2003; Guskey, 2002); and justify the very existence of faculty development centers by providing evidence of their programming impact on faculty, departments, and the institution (Sorcinelli & Stanley, 2011). This potential illustrates a need for a more systematic evaluation of the effectiveness and impact of faculty professional development (Chism & Szabo, 1997; Hines, 2009). Program assessment informs decision making and improves practice, measures impact, helps others understand and value the work, and provides useful information for improvement (Plank & Kalish, 2010).

Online learning, in all its many disruptive variations, contributes to the increased pressure faculty feel to keep current on evolving teaching practices and new technologies. Student expectations of seamless integration of technologies as a part of their learning system and the redefinition and expansion of learning throughout a student's lifetime create new pressures on historically slow-to-change higher education systems to adjust to the times (Lawler & King, 2001). How to decipher the many professional development options and to assess where to invest limited time and energy is of constant concern for faculty members. Some hold their breath and hope they can ride out a few more years without getting caught up in this tsunami of change. Others, experienced and novice alike, embrace the challenges presented by this new and emerging teaching and learning landscape and actively seek ways to find their place. From all these dynamics comes one constant message: "This is not your grandparents' classroom!" Improved and better-appreciated theories of learning, coupled with complex communication systems and services, are fundamentally changing the skills and competencies required for teaching and learning success. Today, maybe more so than any time in the history of education, the role of faculty preparation for success in a variety of teaching formats is critical.

Understanding and addressing the various skills and competencies necessary for teaching success in today's classroom, virtual and face-to-face alike, return dividends far greater than the investment of faculty time and energy. Designing, developing, delivering, and evaluating faculty development opportunities serve the needs of today's instructors by building a foundation of knowledge, philosophy, and approach that can ultimately lead to online student success. The challenges of teaching with new pedagogies and technologies are many. The solutions are also rapidly evolving and need to be communicated and transferred through effective programming of professional development. There should be a deliberate use of theory and education principles in the design and development of faculty professional development programs (Steinert et al., 2006), taking advantage of the advances from research in these areas. Training and support of faculty are consistently cited as critical components of the successful implementation of online teaching programs (Ali et al., 2005; Covington, Petherbridge, & Warren, 2005; Dalziel, 2003; Phipps & Merisotis, 2000; Yang & Cornelious, 2005).

The increased focus on serving faculty professional development needs calls for a renewed attention to quality standards in the design, development, and delivery of faculty development programming. This includes both evaluation—"judging the effectiveness of various services to determine value and improvements"—and assessment—the "determination of the level to which the center achieved its specific outcomes—similar to academic program assessment" (Hines, 2011, p. 1). Although *quality assurance* may be defined in multiple ways, in this context it is the method by which a unit or organization assesses faculty development program impact on teaching behaviors in order to improve student success.

In this chapter, a historical context will be provided as the background for developing a quality assurance strategy for the faculty professional development initiative. Then, an incremental model will be introduced with a range of quality assurance dimensions that need to be considered to determine the effectiveness and impact of faculty professional development programs. The dimensions include an understanding of the characteristics of the faculty audience, the definition of desired skills and competencies, strategies to measure change in teaching behaviors and achievement of student learning outcomes, and an alignment of the faculty development programs' assessment activities with institutional missions and goals.

History of Faculty Development

Faculty professional development had simple beginnings just a few decades ago, when the provision of sabbaticals was the extent of its offerings in the United States. In the 1970s faculty development expanded to include programming in teaching skills and knowledge (Centra, 1976; Lawler & King, 2000) with workshops and seminars focused on attitude change and skill development (Levinson-Rose & Menges, 1981). The mid-1980s saw the establishment of instructional development centers (Elsever & Chauvin, 1998; Lawler & King, 2000). The early 1990s experienced a shift in focus from teaching to student learning, and faculty development centers saw themselves as serving the institution more broadly (Lieberman, 2005). During the 2000s the goals of faculty development included guiding faculty members as they negotiated the challenges affecting institutions in higher education (Langley, O'Connor, & Welkener, 2004); encouraging faculty members to critically examine their habits of mind about teaching in order to better understand what they do, what they believe, and why so that they could consider alternative ways to think about their teaching (Cranton & King, 2003); and developing teaching and motivational skills for face-to-face and online situations (Hampton, Morrow, Bechtel, & Carroll, 2004). Some saw the move to online teaching as an opportunity for faculty members to rethink their beliefs about teaching and learning (McQuiggan, 2007), whereas others suggested the overall goal was to focus on improving student learning (Sorcinelli, Austin, Eddy, & Beach, 2006; Wright, 2002).

The 2000s saw heightened expectations for faculty dealing with funding and accountability pressures (Sorcinelli et al., 2006). The difficult economic times and increased demands for accountability have led to the recent interest in evaluating the effectiveness of faculty development (Hines, 2009, 2011; Plank & Kalish, 2010). In 2010, at the 35th Annual Professional Organizational and Development (POD) Network Conference, assessing the impact of faculty development was identified as a key priority (Hines, 2011).

Although literature on faculty development program success is available (Centra, 1976; Chism & Szabo, 1996; Erickson, 1986; Murray, 2002), it typically does not provide substantial information about how it was evaluated to determine its success. Beyond simple satisfaction surveys and data on usage and who used what services, there still exists a significant lack of rigorous and systematic research evaluating faculty development programs to provide this needed evidence (Chism & Szabo, 1997; Hines, 2009; Steinert et al., 2006). Hines (2009) explained that "program success needs to be reframed to mean quality educational outcomes," rather than only reporting on satisfied users (p. 10). It is important to note that the lack of evaluation has often been tied to an absence of faculty development program goals, and especially goals tied to the institution's mission, highlighting yet another gap in evaluation practices.

The Quality Transformation Faculty Development Assessment Framework

The online teaching and learning environment presents a radically different set of instructional dynamics that require consideration and adoption by the online instructor. A high-quality faculty development program needs to understand all the parameters of these new instructional dynamics and be able to serve the professional development needs of online instructors, novice and experienced alike. According to Brancato (2003), "Faculty development initiatives that are strategically planned, implemented, and sustainable over time encourage a perspective on teaching as a lifelong endeavor and necessitate continuous learning by faculty" (p. 61). Assessing the impact of such a program requires a thoughtful, planned, and measured approach that starts with basic data points such as number of participants and repeat participants and ends with the more behavioral measures of changed teaching practices. A systematic approach to information gathering and analysis of all professional development activities will provide continuous constructive feedback for program assessment and successful professional development efforts (Guskey, 2002; Hines, 2009).

Many faculty development models designed to assist with the preparation of the online instructor have focused on the "transition" from the face-to-face classroom to teaching online. This framework, although comfortable for the instructor because it attempts to build upon already familiar teaching skills, may not serve the long-term developmental needs of the online instructor. Rather, a "transformation" model for online instructor preparation is required. A transformation model represents a marked change in appearance or character of the teaching and learning experience and conveys the message that the online classroom is a new type and style of learning space. According to Hines (2009), "Program success needs to be reframed to mean quality educational outcomes [as] opposed to satisfied users" (p. 10).

So, too, the evaluation of the quality of instructor preparation throughout this "transformation" calls for the consideration of a fresh approach and new strategies. Evaluating the impact of a faculty development initiative has several inherent challenges owing to the nature of professional development for faculty, institutional variables such as promotion and tenure processes, and the willingness of faculty members to expose their potential weaknesses through an evaluation process. These challenges, and the complexity they imply, create the perception of insurmountable barriers to determining the return on investment of faculty professional development programming. Indeed, many individuals in the field will readily admit to not having a good handle on their program assessment techniques or not being as robust in evaluation as they desire.

Four integral sources were considered in constructing a framework for assessing faculty development. The first source is Kirkpatrick's (1994) four steps of evaluation: reaction, learning, behavior, and results. With Kirkpatrick's steps, the most common and easiest evaluation to complete is faculty members' reactions to their professional development experience, often referred to as a happiness index or smile sheets. As faculty developers, we often capture the input of content, learning activities, and resources shared and marginally capture the output of participation and satisfaction. Additionally, we rarely capture the outcomes of faculty professional development activities that include change in teaching behaviors, impact on student learning, or impact on the institution.

Also included in the framework's construction were Guskey's (2002) five critical levels of information: participants' reactions, participants' learning, organizational support and change, participants' use of new knowledge and skills, and student learning outcomes. Guskey (2002) suggests that we look for evidence instead of definitive proof. This could include collecting anecdotes and testimonials, creating meaningful comparison groups, administering pre- and posttest measures, and using time-series designs with multiple measures collected before and after implementation. Although this process does not need to be complicated, it does require thoughtful planning, purposeful questions, and a basic understanding of the strategies for answering those questions (Guskey, 2002).

An additional source (Plank & Kalish, 2010) provided guidance for working through preassessment planning, determining outcomes and measurements, and then reporting the results. In preassessment planning, program goals are defined by identifying what you want to know and why. It is important to link the unit and program goals to the institution's strategic plan to provide value by helping to meet those strategic goals and to ensure that the outcomes remain useful and relevant for the institution. A needs assessment can be completed to determine faculty needs and stakeholders' expectations. Once goals are defined, how to measure achievement of those goals must be determined by identifying sources of data, including the kinds of evidence that reflects the work and the impact of each service offered by the faculty center. Evidence can be collected from faculty development programming from workshops, seminars, and consultations to the receipt of grants and awards, the creation of new resources, and even presentations and publications. Consider the reporting and use of the data both internally to the faculty center and externally to the institution's administration. Internally, data can be used to make decisions about future program planning. Externally, data can be used to make decisions about budget requests, marketing, and performance reviews of the faculty center staff (Plank & Kalish, 2010).

Finally, Hines's (2009) dimensions of quality program assessment, determined by their commonality and recurrence in the literature, were considered in the framework's construction. These dimensions include program assessment that is systematic and goal-directed with benchmarks for success, assessment methods that measure the objectives, multiple measures to collect both formative and summative data, and evidence of a causal relationship. More recently, Hines (2011) provided a description of the match between desired outcomes and assessment: If the purpose of the initiative is to meet the needs of faculty preparation, then the assessment methods would evaluate faculty behavior. If the purpose is to meet needs of the institution, employ methods and metrics that would evaluate institutional impact. If the purpose is to improve academic quality, strategies may include the evaluation of faculty and student learning outcomes. Hines (2011) added, "Evaluation of faculty development programs can be done in an efficient and effective manner by developing a systematic plan designed for staggered, staged-out evaluation that considers staff time and available technology" (p. 5).

By combining the assessment techniques in these four sources—Kirkpatrick (1994), Guskey (2002), Plank and Kalish (2010), and Hines (2009)—the Quality Transformation Faculty Development Assessment Framework was created. Any institution considering the creation or adaptation of the Quality Transformation Faculty Development Assessment Framework should have a thorough understanding of expectations for, and of, their faculty development initiative. The assessment of program success should be aligned with the explicit or implicit purposes of the faculty development program and with institutional goals and values (Guskey, 2002; Hines, 2009, 2011; Plank & Kalish, 2010). The six steps of this framework build incrementally in ease of data collection and complexity and scaffold upon each other to create a comprehensive system of building program effectiveness and impact. Institutions may not be able to use all the suggested methods or approaches but should consider prioritizing and employing those that best match their needs. It is suggested that institutions bring all assessment data, from program attendance and consultations to evaluations and surveys, into a single relational data system. This way, data will need to be entered only once but can be available for a number of outputs and reports, creating a valuable efficiency (Plank & Kalish, 2010).

The key to establishing quality assurance measures and practices is to begin somewhere. Identifying several methods and metrics as a starting point for determining impact, although perhaps not the ideal, is of far greater worth than waiting to "get it perfect." The Quality Transformation Faculty Development Assessment Framework is an organizational model that can adapt and assimilate the best of the existing evaluation models into a practical and doable quality assurance methodology for today's faculty professional development programs. If a faculty center has programming in place but no assessment practices, Step 1 might be the place to start for easy entry. However, if a center has been newly created and is starting new programming from scratch, it might be best to begin with Step 6 and work backward to Step 1.

Step 1: Participation Metrics

Although in no way a guaranteed measure of professional development program impact, recording and tracking the level of faculty attendance and pattern of program participation provide critical baseline data on the level of faculty engagement. If attendance is 80% of the goal, the professional development offerings must address variables that continually track and increase this metric.

With a clear understanding of the characteristics of the target audience, the professional development program can creatively design and deliver learning opportunities that serve faculty needs. For example, if the target faculty members are primarily individuals in an adjunct relationship with the institution, providing professional development programs for self-study and completion in an asynchronous mode will address the problem of finding the right or best time for program delivery. In addition, providing layers of program content may address the needs of novice (introductory information), intermediate (increased best practices), and expert (advanced tips) learners.

The quality of faculty development initiatives is largely, but not solely, based on faculty participation. Having the metrics available and the systems necessary to track faculty participation is the first criterion for an effective professional program. Faculty development staff should collaboratively determine the data categories, what to count and how, and how to use data in their strategic planning efforts (Plank & Kalish, 2010). Assessment efforts should be integrated into the daily work of all faculty development staff, making data collection "regular, timely, accurate, and feasible" (Plank & Kalish, 2010, p. 143).

Table 7.1 provides a sample of desired outcomes and metrics that may be used to establish levels of professional program participation.

The Illinois Online Network (ION) offers a series of online faculty development courses titled Making the Virtual Classroom a Reality (MVCR). Course participants and ION administrators use a web portal that tracks participants' progress, enrollment data, and course completion. This data collection enables the administrators to generate reports on the number of registrants, the percentage of registrants who register for more than one course, and the number of registrants who successfully complete a course (Varvel, Lindeman, & Stovall, 2003).

Data collection for participation in the various Centers for Teaching and Learning at the City University of New York allowed the institution to report that in 2010–2011 it served approximately 2,500 full-time faculty, 850 adjunct faculty, and 650 staff. The report highlighted the need to more fully integrate adjunct faculty into professional development offerings. The university also collected data about the various types of development events and their delivery methods. These data showed that although the university's development programs focus on the impact of technology on teaching and learning, very few of its professional development offerings were provided online (Wilks, 2011).

Step 2: Faculty Input and Satisfaction Metrics

Great caution needs to be applied when considering faculty satisfaction measures as an indicator of the quality of professional development programming. The transformative nature of online teaching and learning generates

TABLE 7.1
Step 1: Participation Quality Assurance Outcomes and Metrics

Sample outcomes	Metrics
Faculty participation	Number of program participants
Percentage of faculty participation	Number of available faculty participants versus actual number of participants
Reengagement	Number of repeat attendees
Course completion	Number/percentage of participants who complete the course
Participation by specific discipline, school, department, or full-time or part-time faculty	Number/percentage of participants broken down by variables

a level of discomfort and uneasiness that is necessary for faculty to achieve some of the program goals and outcomes. In many professional development programs, much attention is given to the degree of customer satisfaction following participation. Did participants enjoy the experience? Did they feel the experience was worth their time? Were they physically comfortable during the program (e.g., was the temperature of the room comfortable), and was the method of program delivery convenient? Indeed, substantial program elements are routinely adjusted to appease the customer and increase the degree of satisfaction. These traditional measures may still be collected; however, interpretation and consideration of customer satisfaction data need to be balanced against the overall, long-term desired changes in instructional behaviors.

It may be more helpful to consider information gathered via satisfaction-based inquiries as input into the design and delivery format, timing, sequencing, and topic aspects of the faculty development program. These inquiries may be less about faculty liking or being comfortable with the course content and more about assessing the most efficient and effective delivery model. Additionally, these inquiries are a method of gaining insights into what topics the faculty members are interested in learning about.

Certainly a quality assurance strategy for a faculty development initiative will include methods that enable the constituent group to provide input and guidance in program design and delivery. Table 7.2 provides a series of sample inquiries that may help to gather input on both program logistics and areas of need for professional development.

For ION's MVCR series of courses, anonymous postcourse evaluation surveys are used to collect data on course design and organization and instructor performance. In one sampling of results, 94% of respondents indicated that the course overall was excellent or good, 83% indicated that they would strongly agree or agree that there was an appropriate amount of participation among classmates, 91% strongly agreed or agreed that the course gave them skills and techniques directly applicable to their jobs, and 96% indicated that they would take an MVCR course again (Varvel et al., 2003).

Step 3: Attitude and Knowledge Metrics

To measure the impact of any educational intervention, one must assess a degree of change in attitude about and knowledge of the subject matter. In the simplest of models, this change in attitude and knowledge would be assessed after the educational or training event has been completed and would be based on a comparison with data obtained before the training occurred. This assessment may use a variety of devices to gather input, including knowledge tests, attitudinal measures, and written learning reflections.

TABLE 7.2
Step 2: Faculty Input and Satisfaction Quality Assurance Inquiries and Metrics

Sample inquiries	Metrics
Was the professional development program offered at a convenient time?	Scaled response rate (very inconvenient to very convenient). Qualitative input: please indicate why this time was inconvenient for you.
Was the duration (number of days or weeks) of the professional development program reasonable for you?	Scaled response rate (very unreasonable to very reasonable). Qualitative input: please indicate why this duration was unreasonable for you.
Which topics offered in the professional development program were most beneficial for you?	Provide checklist that enables faculty to choose topics from program offerings.
What additional topics were not offered in the professional development program that you would have found beneficial?	Provide checklist of other topics (not currently included) for faculty to choose from.
What questions remain?	Provide space for open-ended response.

The content of a faculty development program needs to reflect the local context of the online learning initiative. For example, an institution that defines and implements a synchronous online learning program (e.g., using online video conferencing or streamed lectures) should include strategies to engage learners and evaluation techniques appropriate for this model in its faculty development program. An institution using primarily an asynchronous model of online education, such as may be delivered via a learning management system, will need to include a different set of skills and competencies in its development program. Additionally, the applicability of soft skills, such as serving the needs of the adult learner or military student, may vary from institution to institution.

Ensuring the quality of faculty development programs regarding instilling attitudes and knowledge necessary for online teaching success may include ensuring that the program aligns with the institutional model for online learning. This requires a clear grasp of the required information and soft skills reflected in the institutional model. Table 7.3 suggests several techniques that may be used to ensure faculty development program quality in terms of attitudes and knowledge.

ION used a survey to measure the long-term effects of MVCR training on faculty members who registered for a course in the series. The survey

TABLE 7.3

Step 3: Attitude and Knowledge Quality Assurance Techniques and Metrics

Sample techniques	Metrics
Knowledge quizzes and exams embedded in faculty development program	Standard grading scales and feedback
Postprogram survey instruments (phone interviews, focus groups, online surveys) examining attitudes toward learning environment	Feedback regarding online instructor's preparedness (identify areas requiring additional information or skill development)
Collection of feedback from student complaint and resolution services	Number of complaints; nature of conflicts and resolutions
Midcourse and end-of-course student survey on online instructor's preparedness and teaching practices	Student satisfaction and evaluation of instructor preparedness for teaching online

studied faculty members' confidence in their ability to teach online before and after taking the MVCR course in order to gauge whether their level of knowledge about online teaching was sufficient to instill confidence. ION conducted a *t*-test to determine the differences between participants' responses before and after the MVCR course and found highly significant results showing an increase in faculty confidence after program participation. ION has also used surveys at the completion of its Faculty Summer Institute. One survey question asks, "To what extent did the institute increase your understanding in the following areas?" The answer choices include use of technologies in instruction, student benefits from educational technology, faculty benefits from educational technology, technologies available for teaching, effective online pedagogy, and instructional design (Varvel et al., 2003).

Step 4: Instructor Performance Metrics

The ultimate measure of the quality of a faculty development program for online education is feedback on the online instructor's teaching performance. Measuring and gauging the actual in-classroom behavior of an online instructor directly reflects on the impact of a faculty development program. Examining the degree of transfer of the instructor's learning from a professional development program to the online classroom is critical, however difficult or challenging. The ability to measure teaching behavior or performance is largely informed by the cultural practices and academic policies of the organization. Depending on the degree of access to the online classroom environment, observing teaching performance may be more or less possible. In many cases, as long as institutional policies are adhered to, online instructors may welcome insights, analysis, and feedback on their teaching performance from a trained observer or experienced colleague.

Faculty preparation programs are more challenging to assess because of the complexities of several key variables. Some of these may include the following:

- Lack of evaluation or assessment information prior to the faculty development program
- Lack of definition of the required skills and competencies expected to be taught
- Lack of information regarding skills developed in prior faculty development programming
- Inability to observe and record instructor's teaching ability both before and after faculty development program intervention
- Lack of academic authority and access to instructor teaching performance scores, student ratings, or assessment results

Some of these challenges may require creative alternative or secondary approaches. Several of the strategies for assessing teaching performance may be similar to methods suggested in the attitude and knowledge step of this framework. Instructor self-reflection can provide valuable insights but is dependent upon self-reporting techniques. Another strategy for gathering teaching performance feedback is using a longitudinal survey of instructor-reported transfer of behaviors resulting from professional development programs. Regardless of the approach used, planning and implementing techniques to measure the direct results of faculty preparation programs remains a crucial element of a high-quality faculty development effort.

Although presenting challenges and obstacles for many faculty development programs, assessment strategies to track and measure direct impact of the program on instructor performance remains a valuable and critical dimension of gauging program impact. Table 7.4 provides a sampling of strategies that may assist in this effort.

With the belief that the level of interaction in an online course can be a key indicator of course quality, ION conducted a survey that included questions focused on the level of interactivity among participants in online courses in the MCVR program to determine whether it had increased as a result of MVCR training. The responses indicated a positive result. A postprogram survey of Faculty Summer Institute participants included

TABLE 7.4
Step 4: Instructor Performance Quality Assurance Techniques and Metrics

Sample techniques	Metrics
Postprogram survey instruments (phone interviews, focus groups, online surveys) examining teaching behaviors, conducted either immediately following a program or over a longer period	Description of teaching behaviors and source of new skill (creating a linkage to faculty preparation program)
Midcourse and end-of-course student survey on online instructor's preparedness and teaching practices	Student satisfaction and evaluation of instructor preparedness for teaching online
Collection of feedback on instructor teaching behaviors	Evidence of the application of specific instructional methods and techniques by online instructor

the question, "How likely are you to incorporate aspects of what you learned at the Institute into the classes you teach and support?" Of the 193 respondents, 144 found application to be extremely likely, 47 found application to be somewhat likely, and 2 found application not at all likely (Varvel et al., 2003).

Step 5: Student Performance

The quality of a faculty development program can be linked indirectly to student performance through the adequate preparation of the online instructor. Although there are many mitigating factors impacting student retention and success, certainly the skill and ability of the online instructor to create a learning environment in which the student has a reasonable opportunity for success plays a critical role in the educational endeavor. Great care needs to be used when determining student success in a faculty development program.

A skilled and competent online instructor may improve the student's ability to manage and ultimately succeed in an online class. A faculty development program should consider establishing measures to assess the impact of the program on student performance. This step may include establishing an active relationship with student services units, examining student-faculty problem resolution functions, and establishing a close relationship with the academic unit. Table 7.5 provides sample techniques that may be considered when assessing the impact of faculty development programming on student success.

TABLE 7.5
Step 5: Student Performance Quality Assurance Techniques and Metrics

Sample techniques	Metrics
Examination of student retention within program of study, student progress toward degree, years to program completion	Data gathered from student tracking and record systems
Calculation of number of students achieving passing grade	Program or institutionally defined
End-of-course (or maybe longer-term) student survey regarding online instructor's preparedness and teaching practices	Student report and evaluation of instructor's impact on course success

The LaGuardia Center for Teaching and Learning in the City University of New York collaborates with institutional researchers to collect formative and summative evaluation data using faculty surveys, faculty documentation of innovative practice, and student surveys. The center also uses student outcomes such as attrition, course pass rates, pass rates on standardized examinations, and next-semester retention. These data are then analyzed to inform institutional policy and practice (Wilks, 2011).

Step 6: Return on Investment Metrics

The final analysis in a comprehensive quality assessment of a faculty development program needs to determine the institution's return on its financial investment in terms of the desired outcomes for online learning. This step may include both short-term (postprogram delivery) and long-term (over time) impact evaluation. Although not necessarily an easy or convenient analysis to conduct, this step ensures that the program's overall service to the institution's goals and mission is considered, measured, and analyzed. Institutions are cautioned to avoid using this step as a single data point for determining program value or impact.

To assess the return on investment in faculty professional development programming and support services, a variety of factors should be considered. Primarily, the program needs to be in alignment with the institution's stated outcomes for online programming. In addition, the institution's core principles regarding online education and its models for delivering such education need to be thoroughly reviewed and integrated into the comprehensive faculty development evaluation model. Table 7.6 provides several suggested methods and metrics for assessing return on investment in faculty development programming.

TABLE 7.6
Step 6: Return on Investment Quality Assurance Techniques and Metrics

Sample techniques	Metrics
Analysis of resources invested in faculty development programming	Annual budget, including staff, material, and program delivery costs
Establishment of data points aligned with institutional goals and mission (these may include qualitative as well as quantitative measures)	Assessments of specific institutional records and documents related to online learning
Collection of qualitative data on impact of faculty development on overall institution direction and service to students	Student and faculty evaluations, input from advisory boards, governing bodies, and accrediting agencies

Conclusion

New and rapidly emerging technologies and pedagogies, coupled with an ever-shifting higher education landscape, provide a rich context for faculty development and preparation programs. Not only are institutions examining how they respond to this evolving reality in order to meet the needs and demands of today's educational ecosystem, but they are also considering how to serve the needs of their instructional resources. The vast majority of today's faculty transitioning from face-to-face delivery to an online teaching/learning environment did not experience a virtual classroom firsthand during their academic career. Thus, the need for faculty development is more critical than ever and will continue to be so as the pace of change in higher education either holds steady or slowly increases.

The growth of faculty development programs across delivery platforms and formats highlights the need for institutions to comprehensively assess the efficiency and effectiveness of these initiatives. Assuring quality in the design, construction, and delivery of a faculty development program must be a consideration at the start of the program, not an add-on once the initiative is under way. Beginning with a quality assurance plan requires that the program objectives be clearly stated and strategies to assess these methods be considered and implemented up front.

The Quality Transformation Faculty Development Assessment Framework provides a stepped approach to quality assurance with suggested strategies and metrics at each phase. This model draws from relevant literature, including Kirkpatrick's (1994) four steps of evaluation, Guskey's (2002) five critical levels of information, guidance provided by Plank and Kalish

(2010), and Hines's (2009) dimensions of quality program assessment. The Quality Transformation Faculty Development Assessment Framework does not imply that all institutions must consider implementing all steps in the framework. Rather, based upon a thorough understanding of the institutional goals and outcomes of the faculty development initiative, an institution should identify those strategies and metrics that fit its system. A quality assurance framework does imply, however, that strategies and metrics from each of the six steps be considered in the plan.

Step 1 of the framework includes participation metrics designed to track the level of faculty participation and patterns of faculty development progress. This step provides critical baseline data on the level of faculty engagement. Data collected in this step can inform the program delivery design by highlighting who participates, when, and the method they use to access resources. Matched with a thorough understanding of the target audience, these data can help an institution make adjustments to the program delivery model.

Step 2, faculty input and satisfaction measures, examines general faculty appreciation and satisfaction with their learning experience. Although caution needs to be applied when considering adjustments based on these data, they are a valuable source of input as far as meeting faculty expectations for professional development. Being customer-centered is an important consideration but should be balanced with a clear understanding of the impact of the faculty development program.

The attitudes and knowledge measures contained in Step 3 are directed to assess the participants' change in attitude and knowledge gained. One effective method for evaluating this domain is by measuring attitude and knowledge before and after training and comparing the two. This step needs to reflect the local context of the online learning initiative. Attitudes and knowledge necessary for one educational model may be dramatically different from those necessary for another model.

Step 4 examines instructor performance in the online teaching environment, perhaps the ultimate measure of faculty development impact. This step has been identified as one of the more challenging dimensions of assessment owing to varying cultural practices and academic policies among organizations. Although not a perfect measure, instructor self-reporting is one method for assessing changes in teaching behavior. Peer course review and student feedback may also be input sources for this quality assurance measure.

The student performance measures suggested in Step 5 may be correlated with but not directly tied to the effectiveness of faculty development programming. Increases in student performance, success, and retention may be more significant in programs with faculty who have been adequately trained and prepared for teaching success. Care needs to be used when correlating a faculty development program with student success.

The final step, Step 6, return on investment, suggests that a quality analysis of a faculty development program can be tied to quantitative metrics in a business model that reflects the degree to which the faculty development program matches the institutional needs. A business-based model for measuring institutional impact allows the institution to justify and validate professional development program impact and return on investment of resources. Caution needs to be exercised to avoid using this step as a single data point for determining program value or impact.

Quality assurance of a faculty professional development program can be achieved by carefully matching the desired outcomes of the initiative to the strategies and metrics used to ascertain effectiveness, efficiency, and impact. Analyzing multiple measures increases the reliability of quality assurance and provides breadth as well as depth of information (Sorcinelli & Stanley, 2011). Beginning with a clear understanding of the goals of the program and overlaying selected techniques from each of the six steps of the Quality Transformation Faculty Development Assessment Framework will allow faculty development programs to establish, validate, and verify program contributions through both direct and indirect measures.

Ultimately, the Quality Transformation Faculty Development Assessment Framework must operate within the culture and context of the institution. The best results will be realized when all participants—program developers and online faculty alike—are included in the process of defining, designing, and analyzing program outcomes and subsequent success. In the end, it is the learner who benefits from a well-prepared online instructor whose professional development needs are well addressed through a quality-assured faculty development program.

References

Ali, N. S., Hodson-Carlton, K., Ryan, M., Flowers, J., Rose, M. A., & Wayda, V. (2005). Online education: Needs assessment for faculty development. *Journal of Continuing Education in Nursing, 36*(1), 32–38.

Brancato, V. (2003). Professional development in higher education. *New Directions for Adult and Continuing Education, 2003*(98), 59–65.

Centra, J. (1976). *Faculty development practices in U.S. colleges and universities.* Princeton, NJ: Educational Testing Service.

Chism, N., & Szabo, B. (1996). Who uses faculty development services? *To Improve the Academy, 15*, 115–128.

Chism, N., & Szabo, B. (1997). How faculty development programs evaluate their services. *Journal of Staff, Program and Organizational Development, 15*(2), 55–62.

Covington, D., Petherbridge, D., & Warren, S. E. (2005). Best practices: A triangulated support approach in transitioning faculty to online teaching. *Online Journal of Distance Learning Administration, 8*(1). Retrieved from http://www.westga.edu/~distance/ojdla/spring81/covington81.htm

Cranton, P., & King, K. P. (2003). Transformative learning as a professional development goal. *New Directions for Adult and Continuing Education, 2003*(98), 31–38.

Dalziel, C. (2003). Community colleges and distance education. In M. Moore & W. G. Anderson (Eds.), *Handbook of distance education* (pp. 663–671). Mahwah, NJ: Lawrence Erlbaum.

Elsever, C. B., & Chauvin, S. W. (1998). Professional development how to's: Strategies for surveying faculty preferences. *Innovative Higher Education, 22*(3), 181–201.

Erickson, F. (1986). Qualitative methods in research on teaching. In M. C. Wittrock (Ed.), *Handbook of research on teaching* (3rd ed., pp. 119–161). Old Tappan, NJ: Macmillan.

Guskey, T. (2002). Does it make a difference? Evaluating professional development. *Educational Leadership, 59*(6), 45–51.

Hampton, S. E., Morrow, C. D., Bechtel, A., & Carroll, M. H. (2004). A systematic, hands-on, reflective, and effective (SHORE) approach to faculty development for new and seasoned faculty. *To Improve the Academy, 22*, 156–172.

Hines, S. (2009). Investigating faculty development program assessment practices: What's being done and how can it be improved? *Journal of Faculty Development, 23*(3), 5–19.

Hines, S. (2011). How to evaluate your faculty development services. *Academic Leader, 27*(2), 1.

Kirkpatrick, D. L. (1994). *Evaluating training programs.* San Francisco: Berrett-Koehler.

Langley, D., O'Connor, T. W., & Welkener, M. M. (2004). A transformative model for designing professional development activities. *To Improve the Academy, 22*, 145–154.

Lawler, P. A., & King, K. P. (2000). *Planning for effective faculty development: Using adult learning strategies.* Malabar, FL: Krieger.

Lawler, P. A., & King, K. P. (2001). *Refocusing faculty development: The view from an adult learning perspective.* Paper presented at the Pennsylvania Adult and Continuing Education Research Conference, Indiana, PA.

Levinson-Rose, J., & Menges, R. F. (1981). Improving college teaching: A critical review of research. *Review of Educational Research, 51*(3), 403–434.

Lieberman, D. (2005). Beyond faculty development: How centers for teaching and learning can be laboratories for learning. *New Directions for Higher Education, 2005*(131), 87–98.

McQuiggan, C. (2007). The role of faculty development in online teaching's potential to question teaching beliefs and assumptions. *Online Journal of Distance Learning Administration 10*(3). Retrieved from http://www.westga.edu/~distance/ojdla/fall103/mcquiggan103.htm

Murray, J. P. (2002). The current state of faculty development in two-year colleges. *New Directions for Community Colleges, 2002*(118), 89–97.

Phipps, R., & Merisotis, J. (2000). *Quality on the line: Benchmarks for success in Internet-based distance education.* Retrieved from the Institute for Higher Education Policy website: www.ihep.com/quality.pdf

Plank, K., & Kalish, A. (2010). Program assessment for faculty development. In K. J. Gillespie & D. L. Robertson (Eds.), *A guide to faculty development* (2nd ed., pp. 135–149). San Francisco: Jossey-Bass.

Sorcinelli, M., Austin, A., Eddy, P., & Beach, A. (2006). *Creating the future of faculty development: Learning from the past, understanding the present.* Bolton, MA: Anker.

Sorcinelli, M. D., & Stanley, C. (2011, May 6). *Using assessment to become a non-negotiable asset.* Paper presented in Why Faculty Development Matters: Assessing Impact, Jossey-Bass and POD Network webinar.

Steinert, Y., Mann, K., Centeno, A., Dolmans, D., Spencer, J., Gelula, M., & Prideaux, D. (2006). A systematic review of faculty development initiatives designed to improve teaching effectiveness in medical education: BEME Guide No. 8. *Medical Teacher, 28*(6), 497–526.

Varvel, V., Lindeman, M., & Stovall, I. (2003). The Illinois Online Network (ION) is making the virtual classroom a reality: Study of an exemplary faculty development program. *Journal of Asynchronous Learning Networks, 7*(2), 81–95. Retrieved from http://sloan-c.org/publications/jaln/v7n2/v7n2_varvel.asp

Wilks, K. (2011). *Analysis of CUNY centers for teaching and learning.* Retrieved from the City University of New York website: http://www.cuny.edu/about/administration/offices/ue/CentersTeachingLearning/CTLReport6-15-11.pdf

Wright, D. L. (2002). Program types and prototypes. In K. H. Gillespie (Ed.), *A guide to faculty development: Practical advice, examples, and resources* (pp. 24–34). Bolton, MA: Anker.

Yang, Y., & Cornelious, L. F. (2005). Preparing instructors for quality online instruction. *Online Journal of Distance Learning Administration, 8*(1). Retrieved from http://www.westga.edu/~distance/ojdla/spring81/yang81.htm

8

THE POWER OF A COLLABORATIVE, COLLEGIAL APPROACH TO IMPROVING ONLINE TEACHING AND LEARNING

Leonard Bogle, Scott Day, Daniel Matthews, and Karen Swan

This chapter will demonstrate how online teaching and learning can be enhanced by the collegial efforts of faculty members working collaboratively to analyze and improve their online courses. The focus of this chapter will be a process for improving instruction and learning without alienating faculty members. It will emphasize the collaborative use of the Quality Matters (QM) Rubric to review and revise online course designs and the Community of Inquiry (CoI) survey to iteratively review and revise learning processes in the identified courses.

A description of the program in which these changes were made, the stakeholders affected by these changes, and the focus on continuous improvement will be addressed, as will the application of a collaborative/collegial approach and backward design to assure design quality and implementation. We conclude with practical recommendations and advice for those programs and institutions desiring to make similar improvements in their online courses and programs.

Master of Arts in Teacher Leadership Program

The Educational Leadership (EDL) program at the University of Illinois Springfield provides master's degrees for educational practitioners who desire to become school administrators or teacher leaders. In the past 15 years, the EDL department has grown from a full-time instructional staff of three professors who taught strictly face-to-face classes to an instructional staff of eight full-time professors who teach face-to-face, blended, and fully online courses today. This development from a small department to a nationally recognized online program was the result of visionary leadership and faculty who regularly reviewed and refined course offerings in an environment where sharing information and working collaboratively is not only encouraged, but embraced.

The initial development of the fully online master of arts in teacher leadership (MTL) program focused on what types of content, training, and assessments would result in the greatest amount of change in schools. We believed the online option would offer K–12 educators in rural America greater access to a teacher-focused advanced degree, while expanding the potential for students from other states to take advantage of these offerings. A degree development grant from the Sloan Foundation, which was interested in assisting universities that were trying to offer teacher-oriented degrees online, provided a much-needed impetus for the development of the first two courses in the program. In five years' time, enrollments grew from 30 to nearly 300 students in the program. Today, our students represent 26 states and six countries outside the United States, and the EDL department is one of the largest graduate student departments on campus.

Stakeholders

The systematic changes made to the courses in the MTL program affect all stakeholders—faculty, students in the program, and schools and school personnel across country. Most but not all students in the MTL program are teachers; nonteachers work in a variety of fields, including dental hygiene and store management. Some are academic professionals and coordinators in higher education. The MTL program is designed to meet the needs of those individuals who desire to enhance their leadership skills in an educational setting.

The process by which the MTL program enhanced the design of its courses, increased student satisfaction, and realized student achievement gains can be undertaken by any department at any level. The key elements to realizing these gains are (a) a desire to improve the existing offerings, (b) a willingness to provide access to an existing course for design analysis by other faculty, and (c) a readiness to adjust course designs based on empirical data and peer review. An environment where collaboration is sought and collegiality encouraged is also essential to achieve maximum impact of course changes on student achievement.

Continuous Improvement and Results

The redesign of the MTL program started with a single section of a single course titled Educational Research Methods. We assumed that improved course design based on a peer review using the QM Rubric would result in improved learning processes, which in turn would enhance student learning outcomes. The outcome measures included final course grades as well as scores on the final exam and the major course paper. The initial revision process, which took place in the fall of 2009, was guided by an informal QM review. The CoI survey, which measures learners' sense of engagement, then served as a measure of learning processes. We initially believed that changes in course design would result in improved learning processes, which in turn would result in improved learning outcomes. We were wrong.

The spring 2010 semester outcomes showed a reduction in student perceptions of learning processes (CoI scores) but an increase in student performance (learning outcomes) after the QM redesign (Swan, Matthews, Bogle, Welch-Boles, & Day, 2012). This led to the realization that the QM and CoI frameworks viewed learning from differing perspectives and, as such, measured different things. Because scores on the CoI survey went down after the QM redesign, we began exploring a second, design-based notion, namely, whether iterative changes to the course based on CoI responses could lead to further increases in student performance.

The average spring 2010 CoI scores were reviewed, and changes were made in course design and implementation in the summer 2010 course based on the lowest of these. Similarly, summer 2010 CoI scores were reviewed, and changes were made in the fall 2010 course implementation. This iterative, design-based approach resulted in significant improvements in learning outcomes across four semesters. That is, we found that a QM redesign followed by the iterative "tweaking" of design and implementation factors could meaningfully improve student outcomes (Swan et al., 2012).

The work on this one course has led to the QM and CoI analyses and revisions of other core courses within the MTL program. The analyses of these courses are ongoing and initial findings reflect what was learned from the analysis of Educational Research Methods: Adjustments to course design and implementation based on QM and CoI revisions can result in increased student achievement over time.

A Collaborative, Collegial Approach

Our approach to improving program quality differs distinctly from the traditional, administrative-led change models. We did not have the burden of imposing change or generating buy-in because our approach to change grew primarily from our intrinsic interests as educators in providing high-quality learning opportunities for our students. Our mechanisms for change were, and continue to be, continuous-improvement tools that are available to professional educators everywhere and that we voluntarily adopted and adapted to achieve our course improvement goals.

The catalyst that set in motion our programwide, data-informed course improvement project was the receipt of a small grant from Quality Matters to review and revise one course, Educational Research Methods. The course has been taught by different faculty, including a majority of the authors of this chapter, so the decision to consider the course for modifications coincidentally and fortuitously resulted in creating an impromptu team of collaborators.

Our team brought a range of experience and expertise to the task of responding to the initial QM review. The QM reviews were on two instructors' sections of the course, and both reviews identified the need to generate a list of course goals and learning objectives at the unit level and to make those available to the students themselves. The course instructors worked together to create common course goals and unit-level learning objectives that were then implemented in all sections of the course. Based on these common goals and objectives, the instructors independently modified their own course activities, including lectures, discussions, and formative assessments. Although each instructor's section shares course goals and objectives with other sections, it remains uniquely his or her own, distinctively influenced by the specific instructor.

That initial, onetime QM review and revision directly affected key course design components, including the identification of goals and learning objectives. As online educators, we were also interested in course processes—how our students were experiencing our courses and how those experiences might be improved. To understand those processes, we used the CoI framework (Garrison, Anderson, & Archer, 2000). At the program level, we set up a voluntary system that collects student perceptions of course processes using the CoI survey (Arbaugh et al., 2008; Swan et al., 2008). We set up a routine to analyze CoI data between semesters and to provide instructors with item-by-item averages for scores on each of the Likert-scale survey items. Instructors then used those data to identify specific elements to change within their courses and to implement those modifications.

After a semester of using these processes with a single course shared by multiple instructors, we recognized the potential value of this continuous-improvement process for other courses. We now use this process with virtually all the required courses in the degree program. The result is an ongoing, collaborative approach to programmatic change that incorporates the following key elements:

- a shared interest in initiating change
- agreed-upon frameworks (e.g., QM, CoI) for identifying areas for improvement and for evaluating progress toward change
- faculty independence and responsibility at the course level to creatively generate and implement learning activities that address our shared learning goals

Backward Design

Our collaborative approach to course improvement addresses Wiggins and McTighe's (2005) call for educators to replace content-based design with results-focused design, while maintaining an emphasis on the core value of faculty independence. Our approach is consistent with their argument for a backward-design approach to instruction: "The best designs derive backward from the learnings sought" (Wiggins & McTighe, 2005, p. 14). Wiggins and McTighe suggest that until we are quite clear about which specific understandings we are after and what such understandings look like in practice, it is not possible to determine *how* to teach for understanding or *which* materials and activities to use.

Identify Learning Outcomes and Assessments

The collaborative approach we used is consistent with Wiggins and McTighe's stage 1—identify desired results—and stage 2—determine acceptable evidence—in that, as a result of the QM review, we made explicit the previously implied goals and unit-level learning objectives. Our goals and objectives were developed collaboratively and ranged from specific unit-level objectives to course-level and even program-level goals. From these we collaboratively created general forms of assessment, which were subsequently modified by individual instructors. As a result of the QM review and our work to make our course goals and unit objectives more explicit and available to students, we addressed Wiggins and McTighe's (2005) recommendation that "students be helped to see *by design* the purpose of the activity or resource" and how that activity helps them to meet course goals (p. 17).

Design Learning Activities

Our collaborative approach to identifying learning outcomes and assessments is complemented by the faculty independence we support at the course-design level. That is, each course instructor, even when teaching different sections of the same course, is ultimately responsible for generating and providing learning experiences that he or she determines are appropriate and consistent with our shared goals while addressing the teaching and learning styles of the participants in each course section.

In other words, when we move from Wiggins and McTighe's (2005) stages 1 and 2 to their stage 3—plan learning experiences and instruction— we go from a primarily collaborative, programmatic approach to change to one that emphasizes individual faculty independence, creativity, and responsibility for identifying and implementing change at the course level.

Assuring Design Quality

Too often educators get so caught up in the fine-grained design of course activities that they lose sight of the design of the course as a whole. Thus, it is critically important, especially when addressing quality at the program level, to ensure that all courses meet general standards of design quality. General standards could, of course, be designed locally. Although this might make some sense in specialty programs, such as certain corporate training, in most cases the use of commonly accepted standards is both more effective and more efficient. Commonly accepted standards can always be adapted to meet local needs, but they have the advantage of having been validated through extensive application at multiple institutions.

Several rubrics have been developed to evaluate online course design. Two of the most commonly used are the Chico State Rubric for Online Instruction (California State University–Chico, 2003) and the QM Rubric (Quality Matters, 2011). The Chico State Rubric was specifically designed for self-evaluation, and thus it may not be the best vehicle to use for quality assurance at the program level.

The QM Rubric, in contrast, employs a faculty-oriented, but external and objective, peer-review process (see chapter 6, "A Process to Improve Course Design: A Key Variable in Course Quality"). It is almost certainly the most widely used instrument for assuring quality in online course design. It was the initial measure we used to assess and improve the quality of MTL core course designs. Although the QM Rubric is clearly objectivist in nature, as seen in the importance of module-level objectives to achieving a successful review, what is particularly useful about it is the standardized review process, clear-cut scoring (standards are either met or not), and the review results provided in a numerical score.

In our QM reviews of the MTL core courses, two faculty members served as reviewers, and they were led through the process by the third reviewer, an instructional designer from the university center for online learning

(Matthews, Bogle, Boles, Day, & Swan, 2012). After revisions were made to the courses, the entire MTL core faculty, including the course designer and instructors, met to share revisions and collaboratively decide whether or not the redesigned courses met QM standards. This sharing of course designs also resulted in the exposure of faculty members to many good ideas for the design of their own courses. In addition, the need to explicitly state objectives resulted in faculty discussions of key program goals and objectives and how these were being met within and across MTL core courses.

Ensuring Implementation of High-Quality Learning Processes

It is clear that unless online courses are designed to support particular learning processes these processes cannot occur. For example, unless an explicit provision is made for student discussions, such discussions cannot occur. However, design alone cannot ensure that learning will take place. Thus, it is important to have strategies for assessing the quality of particular course implementations and for assessing the quality of learning processes that occur within specific courses.

There are many ways to assess learning processes in online courses. Because most online learning happens within learning management systems (LMSs), such things as online discussions, instructor feedback, and the online activities of both instructors and students can be accessed quite easily. At least three types of learning processes can be categorized or measured using LMS reports and archived courses: pedagogical approaches, interactions, and forms of assessment.

Pedagogical Approaches

Pedagogical approaches can be categorized as objectivist or constructivist, formal or informal, low touch or high touch, and so on, and their effects studied. Arbaugh, Bangert, and Cleveland-Innes (2010), for example, have found pedagogical differences along these lines between what they identify as hard and soft disciplines in business education. Other pedagogical approaches that might be identified include the use of instructional strategies such as collaborative groups (Benbunan-Fich & Hiltz, 1999) and the incorporation of technologies into instruction (Ice, Curtis, Phillips, & Wells, 2007).

Interactions

Michael G. Moore (1989) identified three types of interactions that take place online: learner-instructor, learner-content, and learner-learner. There are a variety of ways to measure interactions among participants in online courses, many of which can be accessed through LMS reporting functions. Research has shown, for example, that interactions with instructors (Swan, 2001) and interactions among classmates (Jiang & Ting, 2000; Picciano, 2002) enhance perceived and actual learning in online courses.

Forms of Assessment

Assessment itself is another sort of learning process. What is assessed and how it is assessed affect the learning processes and general course outcomes (Swan, Shen, & Hiltz, 2006). Indeed, researchers have shown that how online activities are assessed significantly affects student behaviors (Swan, Schenker, Arnold, & Kuo, 2007).

Other ways of exploring online learning processes include social network analysis (Haythornthwaite, 2002) and content analyses (Shea & Bidjerano, 2010), but what these and the previously mentioned analyses have in common is that they all take an objectivist or quasi-objectivist stance. That is, they approach the learning process from the outside looking in. If one accepts the constructivist perspective, however, learning is uniquely individual and can therefore best be explored through the perspective of individual learners.

Community of Inquiry

One instrument that does just that is the CoI survey (Arbaugh et al., 2008; Swan et al., 2008), and for this reason, we used this survey to guide our efforts to improve the implementation of courses in the MTL program. The CoI survey also has the advantage of being grounded in one of the most widely accepted theoretical models of learning in online and blended environments.

The CoI framework (Garrison et al., 2000) is a collaborative-constructivist model of online learning processes. It assumes that effective online learning requires the development of a community of inquiry (Dewey, 1938; Lipman, 1991). The CoI model represents the online learning experience as a function of the interweaving of three "presences"—social presence, teaching presence, and cognitive presence—and suggests that all three are necessary for learning to take place. *Social presence* refers to the degree to which participants in online communities can project themselves as "real people" and feel socially and emotionally connected with each other. *Teaching presence* is defined as the design, facilitation, and direction of cognitive and social processes for the realization of personally meaningful and educationally worthwhile learning outcomes. *Cognitive presence* describes the extent to which learners are able to construct and confirm meaning through course activities, sustained reflection, and discourse.

The CoI survey is designed to measure student perceptions of the extent to which each of the presences are expressed in online courses. It consists of 34 items (13 teaching presence, 9 social presence, and 12 cognitive presence items) that ask students to rate their agreement on a 5-point Likert scale (1 = *strongly disagree*; 5 = *strongly agree*) with statements related to each of the elements of each of the presences. The survey was validated through a confirmatory factor analysis of survey responses from 287 students at four institutions of higher education in the United States and Canada (Arbaugh et al., 2008), the results of which validated both the survey and the CoI framework itself.

To improve and assure the quality of MTL core course implementations, students in the core courses are asked to complete the CoI survey every semester. We then collaboratively review the scores and brainstorm ways to improve the lowest-rated items. Changes to course design and implementation are then implemented in the next iteration of the course from which CoI scores are collected, low ratings are reviewed, and consequent changes are made. As previously stated, we have found this design-based approach of incremental improvements to be highly effective.

Practical Recommendations

Course Redesign Model

In our redesign efforts, we discovered the importance of a data-driven process. Our goal of improving course processes and learning outcomes is guided by theory, data, and collaboration (see Figure 8.1).

Figure 8.1 illustrates the key elements of our course redesign model. On the right side of the top theory level of the diagram is the CoI framework, the social constructivist approach that provided our team the structure for operationalizing improvements in course implementation and learning processes. On the left side of the theory level is the QM framework, which offered an objectivist theoretical perspective on our redesign efforts with an instructional design focus. Our ongoing course improvement process is informed by both theoretical perspectives.

The data level of the model includes both the initial QM peer reviews of course designs/redesigns and the semester-to-semester student feedback on learning processes obtained through the CoI survey. At the collaboration level at the bottom of the model, the data are analyzed and course modifications are made collaboratively. Although course-level revisions are implemented by the individual instructors, they are discussed collaboratively and strategies are shared among faculty. The collaborative nature of this process ensures that the faculty's course modifications reflect student perceptions

Figure 8.1. Course redesign model.

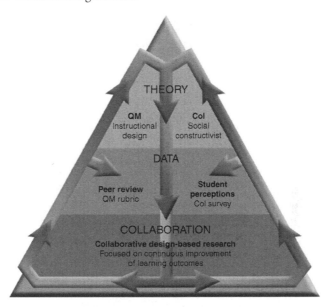

From "Developing Communities of Inquiry in Online Courses: A Design-Based Approach," by D. Matthews, L. Bogle, E. Boles, S. Day, & K. Swan, 2012, in *Educational Communities of Inquiry: Theoretical Framework, Research and Practice*, edited by Z. Akyol & D. R. Garrison pp. 490–508, Hershey, PA: IGI Global. Copyright 2012 by D. Matthews, L. Bogle, E. Boles, S. Day, & K. Swan. Reprinted with permission.

(CoI framework), peer analysis (QM framework), and a programwide vision. The process is situated in a multisemester, iterative cycle that begins again at the top of the model and culminates in continuous data-driven and collaborative improvements focused on learning outcomes.

To ensure the implementation of a collaborative, collegial approach, willing stakeholders must be included as part of an ongoing, iterative cycle. In our view, the first aspect of any change process is to effectively communicate with stakeholders (professors in the department) and obtain their approval before introducing a new plan (Bolman & Deal, 2008). In our case, the bottom-up approach, initiated by two faculty members who were working on the improvement of a single course, was particularly effective because others in the department were attracted to the research project. As faculty members were added to the research team, we found course redesign addressed at multiple stages of QM and CoI reviews and revisions to be useful. Further, this approach allowed us to focus on different aspects of our own courses, through design and then implementation processes.

Although it can be threatening to review a colleague's course content and to be reviewed by one's peers, it has helped us understand more about the degree program and how individual courses fit into the overall program goals. "While a single instructor can improve his or her own courses, programmatic improvements require collaborative efforts" (Day, Bogle, Swan, Matthews, & Boles, 2013, p. 405). We have discovered that improving your own course is enhanced by sharing the responsibility of reviewing courses developed by others. The willingness to work collaboratively has provided an opportunity for unique, informal, and ongoing professional development within our department.

The collaborative approach that facilitated this work emerged from a faculty with a history of working collaboratively well before this research project. The faculty members involved share an underlying sense of trust and respect for their colleagues. In our department, professors value each other's strengths and the collaborative approach and are willing to share instructional strategies and new technology deliveries. From the beginning, faculty members were willing to open their courses for peer review because they understood it was needed to help bring improvements in the overall program.

To ensure that the identified course outcomes are met, select a model or models that reflect the goals for the course or department. This ongoing study employs two of the most commonly used theoretical frameworks in online teaching and learning. It also provides an important outcome-based model for the improvement of online courses and programs. Taken together, the QM and CoI revisions can be linked to improving intended and actual outcomes in ways that (a) can been seen by all stakeholders and (b) are measurable and can be used for ongoing, continuous improvements by instructors and students because they are grounded in well-articulated models that reflect program goals.

To ensure design quality, collaboratively choose a common measure and apply it to essential courses in an open environment of collaboration and trust. Although we were very happy with the QM process and the ways in which its use improved our courses and our program, we think that collaboratively choosing an instrument with which all instructors or course designers are happy is more important than the chosen instrument itself. The selected instrument should provide clear and actionable findings. We also believe that course design issues are best addressed in an open environment where everyone helps each other in pursuit of common quality.

To ensure implementation quality, collaboratively choose a way to assess learning processes and apply it in a design-based, iterative manner. Again, although we found that the CoI survey captured student perceptions of implementation processes in a way that was both meaningful and could be acted upon, we believe it is more important to agree on a measure that all can believe in. Because learning processes are dependent on course participants, they must be assessed in an ongoing manner. Online technologies change over time, and what works for one instructor and a particular group of students may not work for another.

Continuous improvement must be embedded in the culture of the program. Finally, we are convinced that an ongoing, design-based approach is needed to maintain course and program quality. Such an approach is grounded in a collaborative, data-driven, iterative, and continuous cycle of assessment and revision that must become part of the faculty culture if it is to remain strong.

Conclusion

The growth in online course offerings by higher education institutions has necessitated analysis of the quality of those programs. This analysis must be ongoing and developed in a safe environment where instructors collaboratively analyze colleagues' courses, share their findings, and improve their own courses in the process. Doing so ensures that the rigor of the online courses is maintained while the design and student involvement is enhanced. Programs wishing to implement these changes to positively enhance their new or existing courses must select a design-analysis model and a method by which to determine student satisfaction. The models used by our department were the QM (design) and the CoI (student perceptions) frameworks. Others exist and the final selection should be a collaborative decision based on the perceptions of all instructors involved. The process must be ongoing and iterative with all involved instructors dedicated to continuous improvement of their respective courses and the enhancement of the department as a whole. The willingness to develop an environment in which these changes are not only made but encouraged will have positive results for all stakeholders in the online arena.

References

Arbaugh, J. B., Bangert, A., & Cleveland-Innes, M. (2010). Subject matter effects and the Community of Inquiry (CoI) framework: An exploratory study. *Internet and Higher Education, 13*(1–2), 37–44.

Arbaugh, J. B., Cleveland-Innes, M., Diaz, S., Garrison, D. R., Ice, P., Richardson, J. C., . . . Swan, K. (2008). Developing a Community of Inquiry instrument: Testing a measure of the Community of Inquiry framework using a multi-institutional sample. *Internet and Higher Education, 11*(34), 1331–1336.

Benbunan-Fich, R., & Hiltz, S. R. (1999). Impact of asynchronous learning networks on individual and group problem solving: A field experiment. *Group Decision and Negotiation, 8,* 409–426.

Bolman, L., & Deal, T. (2008). *Reframing organizations: Artistry, choice, and leadership* (4th ed.). San Francisco: Wiley.

California State University–Chico. (2003). *Rubric for Online Instruction*. Retrieved from http://www.csuchico.edu/celt/roi/index.shtml

Day, S., Bogle, L., Swan, K., Matthews, D., & Boles, E. (2013). Improving student learning in a fully online teacher leadership program: A design-based approach. In R. Hartshorne, T. L. Heafner, & T. M. Petty (Eds.), *Teacher education programs and online tools: Innovations in teacher preparation* (pp. 392–415). New York: IGI Global.

Dewey, J. (1938). *Experience and education*. New York: Collier.

Garrison, D. R., Anderson, T., & Archer, W. (2000). Critical inquiry in a text-based environment: Computer conferencing in higher education. *Internet and Higher Education, 2*(2–3), 87–105.

Haythornthwaite, C. (2002). Building social networks via computer networks: Creating and sustaining distributed learning communities. In K. A. Renninger & W. Shumar (Eds.), *Building virtual communities: Learning and change in cyberspace*. Cambridge, UK: Cambridge University Press.

Ice, P., Curtis, R., Phillips, P., & Wells, J. (2007). Using asynchronous audio feedback to enhance teaching presence and students' sense of community. *Journal of Asynchronous Learning Networks, 11*(2), 32–35.

Jiang, M., & Ting, E. (2000). A study of factors influencing students' perceived learning in a web-based course environment. *International Journal of Educational Telecommunications, 6*(4), 317–338.

Lipman, M. (1991). *Thinking in education*. Cambridge, UK: Cambridge University Press.

Matthews, D., Bogle, L., Boles, E., Day, S., & Swan, K. (2012). Developing communities of inquiry in online courses: A design-based approach. In Z. Akyol & D. R. Garrison (Eds), *Educational communities of inquiry: Theoretical framework, research and practice* (pp. 490–508). Hershey, PA: IGI Global.

Moore, M. G. (1989). Three types of interaction. *American Journal of Distance Education, 3*(2), 1–7.

Picciano, A. G. (2002). Beyond student perceptions: Issues of interaction, presence, and performance in an online course. *Journal of Asynchronous Learning Networks, 6*(1), 21–40.

Quality Matters. (2011). *Quality Matters rubric standards 2011–2013 edition with assigned point values*. Retrieved from https://www.qualitymatters.org/rubric

Shea, P., & Bidjerano, T. (2010). Learning presence: Towards a theory of self-efficacy, self-regulation, and the development of a communities of inquiry in online and blended learning environments. *Computers & Education, 55*(4), 17211–17731.

Swan, K. (2001). Virtual interactivity: Design factors affecting student satisfaction and perceived learning in asynchronous online courses. *Distance Education, 22*(2), 306–331.

Swan, K., Matthews, D., Bogle, L., Welch-Boles, E., & Day, S. (2012). Linking online course design and implementation to learning outcomes: A design experiment. *Internet and Higher Education, 15*(2), 81–88.

Swan, K., Richardson, J. C., Ice, P., Garrison, D. R., Cleveland-Innes, M., & Arbaugh, J. B. (2008). Validating a measurement tool of presence in online communities of inquiry. *e-Mentor, 2*(24). Retrieved from http://www.e-mentor.edu.pl/artykul/index/numer/24/id/543

Swan, K., Schenker, J., Arnold, S., & Kuo, C. L. (2007). Shaping online discussion: Assessment matters. *e-Mentor, 1*(18), 78–82.

Swan, K., Shen, J., & Hiltz, R. (2006). Assessment and collaboration in online learning. *Journal of Asynchronous Learning Networks, 10*(1), 45–62.

Wiggins, G., & McTighe, J. (2005). *Understanding by design* (2nd ed.). Alexandria, VA: Association for Supervision and Curriculum Development.

9

ENGAGING ONLINE FACULTY AND ADMINISTRATORS IN THE ASSESSMENT PROCESS

Jennifer Stephens-Helm, Karan Powell, and Julie Atwood

Historically there has been friction between individual faculty and the university about how learning is measured. Answering the question, What is good teaching? is as much art as it is science. A faculty member who is considered "great" to a small number of brilliant students may be considered a failure to the rest of the class. Is that bad teaching? Another faculty member may be extremely popular with the students but his or her teaching may be ineffective or not even current with the subject matter. Is that good teaching? Faculty members often resist using data resulting from assessments in the classroom, seeing it as impersonal, intrusive, and not representative of student learning. This resistance has stalled the integration of data into higher education planning and program review and led to a negative perception of data as a tool for tracking consumer behavior, not student learning. The idea of student as consumer is, without a doubt, nothing short of an obscenity in the academy.

There have been attempts to validate entire programs and degrees at the university level. This has led to the use of standardized tests and learning measures that are independent of the faculty teaching experience. These assessment methods are often not popular, as faculty feel that they measure the wrong things and do not account for varieties of pedagogy. Compounding this is the added pressure placed upon colleges and universities to justify their high cost and constant tuition hikes. One of the results is that accreditation standards and validation of student learning have become more prominent and more political in university administration. Colleges often see accreditation and data collection as something negative—something that is foisted on them from the outside and not part of their core function.

The American Public University System (APUS) is an online for-profit university with more than 120,000 students and 1,500 faculty members. We recognize that faculty involvement and voice are essential to providing our students with a high-quality educational experience. Engaging faculty and administrators in ongoing assessment processes at a distance-learning institution can pose unique challenges given that faculty members are geographically dispersed throughout the nation. To overcome these obstacles, we use the following strategies to promote a culture of assessment, continuous improvement, and data-based decision making.

Strategy #1: Develop a Program Review Committee as a Vehicle for Continuous Improvement and to Assure Academic Quality

Every three years APUS conducts a systemwide interdepartmental program review of academic programs that brings together key institutional stakeholders, including administrators, deans, program directors, lead faculty, and research team members. The primary aim of a program review at APUS is to assess student learning and to address the questions, What does this program aim for students to learn? Are students achieving these aims through the program? To address these questions, the objectives of a program review are as follows:

- to assess and validate program content through benchmarking the program against similar programs at other universities
- to obtain feedback from outside evaluators, students, and program advisory councils
- to evaluate student learning through review of graded end-of-course and program assignments, student evaluations, learning outcomes assessments, and outcomes data
- to build common ground across the university by engaging the APUS community, including Admissions, Student Services, Enrollment Management, Marketing, Learning Outcomes Assessment, the registrar, Library and Learning Resources, program faculty, and cross-departmental academic leadership, in the program review process
- to provide strategic direction for continuous improvement of the program content, faculty, and learning experience through the completion of a strategic three-year program development, enhancement, and implementation plan

Program Review Process

The ongoing program review process at APUS consists of six phases:

1. Data collection
2. External review
3. Analysis
4. Program review meeting
5. Three-year plan
6. Follow-up

Phase 1: Data collection and completion of self-assessment by the program director. During the assessment phase, the program director reviews all dimensions of the program and prepares documents and files for others to review. The program is placed under a microscope in the following areas:

- *Benchmarking*: How does this program compare with similar programs at other accredited academic institutions? The courses offered, number of credit hours, cost of the program, student population served, and other related data are obtained and inserted in a detailed spreadsheet that completes a comparative analysis of this program vis-à-vis its competitors.
- *Curriculum and learning*: What are the program-level objectives? Are they current and relevant? In what ways do course-level objectives support program-level learning? What are the methods by which students learn in their classes? What instructional strategies and evaluation strategies are used? Are they varied? Is the level of learning for graduate and undergraduate programs distinct in terms of academic rigor, objectives, and research expectations? What evidence exists to demonstrate that students are achieving program-level objectives? To accomplish this review, all course syllabi are systematically reviewed and audits of classrooms and assignments are conducted.
- *Library, course books, and learning resources*: How frequently is the library used by students in the program? What electronic resources are used in this program and in classes within the program? Evidence of student papers and comprehensive exams are used to demonstrate the level of student learning in the area of research and creative use of learning resources. Cost of books and materials per class are discussed, as are steps taken to advance the use of electronic materials available to students and faculty in the particular discipline or substantive area.

- *Student profile and demographics*: The primary questions that the marketing and academic departments focus on in this area are: Who are the students, and from where do they come? What draws them to this program and why? Are students seeking specific program content that is not covered? What is unique about this program from a marketing perspective, and how does this uniqueness serve the APUS mission of educating those who serve?
- *Faculty*: Who are the faculty in the program area? What are their credentials? What is the student-faculty ratio? How are faculty ensuring student learning? A spreadsheet of faculty and their capabilities and an assessment of their strengths and weaknesses are included in this study.
- *Learning outcomes assessment*: APUS has a robust and integrated learning outcomes assessment process ranging from institutional-level assessments to program-level assessments to individual course, student, and learning assessments. A fact book that contains program-level demographic data; enrollment information; course completion, withdrawal, and persistence rates; grade-distribution data; and other data is examined. Course- and program-level survey data are also reviewed.
- *Three-year plan*: What is the three-year plan for continuous improvement? If a previous three-year plan existed, how were these recommendations met and managed? What was met or not met?
- *Summary report by the program director*: Once the data are compiled, the program director develops a report that identifies the strengths of the program and articulates the areas for development in the program.

Phase 2: Review of the program by an evaluator from outside of the APUS system and community. Concurrent with Phase 1, an external reviewer is obtained to review the program from an objective perspective. This person is a recognized academic leader in the particular field who teaches or is an administrator at another college or university. The review received is a written report, including an assessment and recommendations for change. Some programs have industry advisory councils, a group of individuals who meet one to three times a year to provide guidance regarding the development of the program.

Phase 3: Review of the data and assessment of the program by the school dean. Once the data are compiled, the school dean completes an analysis of the data and the program. His or her summary is provided in a document that is also available to all individuals within the APUS community to read and review.

Phase 4: Engagement of stakeholders from across the university in a formal two-hour review meeting led by the academic dean of APUS. Program review meetings are scheduled regularly throughout the year as part of the APUS calendar and planning cycle. Participating in these review meetings are the program director and school dean, Enrollment Management, Student Services, Transfer Credit, the registrar, Faculty Development, Library and Learning Resources, Learning Outcomes Assessment, Marketing, the provost, and other academic deans and leaders. These meetings are rich learning events for all involved in the university system during which participants openly and honestly discuss the data presented by the program director and their own observations. Not only are program results openly and honestly discussed, but so are challenges to the findings. The result is enhanced learning experiences for APUS students, suggestions for additional resources for program development, and a richer understanding university-wide of the strengths of a particular program.

Phase 5: Establishment of a three-year plan for program and faculty development. Each program director is required to propose a three-year plan for program enhancement and development as part of the review. Following the review, this plan is revised and the program director is held accountable for further development. Given that programs are on a three-year cycle of review, this document becomes a source of analysis for the subsequent reviews: Has the program met its goals? Why or why not? How?

Phase 6: Follow-up by the program director and school dean to ensure program changes and development occurs. This follow-up occurs during the institution's annual strategic planning cycle as each school and program proposes its initiatives for the coming year. This is an ongoing process that allows deans to attend to program attainment of goals on a regular basis.

Strategy #2: Tools and Resources to Support the Program Review Process: Promote Accountability Through the Documentation of Student Learning Outcomes Evidence

The integration of data is a key part of the program review process and enables internal and external reviewers to effectively evaluate program dimensions during each phase. Direct and indirect evidence of student achievement, coupled with information about other dimensions of program and institutional effectiveness, is integrated into the review process. This information includes, but is not limited to, standardized testing results, student satisfaction ratings, book costs, program growth, enrollment history, average class sizes, course completion rates, withdrawal rates, faculty credentials, and faculty performance metrics.

The primary tool used to house the data collection process is an electronic storage repository developed specifically for that purpose (see Table 9.1). This paper-free repository of information allows members from across the university to gain access to program data and information on a shared network drive.

An institution-wide conversation generated from an analysis of the information in the electronic repository ensures that the findings are incorporated into decision-making processes. Following the analysis and evaluation of the program in the formal program review meeting, the academic and school deans make recommendations about the program, and department heads develop a three-year action plan for improvement.

Evidence of Effectiveness

Recommendations and findings from the program review process have influenced our policies, procedures, systems, and services. For example, programs have been streamlined, suspended, or significantly restructured. Faculty training and development needs have been identified, recommendations have been implemented, and faculty evaluation data have been used to affirm positive areas and isolate specific areas of concern.

Since implementation of the program review process, the feedback processes on assessment and quality control measures are more efficient, and we are increasingly more confident about data collected and analyzed. The improvements in our feedback processes have provided a more responsive system, resulting in better data-based decision making and increased student learning. Student satisfaction ratings have increased during the period of continual enrollment growth. We have strengthened the academic quality of our courses and programs, and there has been increased accountability among faculty and program directors. The resulting university-wide awareness and involvement has fostered content ownership and program knowledge, thereby demonstrating APUS's commitment to students and their success.

Lessons Learned

Many lessons were learned throughout the development and implementation of the program review process. First, the interdisciplinary review process is a good tool to help the institution remain focused on its students. Deepening the commitment to and understanding of program outcomes and student learning across the institution has led to higher retention and satisfaction. Second, the process can be costly for the institution in terms of

TABLE 9.1

Types of Data and Information Contained in Each Folder on the Network Drive

1. Library books and resources	*2. Curriculum assessment*	*3. External expert reviewers' feedback*
• Course books and resources • Program assessment of students' writing and research capabilities based upon sample of student work • Observations in classrooms • Student submissions/sample papers	• Program- and course-level objectives • Use of classroom options and level of interaction • Research/learning strategies • Evaluation procedures • Prerequisites • Relationship to other programs and courses • Reviews of programs for redundancy and distinction from graduate to undergraduate level • Assessment of program for graduate-level academic rigor	• Expert reviewer report • Industry advisory council report
4. Faculty	*5. Student profile and demographics*	*6. Learning outcomes assessment*
• Faculty spreadsheet • Analysis of faculty credentials/research and writing	• Enrollment history and growth trends	• Curriculum mapping • Course-level data • Program-level data • Program fact book
7. Program benchmarking	*8. Department chair/program manager summary*	*9. Review findings*
• Program benchmarking with similar programs and institution	• Review and evaluation of findings • Program recommendations • Proposed three-year strategic plan for the program	• School dean's observations • Meeting minutes • Learning outcomes assessment findings and recommendations • Academic dean's observations

time and resources, but the results are well worth the investment considering the improved quality of programs and student learning. Last, an open and honest dialogue is important to the program review process. Conversations can be difficult at times, but this dialogue must be honest if it is to be a true learning event. Incorporating reflection as part of the evaluation of our programs has become a way of doing business for us that is of great value.

Strategy #3: Inform Internal and External Stakeholders About Student Learning Outcomes

To inform external stakeholders about our students' achievements, we have developed a learning outcomes assessment website, available at www.apus .edu/community-scholars/learning-outcomes-assessment. The website serves as a clearinghouse of assessment data. For example, national testing results are posted on the website, thereby allowing the public to compare institution and national norm scores. In addition, the website provides information about assessment resources, learning outcomes, and updates on ongoing assessment initiatives.

Transparency by Design Project

APUS also participates in an initiative called the Transparency by Design (TbD) project. TbD assists adult learners in becoming educated consumers of distance education. The initiative's members make up a consortium of regionally accredited, adult-serving, distance-education institutions. As part of the initiative, participating institutions have launched a website, College Choices for Adults (www.collegechoicesforadults.org), designed to help students make more informed choices regarding their higher education opportunities. The website is designed to help students find what they will learn and how that relates to their career goals. The information on this site will be updated on a regular basis to allow interested parties to measure results, learn outcomes of specific programs, and read student satisfaction survey results (see chapter 5, "Progress Toward Transparency and Quality Assurance").

As part of participation in the initiative, APUS has agreed to abide by the Principles of Good Practice for Higher Education Institutions Serving Adults at a Distance. These established principles were developed to ensure that higher education distance-education courses and programs for adult learning are of high quality and readily accessible. The principles define parameters of excellence, promote transparency of higher education institutions delivering distance-learning programs, and foster dialogue to strengthen and improve the quality of programs and services. The principles facilitate the continuous improvement of adult higher education programs delivered at a distance by establishing benchmarks of quality. All TbD institutional members have pledged to uphold these principles.

Strategy #4: Establish a Reciprocal Relationship Among Stakeholders and the Institution for the Sharing of Data

As a fully online institution, APUS has the ability to collect and review an extensive amount of student data, which we recognize as integral to the continuous improvement of a quality online program. Our challenge is to create a balance between accountability in teaching and learning and faculty comfort with data collection. Our aim is to overcome this challenge, to harmonize the data requirements of the academic administration with the confidence of the faculty and make data collection intrinsic to the needs of both groups. To do this, APUS has aligned data collection and analysis with the three-year program review cycle. Data—including student evaluations of learning, graduation rates, grades, curricula, and program enrollment—are analyzed to make sure we are keeping current with program objectives, core content, and instructional resources and to measure how well our students are learning.

Several standard benchmarking instruments are used to measure teaching and learning, including the following:

- National Survey of Student Engagement (NSSE), which measures how students feel about the value of their education
- Community of Inquiry (CoI), which measures the dimensions of social presence, cognitive presence, and teaching presence in the online classroom
- Educational Testing Service (ETS) Major Field Test (MFT), which compares student achievement to national benchmarks to measure end-of-program knowledge in major fields of study
- Measure of Academic Proficiency and Progress (MAPP), which measures how our graduating seniors compare nationally in areas such as quantitative reasoning and critical-thinking skills

To build a culture of assessment, data collection, review, and reporting at the classroom level is embedded into the core of the program review process. The data team is actively involved in the program review process, meeting with faculty, program directors, and deans throughout. Grade distribution, NSSE scores, MAPP scores, MFT scores, CoI scores, dropout rates, and withdrawal rates are reviewed. The team also works closely with the academic community to understand how these figures represent teaching and learning at the institution.

Working with faculty, program directors, and deans throughout the review process has provided the opportunity to integrate the data into the program review narrative. The result is a collaboratively produced fact book, presenting extensive data and analysis of survey results. The fact-book development process fostered a partnership between our data team and faculty, program directors, and deans. The partnership allowed faculty to better adjust course requirements based on data and to see what programs and courses need to be restructured. This partnership has also shed a positive light on the collection, analysis, and review of data in the APUS academic arena.

Strategy #5: Incorporate Assessment Data Into Daily Decision-Making Processes

APUS regularly provides the public with evidence of student achievement, the soundness of the operation, and the overall effectiveness of the institution. Similarly, the institution listens and responds to the feedback the public provides. Feedback from constituents is used for day-to-day activities and long-range endeavors. In addition to shaping the curriculum, student feedback and assessment data led to a number of policies, procedures, systems, services, and features to accommodate the interests and needs of our constituents. This practice promotes the continuous improvement of teaching and learning and assists in assuring quality at all levels of the institution.

10

DISABILITY AND ACCESSIBILITY

Proactive Strategies to Improve Quality

Barbara A. Frey and Lorna R. Kearns

College student participation in online learning has been on the rise over the last decade. The percentage of students taking at least one online course has increased from less than 10% in 2002 to nearly 33% by 2010. Further, the number of online students has grown from 1.6 million in 2002 to more than 6.1 million in 2010 (Allen, Seaman, Lederman, & Jaschik, 2012). It has been reported that students with disabilities constitute a sizable group of learners in the higher education environment (Newman, Wagner, Cameto, Knokey, & Shaver, 2010), but it is difficult to know exactly how many online learners have disabilities because students are not required to self-identify unless they are requesting an academic accommodation. According to the U.S. Census, in 2005 approximately 18.7% of the general population had some level of disability and 12.0% had a severe disability (Brault, 2008). The *Report of the Advisory Commission on Accessible Instructional Materials in Postsecondary Education for Students With Disabilities* (U.S. Department of Education, 2011) stated that 10.8% of the students in four-year postsecondary institutions had some disability in 2008. Table 10.1 shows the breakdown of these postsecondary students with disabilities by type of disability, based on 2011 data from the Association on Higher Education and Disability (AHEAD) and the National Center for Education Statistics (NCES) (U.S. Department of Education, 2011, pp. 15–16).

The number of students with disabilities may actually be greater than the percentages reported. It is possible that students with disabilities avoid disclosure because of the perceived stigma associated with disabilities. Another concern related to students with disabilities is their graduation rate of 34.8%, which is below the 51.2% for the general student population in a four-year institution (U.S. Department of Education, 2011).

TABLE 10.1
Disability Distributions of Postsecondary Student Population

Disability type	AHEAD %[a]	NCES %[b]
Learning disabilities	28.16	31
ADD or ADHD	20.21	18
Psychological condition	15.59	15
Health impairment	9.25	11
Mobility impairment	6.20	7
Hard of hearing or deaf	3.25	4
Traumatic brain injury	2.79	2
Vision impairment	2.61	3
Intellectual disabilities	2.40	3
Temporary impairment	2.01	N/A
Autism	1.94	2
Speech/language impairment	0.72	1
Deaf-blind	0.09	N/A
Other	4.79	3

a. AHEAD data are from *The 2010 Biennial AHEAD Survey of Disability Services and Resource Professionals in Higher Education,* by D. Kasnitz, 2011, Huntersville, NC: Association on Higher Education and Disability.
b. NCES data are from *Students With Disabilities at Degree-Granting Postsecondary Institutions* (NCES 2011-018), by U.S. Department of Education, Institute of Education Sciences, National Center for Education Statistics, 2011, retrieved from http://nces.ed.gov/pubs2011/2011018.pdf

The goal of this chapter is to describe the need for accessible courses and recommend proactive universal design strategies used by administrators, faculty, and course developers for an inclusive course development process. This proactive approach will lead to high-quality learning experiences for students with disabilities and ultimately enhance their persistence in academic programs. For our purposes, a *disability* is defined as a physical or mental impairment that substantially limits one or more major life activities, including mobility, communication, and learning. The online environment, with anytime and anyplace access, should provide valuable educational opportunities to students with disabilities. After all, the web should be accessible to all users, meaning that students with disabilities can perceive, understand, navigate, interact, and contribute to their web-based courses.

Closely related to the concept of accessibility is universal design, or the design of products and environments so that they are usable by all individuals, to the greatest extent possible, without the need for adaptation or specialized design. In recent years we have seen the term *universal design* broadened from applying only to physical environments to including web and other computer environments as well. This proactive universal design approach to the development of online courses reduces the need for accommodations, or necessary and appropriate modifications, to ensure that individuals with disabilities have access to all course materials. However, even with every effort to make courses as accessible as possible, individual accommodations may be needed. Examples of accommodations in online courses include extended time on exams, note takers, sign language interpreters, and electronic print materials.

Skilled online educators take pride in developing professional relationships with students and forming communities of supportive, interactive learners. Those online students are usually adult learners who develop an online presence as they want others to know them. They choose information to disclose regarding their age, gender, location, position, race, and background. In addition, students choose whether they wish to disclose a disability. Consider that Cameron and Gina described in the following examples may be students in your online course. Would they be successful learners in your course without academic accommodations such as transcripts, captions, or alternative file formats?

Cameron is a 21-year-old male student attending college to earn a bachelor of science degree in psychology. His goal is to become a counselor in a government or higher education setting. Cameron has been blind since birth. With the help of his parents and teachers, he has been successful in finding and using key resources and assistive technologies to access educational opportunities. Cameron uses his computer and smartphone extensively for research, writing, and communication. Currently, he uses a laptop with Job Access with Speech (JAWS) screen-reading software to access web-based resources.

Like many motivated students, Cameron supplements his traditional campus courses with one online course each semester. He likes the anytime and anyplace flexibility of online courses but has faced challenges in retrieving online course information. This semester, he is taking Abnormal Psychology, which is organized into 15 weekly modules. This is the third week of the semester, and he is thinking about dropping the course. The following issues are frustrating to Cameron and are preventing his advancement in the course:

- The course schedule is posted as an extensive unformatted table with five columns and 15 rows. In the column listing course readings, required chapter topics are noted in blue font, optional articles are in red font, and optional website resources are in green font. Unfortunately, Cameron's screen reader does not automatically indicate that there is a change of font color, and he is missing key information.
- Lectures recorded with lecture-capture technology allow Cameron to hear the instructor's presentation, but there is no indication when the slides advance. The slides are not posted as a separate file to supplement the presentation, nor is there a transcript of the instructor's narration.
- Many of the required articles are posted as older PDFs, which are not accessible by Cameron's screen reader. It takes one to two weeks for Disability Services to create the PDFs in an accessible format. To make matters worse, the instructor is developing the course as he teaches it. In other words, course modules are made available to students one week at a time, so Cameron cannot check upcoming readings in advance of needing them.

Gina, a senior at the same university, is majoring in marketing. Because she is deaf, Gina's school provides a sign language interpreter to assist Gina in face-to-face classes. Although Gina is happy that the service is available, it is still difficult to participate in a class discussion that moves quickly. When she enrolled in an online course, Organizational Behavior, she was pleasantly surprised to discover that the text-based nature of the online discussion forum allowed her to understand her classmates' contributions without the mediation of an interpreter. In addition, because online discussion is asynchronous, Gina has more time to reflect on the question prompts and fashion a response that accurately and effectively conveys her ideas.

Although most of the course materials are text based, the instructor has also recorded a series of audio interviews that he conducted with business and nonprofit leaders. Each interview is only about 10 minutes long, but none are transcribed. Gina must rely on her school's Office of

Disability Services to provide a transcript. There have been times when she was not able to fully participate in a discussion forum because she had not yet received the transcription. The instructor also has assigned students several videos on YouTube to watch. Luckily, some are closed-captioned, but not all of them are.

For the midterm and final exams, the instructor conducts optional synchronous teleconferences to help students prepare for the tests. Gina goes to the Office of Disability Services to have a sign language interpreter help her with the teleconferences. She does not feel that she gains much from the teleconferences, however. The discussions are fast-paced, and unlike in the classroom, on the phone she does not have the benefit of seeing the speakers' body language. She spends extra time preparing for the tests to be on the safe side.

Laws and Institutional Policy

Most educators recognize their legal and ethical obligations to provide accessible online course materials for their students. In the United States, the Department of Justice and the Department of Education share responsibility for protecting the rights of students with disabilities. Two major laws relate to accessible online courses: the Rehabilitation Act and the Americans with Disabilities Act (ADA). Interestingly, the Rehabilitation Act was passed in 1973, prior to the introduction of web-based courses. This broad legislation made it unlawful to discriminate against individuals with disabilities in federally assisted programs, services, and employment, which includes higher education institutions. For our purposes, the most important sections of the Rehabilitation Act are Sections 504 and 508. Section 504 includes the statement that "no qualified individual with a disability in the United States shall be excluded from, denied the benefits of, or be subjected to discrimination under" any program or activity that receives federal financial assistance (U.S. Department of Justice, 2009). Section 508 of the Rehabilitation Act was amended in 1998 to require electronic and information technology developed, procured, maintained, or used by federal agencies to be accessible by people with disabilities, including employees and members of the public. A revised version of Section 508 technology guidelines is expected in 2013 (U.S. government, n.d.).

Another key regulation is the ADA, which is civil rights legislation signed in 1990 to prohibit discrimination based on a student's disability. The ADA "prohibits discrimination on the basis of disability in employment, state and local government, public accommodations, commercial facilities, transportation, and telecommunications" (U.S. Department of Justice, 2009). The ADA Amendments Act of 2008 expands the definition of disability to broaden the number of individuals who are eligible for the protections of the ADA, including accommodations for temporary disabilities caused by medical conditions and illnesses such as cancer, diabetes, HIV infection, bipolar disorder, and epilepsy.

In addition to federal and state legislation, higher education organizations need to have institutional accessibility policies (Crow, 2008). A campuswide institutional commitment is essential to developing accessible online programs. In a 2010 Quality Matters (QM) benchmarking study, 98% of the responding QM institutions reported that they had a general institutional disability policy, but only 13% indicated that they had a disability policy for online courses and programs (Frey & King, 2011). A follow-up study (Frey, Kearns, & King, 2012) resulted in development and dissemination of a generic accessibility policy for online courses that can be adapted by online programs. (The policy template can be found at www.qualitymatters.org/accessibility-policy-request.) QM is a nonprofit organization that promotes quality assurance and continuous improvement in online and blended courses.

Since online programs attract students from around the globe, program administrators and educators may want to consider international accessibility standards available through the World Wide Web Consortium (W3C), an international community of experts who work together to develop web standards, and the World Health Organization (WHO). The Web Content Accessibility Guidelines (WCAG) provide recommended standards for web accessibility that are used in many countries (W3C, 2011b). WCAG standards are discussed later in this chapter. In addition, the Convention on the Rights of Persons with Disabilities (United Nations, 2006) provides guidelines to ensure access to information and communication technologies, including the Internet, for people with disabilities.

Disability Services and Accommodations

A proactive universal design approach to course design and development is expected in online courses. Even if a program designer puts in great care and attention to detail, it is unlikely any program will be able to meet the needs of every student with a vision, hearing, motor, speech, or learning disability. Therefore, accommodations or modifications to ensure that individuals with disabilities have access to web-based course materials are likely to be necessary at some point in an online program. Accommodations may involve providing a sign language interpreter or real-time captioning software for an interactive synchronous guest lecturer session or developing extensive descriptions for interpreting visual content, such as maps in a history course or graphs for an economics lecture.

Each online course should include a disability statement. These statements are usually in the syllabus or a specific area of the course website designed for student support and services. The disability statement should include a link to the institution's ADA policy/guidelines and information about how to access the university's disability services. For example, the following statement is required on syllabi for Pitt Online courses at the University of Pittsburgh:

> If you have a disability for which you are or may be requesting an accommodation, you are encouraged to contact both your instructor and the Office of Disability Resources and Services [DRS], 216 William Pitt Union, (412)648-7890/(412)383-7355 (TTY) or visit http://www.drs.pitt.edu as early as possible for more information. DRS will verify your disability and determine reasonable accommodations for this course.

Unlike elementary or secondary public schools, colleges and universities do not have a responsibility to identify students with disabilities. Furthermore, students are not required to disclose their disability unless they are requesting an academic accommodation. Typically, students requesting an accommodation must submit documentation of their disability to the Office of Disability Services. The process of determining reasonable accommodations involves collaboration among the student, the disability specialist, the professional providing the diagnosis, and the course instructor or program director, if necessary. Each course should have a link to the university's Office of Disability Services website. One advantage of making all course materials available to students from the beginning of the term is that they can check modules in advance to ensure that they can open all the documents and media content and, thus, successfully complete all the activities and assignments. This will allow the student to make any requests for materials in alternate formats in advance, rather than after the class has moved on to the next modules.

Assistive Technology

In the Assistive Technology Act of 1998, *assistive technology* (AT) is defined as any technology used to increase, maintain, or improve the functional capabilities of individuals with disabilities. For our purposes, AT is any piece of hardware, software, or equipment that is used to enhance the functional capabilities of students with disabilities. Just as integrating universal design

TABLE 10.2
Examples of Assistive Technology by Type of Disability

Type of disability	Examples of assistive technologies
Visual	Screen-magnification software
	Screen-reader software
	Braille-display software
	Enlarged monitor
	Talking calculators
	Talking books
Hearing	Assistive listening device
	Closed-captioning
	Real-time captioning
	Text-to-speech software
	Text-telephone (TTY) software
	Speech-to-text-to–sign language software
Motor	Adapted mouse (e.g., trackball mouse)
	Adapted keyboard or on-screen keyboards
	Voice-to-text software
Speech	Voice-recognition software
	Text-to-speech software

principles into online courses benefits students with and without disabilities, ATs are reaching users beyond the original audience for which they were developed. For example, screen-reading software and speech-recognition software are being used by students with learning disabilities such as dyslexia and attention deficit disorder (Ofiesh, Rice, Long, Merchant, & Gajar, 2002). Table 10.2 identifies some of the most common ATs used by students with disabilities.

Inclusive Online Course Design

Inclusive course development is an approach to building accessibility into course design from the beginning of the course creation process, rather than implementing costly add-ons at the end of the process. A critical consideration is the accessibility of the learning management system (LMS) or first-generation course accessibility. A statement by the LMS provider and other software applications certifying accessibility should be readily available as a link within each course. This includes supplemental web-based applications, such as conferencing systems, antiplagiarism software, and other licensing agreements that might be used by students or faculty.

Individual course websites should be designed and maintained in conformance with the Web Content Accessibility Guidelines, Version 2 (WCAG 2.0) (W3C, 2011b). WCAG 2.0 is published by the Web Accessibility Initiative, a functional unit of W3C. There are three levels of conformance in WCAG 2.0: A, AA, and AAA. Level A specifies the lowest level of conformance. The guidelines are based on the following four principles:

1. *Content must be perceivable.* Online course content can be delivered in many formats and make use of multiple types of media, including text, images, audio, and video. This principle stipulates that regardless of form, course content should be universally perceivable. For nontext content, a text alternative should be provided. In the case of images, charts, and graphs, the standard alternative is a text-based tag that describes the nontext material. For video and audio, standard alternatives include closed-captioning or a text-based transcript.

   Content should also be distinguishable. For example, visually based content should use high-contrast color schemes that facilitate the differentiation of fonts from background. Content should be created so that foreground sounds are able to be appropriately differentiated from background sounds. Content should also be adaptable—that is, able to be presented in multiple ways without losing information. For example, when a page of text includes sidebars and callouts, these should be designed so that a screen reader reads them in their intended order.

2. *Interface components in the content must be operable.* Web pages should be navigable. The organizational structure of the site should make it obvious to students where they are within a network of web pages and how to move to a different page. When naming hyperlinks, a descriptive phrase such as "Assignment Instructions" is better than a generic phrase such as "Click here." It is important that web pages be navigable using individual keystrokes. This enables people with limited motor control to use the site and ensures that ATs can navigate the pages. Time-based media, such as videos or narrated PowerPoint files, should provide students with a way to pause the advancement of the action.

   Flashing and blinking web page elements may cause seizures in people who have a photosensitive seizure disorder. Although it is acceptable to display an element that flashes less than two times per second, the best practice is to avoid flashing and blinking altogether.

3. *Content and controls must be understandable.* Guidelines based on this principle direct designers to create web pages that are readable and predictable and that provide users with assistance to avoid and correct mistakes. Text-based content should be clear and readable without unnecessary wordiness, abbreviations, idioms, or foreign terms. Italicized, bolded, and highlighted fonts should be limited. The overuse of multiple text styles should be avoided. Tables represent a special case of text-based material. Since screen readers read from left to right and top to bottom, tables should be designed as simply as possible with no split cells. Column and row headings should be clearly labeled. In addition, tables should be used to display data and not for formatting web pages.

Because screen readers and screen magnifiers do not easily convey the overall contents of a web page, design consistency using headers or landmarks is important to help students using such technologies to locate material from one web page to another. Web-based forms should contain clear instructions for use and be designed to minimize misinterpretation of fields that require user input.

4. *Content should be robust enough to work with current and future user agents (including ATs).* Content should be created to be accurately interpreted by any and all ATs. All content should be usable by both PC and Mac platforms, as well as common mobile devices.

Online courses often contain links to external websites. For each external site to which students are directed, the portion of the site intended for student viewing should be reviewed for conformance with the listed guidelines.

Additionally, online courses make extensive use of supplemental documents. Examples of such documents include Adobe PDF files and Microsoft Office files (e.g., Word, Excel, PowerPoint). Sometimes referred to as "second-generation" documents, these materials should conform, where appropriate, to the guidelines listed. Documents created by Microsoft Word or PowerPoint should make appropriate use of heading styles to assist a screen reader in presenting material in a logically structured manner. Adobe PDF files should be character readable (i.e., text should be searchable). Sometimes, older PDF text files are not searchable because of the way they were initially scanned into a digital format. In these cases, the file should be run through the Adobe Acrobat optical character recognition function.

The Georgia Tech Research on Accessible Distance Education (2012) project has developed guidelines for creating second-generation online course materials from several common applications, such as Word, Excel,

PowerPoint, Adobe, and Flash. The University of Washington (n.d.) has also created a set of guidelines for designing accessible Adobe PDF files.

The recommendations in this section apply not only to new courses but also to existing courses. Courses in the path of current students who are known to have disabilities should be given priority for being brought up to standard. Other existing courses should be brought up to standard during the next revision cycle (usually one to two years).

Quality Review Process

Aside from considerations of accessibility, institutions and departments offering online education should have a quality assurance process for both newly designed and recently revised courses. Such a process would subject each course to a thorough technical review before it is offered to students to ensure that pages are in order, links are working, design standards are met, and all course elements are present and functioning. On issues of accessibility, the quality review process should focus on ensuring that courses conform to the recommendations made in the previous section.

A number of web-based tools are available to assist in the quality assurance process. In general, these tools perform an automatic scan of a web page and display a brief report identifying items on the page that are not accessible. Perhaps the most comprehensive of these is the WAVE Web Accessibility Evaluation Tool hosted by Web Accessibility in Mind (WebAIM) at Utah State University (WebAIM, 2012). WAVE is a web-based form into which a user inserts a URL, an HTML file, or even a fragment of HTML code. The tool conducts a check of the page and displays a copy of the page with icons that identify particular items on the page that either pass or fail the accessibility check. W3C (2011a) publishes a comprehensive list of links to a variety of other accessibility evaluation tools, some of which are similar to WAVE. Examples of additional tools include those that evaluate color contrast, measure flickering rate, identify color blindness issues, simulate how a page would be rendered by various assistive devices, and report on the reading level of a page of text.

Applications used to create second-generation documents often include an accessibility checking tool. For example, Microsoft Word, Excel, and PowerPoint 2010 include an accessibility checker that identifies and repairs accessibility issues. Adobe Acrobat X Pro's tool checks for document structure tags, searchable text, and appropriate security settings.

A caveat should be mentioned here: Although the information provided by the tools can be extremely helpful during a quality assurance check for online courses, it should not be used as a substitute for human judgment.

As stated on the Web Accessibility Initiative site (W3C, 2012, para. 3), "Web accessibility evaluation tools cannot *determine* the accessibility of Web sites, they can only *assist* in doing so." Their use is most appropriate as a complement to the regularly conducted technical course reviews mentioned at the beginning of this section.

A final recommended practice for conducting quality reviews of accessibility is to involve people with disabilities in the review process to point out areas that warrant close inspection during the regular reviews. A sighted person working with a set of accessibility evaluation tools may identify accessibility problems that are obvious and even some that are not, but a blind student using a screen reader to advance through an online course will detect *every* barrier that exists to his or her successful navigation of the course.

Faculty and Staff Training

A prominent theme in the accessibility literature is the need for centralized faculty and staff training to enhance understanding of accessibility and universal design practices (Frey & King, 2011; U.S. Department of Education, 2011). Depending on the institutional model for building online courses, a number of people may be involved in online course design, including faculty, instructional designers, and instructional technologists. Anyone who designs, builds, teaches, or reviews online courses should have the opportunity to receive training on a number of topics related to accessibility for online learning. Topics should include, but are not limited to, the needs of disabled online students, the variety of ATs that may be used by online students, standards and guidelines governing the design of online courses, techniques for developing accessible materials (both first and second generation), the use of accessibility evaluation tools, and factors that impact decision making about accessible course activities.

Conclusion

Accessibility is a key standard of excellence in online courses. Inclusive universal design benefits a broad range of learners by increasing access, enhancing flexibility, and providing options. On an institutional level, a strong accessibility policy demonstrates a commitment to quality, supports diversity at all levels, and exemplifies institutional values. An active, enforced policy preempts the need for an assortment of ad hoc accommodations and responds proactively to the variety of emerging mobile devices and software applications with which students arrive on campus. Furthermore, the policy and its effects are likely to be viewed positively by accreditation teams.

Vanderheiden (1996, para. 7) notes, "Good universal design benefits everyone, but to do this, it needs to take the needs of everyone into account." Universal design of online courses not only provides benefits to all learners. It also provides valuable opportunities for instructors and instructional designers to think about, envisage, and respond to the needs of their students.

Additional Information on Cited Resources

Universal course design is a dynamic process in that technology is continually changing and improving. The following references are provided as key resources for accessibility issues and practices related to technology and online learning.

Access E-Learning is an online tutorial published by the Georgia Tech Research on Accessible Distance Education project. It includes 10 modules with tips and assistance to faculty members seeking to make Word, Excel, Flash, and other file types accessible to people with disabilities. URL: www.accesselearning.net

The *Center for Applied Special Technology (CAST)* is a nonprofit research and development organization that works to expand learning opportunities for all individuals, especially those with disabilities, through Universal Design for Learning. URL: http://cast.org

The *Disabilities, Opportunities, Internetworking, and Technology (DO-IT) Center* at the University of Washington promotes the success of individuals with disabilities in postsecondary education and careers. URL: www.washington.edu/doit

Equal Access to Software and Information (EASI) is an organization that provides online training on accessible information technology for people with disabilities. The EASI website contains informational resources, webinars, and other learning opportunities. URL: www.easi.cc

The *National Center for Accessible Media (NCAM)* is dedicated to achieving media access equality for people with disabilities. NCAM has created the Media Access Generator Tool (MAGpie) for adding captions to multimedia content. You can download the software free of charge from the website. URL: http://ncam.wgbh.org

The *Division of Information Technology (DoIT)* at the University of Wisconsin–Madison has developed resources for learning about accessibility and applying tools and techniques to content on the web. Its website includes videos describing the experiences of people with disabilities. In one video, a blind individual discusses how he uses a screen reader to access web content. URL: www.doit.wisc.edu/accessibility

WebAIM is an initiative from Utah State University. This organization's website has great information about web accessibility, including a tutorial and the accessibility evaluation tool WAVE. URL: www.webaim.org

The *World Report on Disability* by WHO provides information and recommendations on health, rehabilitation, assistance and support, enabling environments, education, and employment to improve the lives of individuals with disabilities. URL: www.who.int/disabilities/world_report/2011/report/en

W3C is an international organization that leads the development of web standards. Its Web Accessibility Initiative was launched to promote web functionality for people with disabilities. URL: www.w3.org

References

Allen, I. E., Seaman, J., Lederman, D., & Jaschik, S. (2012). *Conflicted: Faculty and online education, 2012*. Retrieved from the Inside Higher Ed website: http://www.insidehighered.com/news/survey/conflicted-faculty-and-online-education-2012

Assistive Technology Act. (1998). Retrieved from http://www.section508.gov/docs/AssistiveTechnologyActOf1998Full.pdf

Brault, M. W. (2008). *Americans with disabilities: 2005*. Retrieved from the U.S. Census Bureau website: http://www.census.gov/prod/2008pubs/p70-117.pdf

Crow, K. L. (2008). The legal environment of accessible postsecondary online learning. *Quarterly Review of Distance Education, 9*(2), 169–170.

Frey, B. A., Kearns, L. R., & King, D. R. (2012, October). *An accessibility policy for online programs.* Paper presented at the Fourth Annual Quality Matters Conference, Tucson, AZ.

Frey, B. A., & King, D. R. (2011). *Quality Matters accessibility survey: Institutional practices and policies for online courses.* Retrieved from ERIC database. (ED520903)

Georgia Tech Research on Accessible Distance Education. (2012). *Guidelines for accessible distance education.* Retrieved from the Center for Assistive Technology and Environmental Access website: http://www.catea.gatech.edu/grade/guides/introduction.php

Kasnitz, D. (2011). *The 2010 biennial AHEAD survey of disability services and resource professionals in higher education.* Huntersville, NC: Association on Higher Education and Disability.

Newman, L., Wagner, M., Cameto, R., Knokey, A. M., & Shaver, D. (2010). *Comparisons across time of the outcomes of youth with disabilities up to 4 years after high school.* Menlo Park, CA: SRI International.

Ofiesh, N. S., Rice, C. J., Long, E. M., Merchant, D. C., & Gajar, A. H. (2002). Service delivery for postsecondary students with disabilities: A survey of assistive technology use across disabilities. *College Student Journal, 36*(1), 94–108.

United Nations. (2006). *Convention on the Rights of Persons with Disabilities.* Retrieved from http://www.un.org/disabilities/convention/conventionfull.shtml

University of Washington. (n.d.). *PDF accessibility.* Retrieved from http://www.washington.edu/accessibility/pdf.html

U.S. Department of Education. (2011). *Report of the Advisory Commission on Accessible Instructional Materials in Postsecondary Education for Students With Disabilities.* Retrieved from http://www2.ed.gov/about/bdscomm/list/aim/publications.html

U.S. Department of Education, Institute of Education Sciences, National Center for Education Statistics. (2011). *Students with disabilities at degree-granting postsecondary institutions* (NCES 2011-018). Retrieved from http://nces.ed.gov/pubs2011/2011018.pdf

U.S. Department of Justice. (2009). *A guide to disability rights laws.* Retrieved from http://www.ada.gov/cguide.htm

U.S. Government. (n.d.). *Resources for understanding and implementing Section 508.* Retrieved from http://www.section508.gov

Vanderheiden, G. C. (1996). *Universal design: What it is and what it isn't.* Retrieved from the Trace Center website: http://trace.wisc.edu/docs/whats_ud/whats_ud.htm

Web Accessibility in Mind (WebAIM). (2012). *WAVE web accessibility tool.* Retrieved from http://wave.webaim.org

World Wide Web Consortium (W3C). (2011a). *Web accessibility evaluation tools: Overview.* Retrieved from http://www.w3.org/WAI/ER/tools/Overview.html

World Wide Web Consortium (W3C). (2011b). *Web Content Accessibility Guidelines (WCAG) overview.* Retrieved from http://www.w3.org/WAI/intro/wcag.php

World Wide Web Consortium (W3C). (2012). *Web Accessibility Initiative (WAI).* Retrieved from http://www.w3.org/WAI

11

ASSURING QUALITY FOR AN EXPANDING POPULATION OF CULTURALLY DIVERSE STUDENTS

Kay Shattuck, Jennifer A. Linder-VanBerschot, Janice Maloney High, Carrie Main, Li Wang, and David Black

This chapter addresses the impact of culture in relation to the design and delivery of distance education for colleges and universities. Convenient and flexible access to education in an electronically connected interdependent world drives the need to assure quality and accessibility for culturally diverse students. Most regionally based institutions in the United States are in the middle of the growing global e-learning market, estimated to reach $107.3 billion by 2015 (Global Industry Analysts, 2010). Simultaneously, the same institutions are attempting to increase the graduation rate of racial/ethnic minorities (Nguyen, Bibo, & Engle, 2012) and can expect that by 2020 minority students will represent 45% of students graduating from high school who are potentially headed toward higher education (Western Interstate Commission for Higher Education, 2012). Institutions can approach these 21st-century realities either from a second-language perspective when dealing with nonnative speakers (Ofulue, 2011; Parrish & Linder-VanBerschot, 2010) or from a cultural-hegemony perspective when dealing with culturally based conflicts in teaching/learning expectations and traditions (Shattuck, 2005; Uzuner, 2009). Consequently, assuring quality of education for culturally diverse learners is an ethical, educational, and economic necessity for online distance-education programs and institutions.

The impact of culture and diversity on the quality of online learning has been researched and discussed in the online distance-education literature for more than a decade (Gunawardena & LaPointe, 2008; Gunawardena,

Wilson, & Nolla, 2003; Shattuck, 2005; Uzuner, 2009). McLoughlin (2001) called the ability "to teach effectively online to a multi-cultural group of learners an imperative" and described technology as a "cultural amplifier" (p. 9). Therefore, it is important to increase instructors' awareness and to design culturally inclusive online courses in order to reach students who bring with them culturally influenced learning traditions and expectations of the learning process (Gunawardena & LaPointe, 2008).

Impact of Culture on Online Distance Education

S. Hall (1986) noted that the concept of *culture* is rooted in anthropology and has been endlessly debated; however, a good general definition comes from Kroeber and Kluckhohn (1952):

> Culture consists of patterns, explicit and implicit, of and for behavior acquired and transmitted by symbols, constituting the distinctive achievement of human groups, including their embodiment in artifacts; the essential core of culture consists of traditional (i.e., historically delivered and selected) ideas and especially their attached values; culture systems may, on the one hand, be considered as products of action, on the other as conditioning elements of future action. (p. 181)

In relating culture to online distance education, Shattuck (2005) suggested that culture is "a system of socially and historically created traditions, including educational and pedagogical traditions" (p. 59). These culturally influenced traditions of teaching and learning are especially important as they can cause what Wilson (2001) identified as cultural discontinuities—that is, differences that can interfere with learning when a course is designed and taught from one cultural perspective to students from different cultural perspectives. These discontinuities can take the form of culturally specific concepts and knowledge that do not translate well, linguistic intrusions of the learner's first language into comprehension of the course content, and confusion during the cognitive process of "putting together the new information in a way that allows it to be woven into existing knowledge" (Wilson, 2001, p. 52).

Addressing the impact of learners' sociocultural norms is crucial in making learning online accessible to cross-cultural students. Gunawardena et al. (2003) and Gunawardena and LaPointe (2008) provided an outline of factors to be considered when promoting accessibility of learning opportunities to students learning across cultures. Online instructors and institutions with online courses should consider diverse educational expectations, learning preferences, sociocultural environments, communication styles, language issues, and interpretation of design elements as they design online courses.

were frustrated by the nonauthoritative presentation by an instructor: "I am from the country where teachers are supposed to 'teach,' I have some Hong Kong influence, so I 'pay' for education because I expect that teachers teach me the things I want to know" (Shattuck, 2005, p. 152).

Reflecting on their experience teaching synchronous English courses to Chinese students, Gunawardena and LaPointe (2008) observed,

> American teachers were initially uncomfortable with the long, reflective pauses in the synchronous voice communication. The Chinese respect for authority conditioned learners to wait for an explicit invitation rather than make the impolite gesture of raising a question or criticizing someone else's work. (p. 63)

Cross-cultural students in an online classroom create a learning environment for the teacher too—everyone has to work together to create a positive learning environment.

Perceptions of authority and practices that reflect such perceptions differ across cultures. Such differences not only influence communications but also impact the implementation of academic policy, for example, appropriate citations. In Western countries, modeling one's work on that of an authority is considered plagiarism, whereas such practice is perceived as appropriate and has been a well-established method of studying and demonstrating respect in many Asian countries (Ko & Rossen, 2010).

Course Design Considerations

Higher education can no longer be considered geographically bound. Learners from a myriad of educational traditions and culturally influenced expectations are increasingly participating in online higher education courses. This comes at a time when online instructors and instructional designers are still relatively new to the process of designing online courses. Although some faculty may be experienced in teaching students from multiple cultures within the traditional classroom setting, the nuances of working virtually across cultures requires additional course design attention.

It is important for instructors to be cognizant that design is not culturally neutral. First, the learning content should be specific and culturally relevant (Kinuthia, 2007). Although the knowledge is embedded in the mainstream, instructors need to consider the learners who are not native to the culture of instruction and avoid situations in which mainstream cultural references are difficult for these diverse students to understand (Uzuner, 2009). For example, when American students discuss the popular television shows from their childhood or favorite characters in children's literature, instructors should ensure that the foreign students understand the references and provide background information for them.

According to Hannon and D'Netto (2007), educational institutions are taking courses to the online environment with minor changes to the traditional face-to-face course design. Without making changes based on the learner population, institutions are potentially losing interested students and, more important, not serving their students to the greatest degree possible. In a survey of 241 students, Hannon and D'Netto (2007) found that cultural differences affect learner satisfaction. These findings suggest that high-quality online instruction and design must include culturally inclusive content and approaches. Interestingly, learners reported such a preference for the convenience of online education that they are willing to overlook quality in the final product. Although learners are willing to accept a mediocre course for the convenience of learning at their own pace, instructors should not use that as an excuse to use mediocre course design standards.

Design elements such as text, date formats, symbols, and flow and functionality of text are used differently in different cultures (Mercado, Parboteeah, & Zhao, 2004). For example, the same color holds different meaning in different cultures (Kinuthia, 2007). In some cultures, colors have religious and political connotations. For example, yellow is the color of death in Korea and therefore is infrequently used in academic and professional settings (Khan, 2005). The authors of a survey of images and icons conducted in the United States, Morocco, and Sri Lanka (Knight, Gunawardena, & Aydin, 2009) concluded, "Designers must incorporate research in the early stages of the design process that investigates the various sociocultural contexts and perspectives of users" (p. 33).

Setting Expectations

Providing guidelines is important to help students avoid feeling confused. This is particularly true for students studying in a cross-cultural course. Stating rules will likely improve the students' chance of success. Social presence, considered the key to success for context-dependent students (Ku & Lohr, 2003; Morse, 2003; Tu, 2001), should be a primary consideration for instructors and can be addressed through the inclusion of various design components, such as personal profiles with pictures (Thompson & Ku, 2005). Instructors should also be cognizant that students' cultural values contribute to their success (Hannon & D'Netto, 2007). For students from cultures in which people perceive instructors as the authority, cultivating an open-ended and constructivist learning environment can be confusing and isolating (Shattuck, 2005). To maximize the learning experience of these students, instructors should consider a variety of learning activities and assessments that accommodate various learners' preferences.

Strategies for Addressing Cultural Inclusion

As the frequency and range of culturally influenced expectations and traditions brought into online courses has expanded, online educators have become interested in developing "cultural sensitivity" (Powell, 1997, p. 6) and "cultural inclusivity" (McLoughlin, 2001, p. 12). The following sections offer research-based practical strategies and recommendations for addressing cultural inclusion.

Global Learning in the Online Classroom

The various theories of culture discussed in the first half of this chapter offer theoretical validation for something that instructors know intuitively—that the classroom, online or face-to-face, is a laboratory for diversity. Diversity can include ethnicity, race, religion, gender, sexual orientation, learning preferences, political differences, or just the natural variability in human nature. It is an educator's responsibility to maximize the space for diversity, while also offering gentle guidance so that the conversation remains sensitive, respectful, and enlightened.

Met with so much intriguing theory about diversity and culture in online distance education, what is an instructor to do? One answer comes from Shared Futures, a global learning initiative launched by the Association of American Colleges and Universities (AAC&U, n.d.). The Shared Futures initiative views global learning doctrine as a rethinking of traditional liberal education to embrace both Western and non-Western experience and thereby equip students for the new verities of 21st-century life. "Global learning," wrote Kevin Hovland (2009), AAC&U's program director for Global Initiatives, "[is] a vehicle for integrating multiple disciplinary perspectives and weaving together existing commitments to explore diversity, build capacity for civic engagement, and prepare students to take responsibility for common global problems" (p. 5). The guiding principles of Shared Futures include a curriculum defined by intercultural competence, conflict resolution, social responsibility, and practical engagement with global problems. Diversity is also a vital part of the initiative. As Hovland (2009) memorably concluded, "Diversity is about everything, and global is about everywhere" (p. 7).

Those involved with education delivered through worldwide online technologies welcome diversity and acknowledge it as a great educational tool. They recognize that the online classroom is not merely a microcosm of a diverse world but a place where digital technologies merge identity and culture to create startling new forms—if anything, this process makes diversity itself more diverse. The online classroom positions the instructor not as a transcendent arbiter within a group of learners but as a fellow global citizen.

Instructors can translate global learning into practice in the following ways:

- Feature exam questions and exercises in which students are invited to take the perspective of someone living in a different part of the world.
- Offer readings from authors outside the U.S. and Western European canons, as well as examples drawn from a variety of cultures worldwide.
- Encourage global citizenship and invite students to see their civic lives as extending past their national identities, to assume a point of view associated with cosmopolitanism.
- Include what are identified in the global learning literature as "global skills"—such as practicing adaptability, coping with complexity, understanding ethics, sustaining business relationships across cultures, viewing a problem from multiple perspectives, and being aware of context (Bourn, 2011; Newell-Jones, 2007)—in course design and teaching.

By adopting even one of these practices, instructors can make their classes more accessible to all learners, regardless of their backgrounds.

Culturally Responsive Teaching

For instructors, discovering the impact of culture in education practice begins with establishing a baseline for their own current practices. One useful tool is Culturally Responsive Teaching (Wlodkowski & Ginsberg, 1995), a framework that encourages instructors to examine their own teaching for matters that should be considered from multiple cultural viewpoints. The framework helps instructors to determine whether they include and value multiple perspectives and ways of knowing; emphasize collaboration and cooperation; allow students to share their perspectives and knowledge; encourage discussion of relevant experiences; and incorporate assessments that are connected to students' learning modalities, perspectives, or ways of knowing. With this increased awareness of current pedagogical practices, instructors can identify areas that require change and commit to making at least one change or addition each semester. Changes and modifications can be tracked as needed each semester and may include the following:

Incorporating culture during the planning of an online course. Instructors should consider aspects of human nature and individual personality (Hofstede & Hofstede, 2005). We recommend that instructors plan their courses with this complexity in mind:

- Identify the impact of language in the design of content and activities.
- Use clear and direct language in course structure and organization; save creativity for the content.
- Include a language-courtesy statement in the syllabus.

- Work with your Student Services Office to learn more about the cultural diversity at your institution and to get planning suggestions.

Considering culture during the implementation of an online course. Although instructors may not have consciously incorporated cultural diversity components in their online courses, they probably have already been intuitively doing so by employing a variety of teaching strategies. Take, for example, the inclusion of a group project in the syllabus. Group work requires a high degree of collaboration, which addresses E. T. Hall's (1981) high-context cultural dimension. Hofstede (1983) also referenced collaboration; he saw it as a cultural dimension of collectivist culture. Parrish and Linder-VanBerschot (2010) included collaboration in their CDLF as a nurturing aspect of their social relationships dimension.

Using a variety of teaching strategies addresses the presence of students with multiple learning preferences in an online course. No single definition of learning preferences or list of learning styles has been agreed upon. Although the academy is divided on the efficacy of learning preferences (Santo, 2006; Zapalska & Brozik, 2006), there is a growing view that learning preferences and culture are related (Raza, 2012). Thus, by employing a variety of teaching strategies, the instructor is acknowledging the value of learning preferences, and thus the value of culture. The instructor responds to the need for different learning strategies through a mix of tasks, including text/audio/ video modalities, individual/group activities, competitive/collaborative assignments, graded/not graded work, objective/essay assessments, and instructor-guided/student-guided discussions.

Effective use of language is as important during the implementation phase as it is during planning. The following recommendations can be applied during a course:

- Use global English (with its focus on general commonalities rather than on local distinctions) in communication.
- Avoid the use of jargon and culturally based references, which may cause unnecessary confusion.
- Encourage students to adhere to the same standards when they communicate with each other online.
- Use emoticons to help clarify the intent of online communication when there is potential for confusion (LaPointe, Greysen, & Barrett, 2004).

In addition, we recommend periodic culture checks, which can help instructors adjust course teaching strategies throughout the semester:

- At the start of the semester, remind students that the more they share about their learning preferences, their background, and their culture, the more their perspectives can be incorporated into the course.

- As students exchange initial introductions, encourage them to share their background and culture to the extent they are comfortable.
- Include assignments in which students are encouraged to incorporate their own background and cultural perspectives in their responses.
- Include at least one question about culture in the midsemester and end-of-semester course review surveys.
- Review course feedback from students each semester, make changes to the course every semester based on the feedback, and address those changes in the syllabus or in a class session.

Considering culture at the institutional level. Institutions are encouraged to adopt recommendations and guidelines from expert groups. One such group is the Organisation for Economic Co-operation and Development (OECD). Although they address cultural diversity from an international perspective, the OECD cross-border guidelines (Vincent-Lancrin & Pfotenhauer, 2012) certainly are applicable for any institution that crosses cultural borders on a smaller scale, even within a single campus. OECD recommends that institutions do the following:

- Recognize that high-quality teaching and research is made possible by high-quality faculty and working conditions that foster independent and critical inquiry.
- Develop, maintain, or review current internal quality management systems so that they make full use of the competencies of stakeholders.
- Share best practices by participating in sector organizations and interinstitutional networks (Vincent-Lancrin & Pfotenhauer, 2012).

We recommend that instructors serve on relevant institutional committees and in other ways make their voices heard so that the institution takes the following actions:

- Subscribes to a quality assurance program
- Subscribes to relevant scholarly and pedagogical publications
- Provides training from a cultural perspective on the technologies associated with the institution's learning management system
- Provides professional development funding for culture-related opportunities

Considering culture at the student level. Students are also partly responsible for creating a culturally appropriate learning environment. Instructors and institutions should provide opportunities for learners to create more desirable online learning communities. We offer several suggestions:

- Students should be aware that the more they share about their learning preferences, their background, and their culture, the more their instructors will be able to incorporate those perspectives into the course. As students exchange initial introductions, they should include their background and culture to the extent they are comfortable.
- Students can seek to incorporate their own background and cultural perspectives into their assignments.
- Students can raise cultural issues in the midsemester and end-of-semester course review surveys.
- Students can be asked to review the course as it is updated and revised.

By making their diverse voices heard, students can become not only an integral but the most important part of a culturally responsive online education.

Conclusion

Online teaching has the effect of obscuring visual markers of personal identity; it also blurs the roles that distinguish teacher and student in the face-to-face classroom. It is obviously more difficult to know a person's race, gender, culture, or creed when everyone's persona is digital or to readily acknowledge the difference in power between teacher and those taught. The result is that online teaching, as much as the Internet itself, has a kind of relativizing force, which alters the pedagogical balance of power in often positive ways. It brings students and instructor together in an ambiguous space, one that amplifies their sense of proximity and mutual experience while casting everyone's words and deeds into bold relief. The best online courses are thus both high-tech and, given how intimate and immersive they are, "high-touch" (Aspden & Helm, 2004, cited in Baran, Correia, & Thompson, 2011, p. 103).

According to the Open Doors report (Institute of International Education [IIE], 2011), which is published annually by IIE in partnership with the U.S. Department of State's Bureau of Educational and Cultural Affairs, "The number of international students at colleges and universities in the United States increased by five percent to 723,277 during the 2010/11 academic year" (para. 1). To embrace a student population that is becoming steadily more diverse, educators, including faculty and administrators, should increase their own cultural awareness and assure quality for the expanding number of culturally diverse students at all possible levels.

References

Aspden, L., & Helm, P. (2004). Making the connection in a blended learning environment. *Educational Media International, 41*(3), 245–252. doi:10.1080/0952380410001680851

Association of American Colleges and Universities (AAC&U). (n.d.). *Shared Futures: Global learning & social responsibility.* Retrieved from http://www.aacu.org/SharedFutures/documents/SharFutFinal2.pdf

Baran, E., Correia, A. P., & Thompson, A. (2011). Transforming online teaching practice: Critical analysis of the literature on the roles and competencies of online teachers. *Distance Education, 32*(3), 421–439. doi:10.1080/01587919.2011.610293

Bourn, D. (2011). Global skills: From economic competitiveness to cultural understanding and critical pedagogy. *Critical Literacy: Theories and Practices, 5*(2). Retrieved from http://criticalliteracy.freehostia.com/index.php?journal=criticalliteracy&page=article&op=viewArticle&path[]=99

Collis, B. (1999). Designing for differences: Cultural issues in the design of WWW-based course-support sites. *British Journal of Educational Technology, 30*(3), 201–221. doi:10.1111/1467–8535.00110

Global Industry Analysts. (2010, September 20). Global eLearning market to reach $107.3 billion by 2015, according to new report by Global Industry Analysts, Inc. [News release]. Retrieved from PRWeb Online Visibility from Vocus website: http://www.prweb.com/releases/elearning/corporate_elearning/prweb4531974.htm

Gunawardena, C. N., & LaPointe, D. (2008). Social and cultural diversity in distance education. In T. Evans, M. Haughey, & D. Murphey (Eds.), *International handbook of distance education* (pp. 51–70). Bingley, UK: Emerald Group.

Gunawardena, C. N., Wilson, P. L., & Nolla, A. C. (2003). Culture and online education. In M. G. Moore & W. G. Anderson (Eds.), *Handbook of distance education* (pp. 753–775). Mahwah, NJ: Lawrence Erlbaum.

Hall, E. T. (1981). *Beyond culture.* New York: Random House.

Hall, S. (1986). Cultural studies: Two paradigms. In R. Collins (Ed.), *Media culture and society: A critical reader* (pp. 33–48). London: Sage.

Hannon, J., & D'Netto, B. (2007). Cultural diversity online: Student engagement with learning technologies. *International Journal of Educational Management, 21*(5), 418–432. doi:10.1108/09513540710760192

Henderson, L. (1996). Instructional design of interactive multimedia: A cultural critique. *Educational Technology Research & Development, 44*(4), 85–104.

Hofstede, G. (1983). The cultural relativity of organizational practices and theories. *Journal of International Business Studies, 14,* 75–89. Retrieved from http://www.mty.itesm.mx/etie/centros/cia/comp_org/archivos/Cultural_relativity.pdf

Hofstede, G., & Hofstede, G. J. (2005). *Cultures and organizations: Software of the mind* (2nd ed.). New York: McGraw-Hill.

Hofstede, G. H., Hofstede, G. J., & Minkov, M. (2010). *Cultures and organizations: Software of the mind: Intercultural cooperation and its importance for survival.* New York: McGraw-Hill.

Hovland, K. (2009). Global learning: What is it? Who is responsible for it? *Peer Review, 11*(4), 4–7.

Institute of International Education (IIE). (2011, November 14). Open doors 2011: International student enrollment increased by 5 percent in 2010/11 [News release]. Retrieved from http://www.iie.org/Who-We-Are/News-and-Events/Press-Center/Press-Releases/2011/2011-11-14-Open-Doors-International-Students

Khan, B. H. (2005). *Managing e-learning: Design, delivery, implementation, and evaluation.* London: Information Science Publishing.

Kinuthia, W. (2007). African education perspectives on culture and e-learning convergence. In A. Edmundson (Ed.), *Globalized e-learning cultural challenges* (pp. 60–73). Hershey, PA: Information Science Publishing.

Knight, E., Gunawardena, C. N., & Aydin, C. H. (2009). Cultural interpretations of the visual meaning of icons and images used in North American web design. *Educational Media International, 46*(1), 17–35.

Ko, S., & Rossen, S. (2010). *Teaching online: A practical guide* (3rd ed.). New York: Routledge.

Kroeber, A., & Kluckhohn, C. (1952). *Culture.* New York: Meridian Books.

Ku, H. Y., & Lohr, L. L. (2003). A case study of Chinese students' attitudes toward their first online learning experience. *Educational Technology Research and Development, 51*(3), 95–102.

LaPointe, D. K., Greysen, K. R. B., & Barrett, K. A. (2004). Speak2Me: Using synchronous audio for ESL teaching in Taiwan. *International Review of Research in Open and Distance Learning, 5*(1). Retrieved from http://www.irrodl.org/index.php/irrodl/article/viewArticle/166/386

Levine, R. (1997). *A geography of time.* New York: Basic Books.

Lewis, R. D. (2006). *When cultures collide: Leading across cultures* (3rd ed.). Boston: Nicholas Brealey International.

McLoughlin, C. (2001). Inclusivity and alignment: Principles of pedagogy, task and assessment design for effective cross-cultural online learning. *Distance Education, 22*(1), 7–29. doi:10.1080/0158791010220102

Mercado, S., Parboteeah, K. P., & Zhao, Y. (2004). On-line course design and delivery: Cross-national considerations. *Strategic Change, 13*, 183–192.

Morse, K. (2003). Does one size fit all? Exploring asynchronous learning in a multicultural environment. *Journal of Asynchronous Learning Networks, 7*(1), 37–55. Retrieved from http://sloanconsortium.org/sites/default/files/v7n1_morse_1.pdf

Newell-Jones, K. (2007). *Global skills and lifelong learning.* London: Development Education Association.

Nguyen, M., Bibo, E. W., & Engle, J. (2012, September). *Advancing to completion: Increasing degree attainment by improving graduation rates and closing gaps for African-American students.* Retrieved from the Education Trust website: http://www.edtrust.org/sites/edtrust.org/files/Advancing_AfAm.pdf

Nisbett, R. E. (2003). *The geography of thought: How Asians and Westerners think differently . . . and why.* New York: Free Press.

Ofulue, C. I. (2011). Literacy at a distance in multilingual contexts: Issues and challenges. *International Review of Research in Open and Distance Learning, 12*(6). Retrieved from http://www.irrodl.org/index.php/irrodl/article/view/981/1957

Parrish, P., & Linder-VanBerschot, J. A. (2010). Cultural dimensions of learning: Addressing the challenges of multicultural instruction. *International Review of Research in Open and Distance Learning, 11*(2). Retrieved from http://www.irrodl.org/index.php/irrodl/article/view/809

Powell, G. C. (1997). On being a culturally sensitive instructional designer and educator. *Educational Technology, 37*(2), 6–14.

Raza, S. (2012). *Learning styles and culture.* Manuscript submitted for publication.

Santo, S. A. (2006). Relationships between learning styles and online learning: Myth or reality? *Performance Improvement Quarterly, 19*(3), 71–86. Retrieved from http://www.academia.edu/attachments/863960/download_file

Shattuck, K. (2005). *Cultures meeting cultures in online distance education: Perceptions of international adult learners of the impact of culture when taking online distance education courses designed and delivered by an American university* (Unpublished doctoral dissertation).

Thompson, L., & Ku, H. (2005). Chinese graduate students' experiences and attitudes toward online learning. *Educational Media International, 42*(1), 33–47. doi:10.1080/09523980500116878

Tu. C.-H. (2001). How Chinese perceive social presence: An examination of interaction in online learning environment. *Educational Media International, 38*(1), 45–60. doi:10.1080/09523980010021235

Uzuner, S. (2009). Questions of culture in distance learning: A research review. *International Review of Research in Open and Distance Learning, 10*(3). Retrieved from http://www.irrodl.org/index.php/irrodl/article/view/690/1305

Vincent-Lancrin, S., & Pfotenhauer, S. (2012). *Guidelines for quality provision in cross-border higher education: Where do we stand?* Paris: OECD Directorate for Education.

Western Interstate Commission for Higher Education (WICHE). (2012, December). *Knocking at the college door: Projections of high school graduates* (8th ed.). Retrieved from http://www.wiche.edu/info/publications/knocking-8th/knocking-8th.pdf

Wilson, M. S. (2001). Cultural considerations in online instruction and learning. *Distance Education, 22*(1), 52–64. doi:10.1080/0158791010220104

Wlodkowski, R. J., & Ginsberg, M. B. (1995). A framework for culturally responsive teaching. *Strengthening Student Engagement, 53*(1). Retrieved from http://www.ascd.org/publications/educational-leadership/sept95/vol53/num01/A-Framework-for-Culturally-Responsive-Teaching.aspx

Zapalska, A., & Brozik, D. (2006). Learning styles and online education. *Campus-Wide Information Systems, 23*(5). doi:10.1108/10650740610714080

PART THREE

PROCESSES FOR ASSURING QUALITY AT RESOURCE AND PROGRAM LEVELS

12

ETHICS MATTERS

Assuring Quality at the Academic Program Level

Melody M. Thompson and Gary W. Kuhne

> *Some people apparently believe that if only someone would write down a set of explicit rules that would tell them how to act in every circumstance, they would become comfortably ethical and right in their behavior. There would be no perplexing decisions, no painful wondering what is the right thing to do. (Godbey, 1992, p. 57)*

Quality Matters (QM), the well-known program for promoting high standards for online courses, communicates a double meaning: a promise to address "matters," or topics relating to quality, and an assertion that program quality "matters," that it is significant or important. We are using our title to communicate a similar double meaning: we will be discussing matters related to the ethics of online programming, and we will be doing so because we believe that this topic is one that not only matters but is crucial to the development and delivery of high-quality programs.

We agree with Mariasingam and Hanna (2006) that

> the structure and features of any framework used for measuring quality will depend on the concept of quality it is designed to measure. Therefore, it is critical to define first the concept of quality from multiple perspectives, at different levels of analysis, and with a view of quality that incorporates multiple measures. (p. 4)

Standardized approaches are particularly useful in assessing aspects of program quality that are amenable to measurement, thereby providing institutions with information important in assuring program sustainability (one quality factor). We base our discussion in this chapter on the belief that these approaches—while addressing many important matters—omit a significant level of analysis: consideration of more intangible elements that are as important as technological and instrumental elements in assuring high programmatic quality. Our discussion in this chapter focuses on one of those intangibles: the ethical dimensions of program quality.

Finally, a caveat: Morris (2008, p. 2) notes that since definitions of "ethical" make clear that ethical questions "deal with matters of moral accountability related to 'doing the right (good) thing' or 'doing the wrong (bad) thing,'" while non-ethical problems are ones where this dimension is not relevant," it can be tempting to view the distinction as clear-cut. However, different worldviews and perspectives create differences in how the same issue is categorized; where one person sees an ethical issue, another may see a power issue, philosophical difference, or methodological concern. What we have labeled ethical considerations for the purposes of our discussion may not have that interpretation for others. Even in the face of such possible differences in interpretation, a focus on ethics can generate important discussions about several essential dimensions of program quality.

The Heart of the Matter: Ethical Considerations in Program Quality

An academic program is the result of decisions about goals, audience, technology, instruction, assessment, and evaluation, among other things. For academic programs in higher education, these decisions are usually made by the academic program faculty and administrator (e.g., department head) and mediated by other influences, such as university policy and institutional support units. These decisions are never neutral in their impact on participants, and the differential impact that results from one decision over another has distinct ethical dimensions (Thompson & Wrigglesworth, 2013).

Standardized frameworks of quality criteria provide guidance by suggesting recognized ways of dealing with various pragmatic and quantifiable elements of practice, but they are often decontextualized from the values and worldviews of those who make decisions about program quality. They focus primarily on the whats and hows of an academic program but less frequently on the whys: why our program has these goals, why we target this audience, why we choose to use these technologies, why we choose and support faculty in this particular way, why we use these criteria for program evaluation, and why program decisions are made by this particular process.

These questions get to the heart of program quality; they reflect the values, beliefs about right behavior, and worldviews of those who develop and deliver the programs. As Godbey (1992) puts it, such decisions are about "'making up our should,' not just making up our minds" (p. 57).

Morris (2008) concurs, noting that ethical questions

are closely linked to judgments of moral accountability. . . . Words like "should," "ought," and "must" enter into the conversation. Thus, it is not surprising that discussions of ethics have the ability to make us nervous, defensive, and annoyingly self-righteous. (p. 1)

Standardized frameworks, by their very rationality, offer a comfortable—if erroneous—metaphorical assurance that all bases have been covered and all boxes checked. Consideration of ethical questions, in contrast, can be anything but comfortable since "by their very nature, ethical analyses impose a moral burden" on those involved, whereas "analyses that are not couched in ethical terms impose no such burden" (Morris, 2008, p. 3).

Although consideration of the ethical dimensions of quality at the program level may at times be uncomfortable, such analyses can help program decision makers ensure a good match among what they are doing, how they are doing it, and why they are doing it. Such a match is a necessary element of professional and institutional integrity, that is, the integration of beliefs and practice. Just as the QM principle of alignment—the idea that all elements within an individual course work together toward the learning objectives of that course—underlies the technical and instrumental quality of courses (Quality Matters, 2010), so does integrity—the integration of values, goals, and practices—underlie the ethical quality of a program.

Among the many possible foci for an ethics of program quality, we have chosen in this chapter to examine two major program elements that are receiving considerable attention in current discussions about the "redefinition" of higher education—program purposes and goals and faculty selection and support—and to discuss several ethical dimensions of each. We also will discuss the importance of their integration toward the goal of offering programs that are not merely sustainable in the pragmatic sense, but also sustaining, that is, that support and strengthen the learning projects of individuals, groups, and communities as a reflection of a just society (Thompson & Kearns, 2011). Considering these elements at the program level offers a useful addition to the literature on ethical considerations at the course level since a program by nature should be more than the sum of its parts. For the purposes of our discussion, we define an *academic program* as a cohesive combination of higher education courses and experiences designed to accomplish established objectives leading to a degree, diploma, or certificate. *Program* may also refer to the administrative unit that develops and offers these activities.

Programs are at the nexus of decision making and practice between the course level and upper-level administration. Although our main focus in this chapter is on quality at the program level, this outcome must be negotiated "within a broad context of reciprocal influence and utilization, highlighting the myriad opportunities for ethical difficulties to arise" (Morris, 2008, p. 1). For example, an academic program is planned and developed by academic departments, but it is approved (or rejected) by administrative bodies, such as a university's faculty senate or graduate school, and supported by technical and student services units. Similarly, teaching occurs at the course level but is influenced by decisions made at the program level, as well as by policies at the level of the institution. As we go through the chapter, we will identify some of these connections, particularly when they involve ethical tensions that need to be resolved or negotiated. We are not suggesting specific answers to the questions we raise because we recognize that educators are likely to come to different well-reasoned conclusions based on the interplay of personal, professional, and contextual factors that characterize specific situations. We are, however, insisting on the importance of asking such questions as part of the decision-making process for online academic programs.

Establishing Program Purposes and Goals: What Matters? Who Matters?

Thompson and Wrigglesworth (2013) discuss the ethical dimensions of what has been termed the *commodification* of higher education, "the apparent shift from learning as a way to become more fully human to learning with the goal of becoming a skilled worker able to contribute to a strong economy" (p. 407). They review the ideas of a number of educators concerned about the narrowing of higher education goals in general, and in online programs in particular. Carr-Chellman (2005), for example, charges that online higher education programs that promote narrowly vocational goals do so at the expense of "liberation, democracy, diversity, and community" (p. 157). Russell (2009) concurs, noting that educators in open- and distance-learning environments are under increasing pressure to narrowly tailor programs to reach goals driven by a globalized economy, with little or no concern for more affective dimensions related to social or cultural contexts. He contends that program decision makers are ethically responsible for providing programs that recognize the importance of other factors and goals.

Tait (2009) argues that although the field of distance education began as an instrument of social justice, current external forces are pressuring institutions to adopt human capacity goals for their programs as a means of "international economic survival" (p. xv). Recognizing the inescapable tension that results from these pressures, he asks, "How do we ensure that the needs for organizational survival in a competitive landscape do not obscure but can be brought to serve the ethos of social justice?" (p. xvi). Tait concludes that the flexibility and commitment to innovation that characterize distance education provide the potential for effectively engaging with core ethical issues, but further suggests that realizing this potential necessitates "that organizational purposes framed within ethical understandings are not suborned" (p. xvi) by competing organizational priorities driven by external forces.

Perhaps the most salient ethical question in relation to establishing a program's purpose, and the subsequent setting of commensurate educational goals, is, Who *should* decide? Most online higher education students are adults. Thompson and Wrigglesworth (2013) note that a core principle in the adult education literature is the ability of adult students to identify what they want and need to learn, and the authors then ask questions that reflect an inherent tension among competing viewpoints:

> What is the role of faculty expertise in deciding what students need to learn? What is the role of "consumer choice"? What if students are not interested in Carr-Chellman's objectives of "liberation, democracy, diversity, and community"? This tension may be one of conflicting "academic freedoms," with students wanting to learn what *they* want to learn and teachers wanting to teach what *they* want to teach. (p. 408)

A recent publication of the Association of American Colleges and Universities (AAC&U) suggests that the rhetoric of "choice" is itself misleading, noting that in today's economic climate, educational choices are seldom freely made on the basis of a broad range of potential educational benefits. Instead, "powerful social forces, reinforced by public policies, pull students—especially first generation and adult students—toward a narrowly instrumental approach to college." The report strongly urges educators "to resist and reverse that downward course" (AAC&U, 2007, p. 17).

Of course, programs can be intentionally designed to meet multiple stakeholder "needs." Mariasingam and Hanna (2006, Table 1) suggest that program quality criteria should include both goals: preparing graduates "for good citizenship with social responsibility, civic participation, and social and cultural understanding" and for making human resource contributions to meet societal needs. The AAC&U (2007) publication, although warning against a too narrow focus on "marketable" college programs, does not denigrate the importance of preparation for work. Rather, it suggests that "what matters in college" is preparation for life in a world "being dramatically reshaped by scientific and technological innovations, global interdependence, cross-cultural encounters, and changes in the balance of economic and political power" (AAC&U, 2007, p. 2). Such preparation can be achieved effectively only by programs with broad goals "keyed to work, life, and citizenship" (AAC&U, 2007, p. 2).

Finding a balance between what students "want" because of social and economic pressure and what they might choose were they aware of the benefits of broader options presents an ongoing challenge for those developing online programs. Might engagement of learners in the planning process—authentic engagement that goes beyond merely asking what they want—provide insights to guide program planning? Is there an ethical imperative to foster such engagement?

A frequent quality criterion in the literature on online programming is the participation of stakeholders in program planning. Space constraints do not allow consideration of the ethical questions relating to each constituent group: instructors, designers, students, administrators, support staff, employers, government, and so on. We have chosen to focus on the one group that, next to faculty, is most directly and immediately affected by decisions about program goals: the students in the program. The principle of learner participation in program planning has a long history within the field of adult education, itself the "parent" field of distance education. Brookfield (1986) offers a representative perspective on the pervasiveness of this principle among adult educators: "Few educators or trainers of adults would publicly subscribe to any program development model that seemed to exclude adult learners from some kind of involvement in planning curricula" (p. 207).

One argument for learner participation is based on the idea that democratic principles mandate participatory planning, that the autonomous nature of adults in a free society argues against the external imposition of goals. Instead, planning should include those who are most directly affected by the program: students. Sork (2010) observes that there "is growing sensitivity about diversity and inclusion in society in general and education in particular. Expectations are high that when programs are planned, those with a stake in the program will have their views heard" (p. 158).

However, although most online higher education students are adults, not all educators who plan online programs think of themselves as adult educators or subscribe to adult education principles. Many educators firmly ensconced within traditional higher education contexts would likely sympathize with this view from an earlier time:

> The most pernicious doctrine in adult education is that democracy demands that the adult educator abdicate his professional authority. Education is not democratic. It must be directed by those who are already educated. . . . Those who stray into university programs . . . should not be allowed to pervert the program. (Petersen & Petersen, 1960, pp. 50, 72)

Evidence of the "trust the expert" perspective continues to be found throughout higher education rhetoric and practice, although couched in more reasonable terms (Goho, MacAskill, & McGeachie, 2003). To some extent, this perspective may reflect a lack of awareness of the changing demographics in higher education and the internal changes necessary to effectively serve adults who, as the new majority of higher education students, exhibit learning strengths and needs quite different from those of yesterday's traditional-aged student. It may also reflect an assumption that disciplinary expertise confers pedagogical and planning expertise. However, most higher education faculty who develop and administer academic programs receive no training in pedagogy or program planning but rather in the content and research methods of their disciplines. Used to being the experts in this realm, they may not recognize that adult students can bring valuable resources and perspectives to the planning table. There may also be concern that an "uncritical" acceptance of this premise can itself have unethical consequences (Ewert, 1982).

Sclove (2010), in discussing a similar question about the value of citizen participation as a complement to expert deliberation in technology planning and assessment initiatives, notes specific ethics-related contributions that lay participants are more likely to make than are narrowly focused experts: "Laypeople excel in articulating ethical concerns and moral and social values, making and explaining value judgments and developing normatively informed insights and analysis" (p. 24). For Cervero and Wilson (2005), inclusive participation is important not only for what a particular group brings to the table but also as an ethical principle that reflects a justice-based answer to the question of "whose interests matter enough to be represented at the planning table" (p. 92).

The tension reflected in differing ideas about purposes, goals, and planning plays out within the context of the overarching institutional mission and the relationship of online programs to the larger university, suggesting both a clear quality factor and a potential ethical challenge. Quality standards for online programs frequently suggest the need for close integration of the online and "traditional" sectors of an institution. We ask, however, To what extent should the goals established by online programs—and the planning process for establishing those goals—be merely a reflection of those of the larger university within which they operate? Mariasingam and Hanna (2006) note that online programs enhance institutional quality and should be recognized for this contribution in a university's mission statement. Does the contribution to institutional quality offered by online programs suggest that their direct participants, both faculty and students, are entitled to—are, perhaps, even ethically responsible for—active participation in redefining their universities' purposes and goals in a changing social context?

A program's answers to ethical questions about purposes and goals— Where should we go?—lead naturally to a further question—How should we get there? In the following section, we address this question as it relates to specific aspects of faculty selection and support.

Faculty Selection and Support: What's the Matter With Adjuncts?

The topic of faculty selection and support has many dimensions. Early discussions in the literature focused primarily on an institution's obligation to provide appropriate professional development opportunities and ongoing support to traditional faculty transitioning from classroom instruction to online teaching. Provision of such support is an important quality factor but has been well covered in other publications. Less frequently discussed is the issue of programs' reliance on adjuncts as instructors in many online courses. The presence of this category of instructor—both online and in resident instruction—is increasing in higher education today. How does the reliance on adjuncts relate to the quality of online programs, and what ethical questions does it raise?

Here we delve into yet another meaning of *matter*: the sense that there is a difference of opinion about the rightness or wrongness of an action—as in "What's the matter with hiring illegal immigrants?"—or that someone is in a disturbed state—as in "What's the matter with John?" In this section, we will discuss the use of online adjunct instructors in all three senses of the word *matters* that we have introduced in this chapter: as a topic, or matter, for discussion; as a topic that matters; and as a practice that should be examined from an ethical perspective to determine whether—or under what circumstances—there might be something the matter.

Discussing adjuncts as online instructors matters because this category of faculty member increasingly bears the responsibility for teaching in higher education, both in resident programs and online. In 2008, 48% of those teaching in degree-granting institutions were adjuncts. When other categories of "contingent" faculty (e.g., part-time or full-time fixed-term) are included, the proportion exceeds 70% (American Association of University Professors [AAUP], 2010; Pullias Center for Higher Education, 2012a). Although current data collection requirements do not separate resident from online instruction when tracking the proportion of faculty with adjunct appointments, a number of trends and economic pressures suggest that the use of adjuncts in online programs exceeds that in resident programs, and at many for-profit institutions, 100% of the faculty are likely to be adjuncts. Given the close connection between perceptions of quality and the performance of faculty (Hussman & Miller, 2001; Kezar & Gehrke, 2012), this category of faculty inarguably matters.[1]

The scholarly literature and other sources of professional opinion (e.g., professional associations) reflect mixed responses to the idea of adjuncts teaching online courses and raise questions about the relationship between academic programs or institutions and adjunct faculty who teach for them.

On the one hand, the practice has been viewed positively as a way for institutions to minimize instructional costs, as a means to extend the reach of
educational programming to unserved or underserved populations by
increasing faculty capacity, and as a factor that enhances learning by bringing the real-world expertise of practicing professionals into the classroom.
On the other hand, the practice has been criticized as undermining university governance structures, putting student learning at risk, and abusing
an "underclass" of teaching professionals. Both perspectives matter in our
discussion of ethical dimensions of program quality.

Brockett and Hiemstra (1998), in their discussion of ethical considerations in program planning, distinguish between deontological ethical
approaches based on duty and teleological approaches, which focus on
consequences. Duty-based questions include, To whom does the program
have a duty or responsibility? What actions are necessary for us to fulfill our
responsibility to those constituents? A teleological orientation attempts "to
create a result that produces the greatest good and the least harm" (p. 126).
Consequence-focused questions include, Who benefits from this decision?
Who is harmed? On what basis are benefits and harms allocated? Both of
these perspectives are helpful in identifying ethical questions related to
adjuncts as online instructors.

Given the contextually embedded nature of academic programs, the duty
element is multidimensional. Programs may perceive a duty to students, to
the parent institution, to the profession associated with the program, to society, and to their own program personnel. In relation to our focus in this section, we suggest that a specific important question is, What level and types of
responsibility does a program or an institution have toward its adjunct faculty?

A considerable body of literature suggests that given adjuncts' core role
in online program quality, institutions have a responsibility to provide them
with a variety of professional development and support services; orientation to and integration into the institution, training related to the online
environment, mentoring, access to institutional resources and staff support,
and ongoing professional development opportunities are mentioned consistently in the literature (e.g., Hill, n.d.; Shelton, 2011; Tipple, 2010). Other
sources suggest that adjuncts should be involved in the design of the courses
they teach and have representation in institutional governance, based on the
idea that people have a right to participate in decision making that directly
affects them (Pullias Center, 2012d; Puzziferro & Shelton, 2009). A very few
sources mention a responsibility to offer appropriate compensation or job
security (Pullias Center, 2012d; Snitzer & Crosby, 2003).

Accrediting bodies, charged with monitoring the quality of higher
education programs, require an institution's adjunct faculty to "meet the same

educational, professional and scholarly requirements and standards as their full time counterparts" (Snitzer & Crosby, 2003, "Administrative Organization," para. 1). As a result, the regional associations stipulate an institutional responsibility to provide all faculty—whether teaching full-time or part-time, face-to-face, or online—with support and development opportunities. The Middle States Commission on Higher Education (2006) makes a specific reference to adjuncts and other contingent faculty in this respect: "The greater the dependence on such employees, the greater is the institutional responsibility to provide orientation, oversight, evaluation, professional development, and opportunities for integration into the life of the institution" (p. 38).

These statements of responsibility clearly communicate a belief that a duty to adjunct faculty members exists. The logical follow-up question from an ethical perspective is, Are actions taken to fulfill this responsibility; that is, are beliefs and actions integrated?

Snitzer and Crosby (2003), in their argument for the importance of institutional and program support for adjuncts who teach online, cite a number of sources as the basis for concluding that "the literature on part time faculty is replete with reports of abuse, poor working conditions, and cases of labor law issues" and "disadvantages such as lack of advancement, job security, benefits and . . . disengagement from the traditional campus culture" ("Administrative Organization," para. 2). More recently, the Delphi Project on the Changing Faculty and Student Success, an ongoing project of the Pullias Center for Higher Education at University of Southern California's (USC) Rossier School of Education, has published findings of its ongoing review of studies that document "poor working conditions" for contingent faculty throughout higher education as well as "exploitative employment arrangements characterized by a growing number of faculty who cannot make enough money to survive, have no benefits, and who lack a career path with opportunities for promotion" (Pullias Center, 2012c, p. 4).

Further evidence of the gap between what are believed to be important quality factors and actual institutional action comes from a recent study of values versus practices related to higher education administrators' hiring and faculty-support decisions, reported at the 2012 meeting of the Council of Colleges of Arts and Sciences (CCAS). Table 12.1 highlights several of these disparities.

Returning to the idea that programs and institutions have duties or responsibilities to multiple constituencies, the misalignment of values and practices reflected in the literature may in some cases represent a trade-off: a lower-priority value or constituency is traded off for one deemed more important. For example, whereas only 16% of respondents in the Kezar and Gehrke (2012) report agreed or strongly agreed that using part-time faculty

TABLE 12.1
Differences in Values and Practices of Deans at CCAS Institutions

	Percentage who strongly agree or agree	*Percentage whose institutions offer such support*
Part-time faculty should be provided with a formal orientation	91	64
Part-time faculty should be provided with structured mentoring	78	31
Part-time faculty should have access to professional development related to teaching	66	53

Note. Adapted from *Report of Findings From Values, Practices, and Faculty Hiring Decisions of Academic Leaders Study for CCAS Leadership*, by A. Kezar and S. Gehrke, 2012, retrieved from http://www.uscrossier.org/pullias/wp-content/uploads/2012/12/DELPHI_Deans_Study_Report_CCAS.pdf

improves teaching quality, 81% agreed or strongly agreed that the practice solves budgetary problems.

The idea of using adjuncts to meet budgetary responsibilities is reflected widely in the literature, with references to hiring adjuncts as a cost-effective strategy or good business model for universities (Liu & Zhang, 2007; Puzziferro & Shelton, 2009). The National Education Association (NEA) notes that "savings to colleges and universities are considerable" since contingent faculty are paid "a fraction of what tenure system faculty earn" and receive no health care and retirement benefits (NEA, 2012, para. 3). Thus, savings appear to be a natural result of both lower compensation packages and institutions' choice to not provide faculty development opportunities, and may thereby represent an instance of fulfilling a program's or an institution's felt duty to "save on labor costs and to smooth the flow of resource exchange with their constituencies" (Liu & Zhang, 2007, p. 7).

What are the ethical dimensions of such trade-offs? Adding a teleological perspective—one that takes into account the consequences of particular actions—provides additional insights. Based on the picture that emerges from the literature reviewed, we might ask, Who benefits? Who is harmed? On what basis are benefits and harms assessed and allocated?

The literature suggests many positive consequences of hiring adjuncts to teach online. Authors state that the practice brings real-world perspectives into a course; will "maximize the educational quality and institutional effectiveness" (Tipple, 2010, "Abstract"); and contributes to "flexibility and the ability to adapt to the changing demands of learners, the new promise of technology, and the new competitive landscape of higher education" (Puzziferro & Shelton, 2009, "Abstract"). However, such beliefs seem largely based on assumptions; no citations are offered to support the claims. In their summary report of the study of academic administrators' beliefs and practices with respect to contingent faculty, Kezar and Gehrke (2012) comment,

> When we examine the beliefs that participants have about NTTF [non-tenure-track faculty], we are struck by the predominantly positive perceptions. . . . While acknowledging the special expertise they bring and the benefits . . . we wonder if a more balanced picture of some of the drawbacks to overly relying on NTTF should be examined more? What proof is there that the use of NTTF has largely positive outcomes? . . . [I]t may be necessary for campuses to consider collecting data about both the costs and benefits so that they are able to address this issue based on data not anecdote. We suspect the cost may be higher than they anecdotally understand given research nationally about negative outcomes. (p. 5)

In his discussion of reading the education literature critically, Brookfield (1995) suggests that readers of academic literature should ask whose voices are heard in discussing a particular idea, practice, or experience. Do people speak for themselves or are they "spoken for" or "spoken about"? Until recently, the voices in the literature about adjuncts were primarily those of scholars and administrators—those with ready access to academic publishing channels—positing what should be the case when "using," "training," "supporting," or "managing" those in this faculty category. Within the last several years, however, adjuncts and other contingent faculty have used the openness and reach of new technologies to express their own ideas about their experiences in the higher education workplace. Additionally, several academic studies have more rigorously examined the alignment—or misalignment—between what the literature reports as consequences for students, institutions, and the faculty themselves and what research evidence shows those consequences to be.

The New Faculty Majority (NFM) was founded in 2009 by contingent faculty with the goal of improving higher education quality "by advancing professional equity and securing academic freedom for all adjunct and contingent faculty. . . . NFM is committed to creating stable, equitable, sustainable, non-exploitative academic environments that promote more effective teaching, learning, and research" (NFM, 2012).

A recent NFM project, undertaken in conjunction with the Center for the Future of Higher Education (a virtual think tank of the Campaign for the

Future of Higher Education [CFHE]), gathered quantitative and qualitative data (in the form of narrative responses) from contingent faculty themselves on their perceptions of the consequences of common hiring and professional support practices in higher education. In this exploratory survey of 500 contingent faculty members, instructors noted that their experiences with just-in-time hiring practices, lack of institutional support, and expectations to perform common instructor duties without pay were injurious to student learning and to their own sense of self-efficacy and personal security. In other words, they believe that something is seriously the matter (NFM, 2012).

Almost 20,000 faculty members responded to a 2012 survey conducted by the Coalition for the Academic Workforce (CAW) that examined demographics, assignments, compensation, and institutional support for part-time faculty. The report highlights low compensation (and even 20% lower for online teaching than for resident instruction), widespread lack of institutional support for teaching, and failure to integrate part-time faculty into institutions in any comprehensive way:

> The respondents paint a dismal picture, one that clearly demonstrates how little professional commitment and support part-time faculty members receive from their institutions for anything that costs money and is not related to preparing and delivering discrete course materials. The findings also reflect a lack of processes and resources to include part-time faculty members in the academic community of the college or university. (CAW, 2012, p. 13)

For example, although 71.6% of part-time faculty are given a mailbox and 71.3% are granted library privileges (two items that cost the institution little, if anything), only 26.7% reported being offered teacher development workshops, 18.8% reported receiving regular salary increases, and 1.8% reported receiving priority for tenure-track openings. Additionally, 60.6% reported that their office hours for discussions with students are unpaid. The AAUP (2010) suggests that these working conditions have "turned the professoriate into an irrational economic choice, denying the overwhelming majority of individuals the opportunity to consider college teaching as a career" (para. 8).

Another concern focuses on consequences related to student learning. The Delphi Project on the Changing Faculty and Student Success has studied the extent to which institutional policies and practices "negatively impact equity and morale" (Pullias Center, 2012a, p. 1) among contingent faculty, as well as connections between these factors and student learning. This project examines four common policies and practices—last-minute hiring and contract renewal, lack of access to professional development, exclusion from curriculum design and decisions, and lack of access to institutional resources—and provides extensive research evidence of negative implications for student learning (Pullias Center, 2012a).

Finally, several studies note the lack of evidence behind institutional discourse that justifies a trade-off between managerial flexibility and budgetary savings, on the one hand, and better working conditions and support of adjuncts, on the other: "Not only is there scarce campus or system level data to support the claims, little or no effort is being made by college administrators or policy makers to gather such data" (Street, Maisto, Merves, & Rhoades, 2012, p. 15). Another study presents bottom-line data of the direct, opportunity, and indirect costs to a program because of high levels of online faculty turnover and attrition. The authors assert that these costs "can be ten times the amount or greater than the actual payment [for teaching]" (Betts & Sikorski, 2008, "Indirect Costs," para. 4). For this reason, Betts and Sikorski (2008) caution program administrators to base decisions about faculty support, not on unexamined assumptions about budgetary implications, but rather on informed understandings of both the benefits of recruitment, retention, and incentive strategies and the costs associated with faculty/adjunct turnover and attrition.

Recommendations and Conclusion

As noted previously, our intention has not been to provide answers but rather to reflect David Naugle's (2002) insight that "human life is largely carried out in the interrogative mood" (p. 83). Coming to understand what we do and why we do it is very much a process of asking questions and then searching for the answers. Although the questions we raise have relevance across programs and institutions, we know that the answers will likely vary based on a number of interconnected factors. Additionally, we recognize that ethical questions similar to those we raise about program goals and faculty support could be raised for other aspects of online programming: course design, technology choice, learner support, and evaluation. For this reason, our recommendations focus on the necessity for those in charge of and working in all online academic programs to actively engage in an intentional process for asking ethical questions and to commit to developing informed answers.

Sork (2010) suggests that the "quaint image of a small group of like-minded people sitting around a table planning an educational activity" (p. 158) is fading owing to the culturally diverse and globalized nature of program providers and learner populations, as well as the availability of multiple ways to communicate across distances. Although his concern about expanding perspectives on and participation in planning is one we share, in concluding our discussion we would like to focus on a somewhat different aspect of the picture he describes: that of people actually coming together—whether virtually or in person—to engage in focused communication about program quality, including the ethical aspects of such quality. We suggest that, too often, the response to a changing higher education environment and the programmatic challenges that come with such change is a form of "lazy consensus" (Nowviski, 2012):

> Lazy consensus has already been working against us in every case where we don't engage. . . . It kicks in and becomes a factor in any set of decisions where we . . . get so busy that we go completely heads-down and become oblivious to larger trends and directions. When that happens, we end up not having a voice. We end up being the people who don't speak up even though we're nominally represented, and no matter what we may really think, we are therefore assumed to be [in agreement].

In some programs, lazy consensus will result in business as usual, with no consideration of changes that might enhance program quality, particularly in its ethical dimensions. In other programs, it might result in unconsidered reactions to widely trumpeted but poorly supported exhortations for radical change. In a few cases, it might even result in the ability of a small group to make positive, well-considered changes under the radar of higher-level decision makers. We believe, however, that the most effective approach is for those responsible for the quality of programs to actively engage with others in discussions and decisions about quality factors, including ethical factors.

Such discussions would greatly benefit from moving beyond standard academic arenas into more open venues, such as that provided by the CFHE (http://futureofhighered.org). The goal of CFHE is to "reframe the debate" about higher education quality by engaging "faculty, students and our communities, not just administrators, politicians, foundations and think tanks" in discussions of higher education change (CFHE, 2012). Although extending the discussion beyond the more usual expert and stakeholder groups will be uncomfortable to traditionalists, broader participation has the potential to enrich analysis through the addition of life experiences and other social knowledge. Such input may contribute a broad range of ethical considerations and consequences "that expert analysis omits or undervalues" (Sclove, 2010, ix).

Effective engagement in decisions about program quality depends on informed judgments based in evidence, not in unsupported beliefs. It also depends on a willingness to go beyond merely instrumental and technical aspects of a program to consider the equally important, if less obvious, ethical aspects. Understanding the interconnectedness of different aspects of the organization becomes crucial in this effort. Taking the time necessary to study and consider the internal and external contexts of a program as well as the ways in which they are connected and influence each other can provide information and perspectives necessary for ethically aware decisions. Such awareness is enhanced by listening to those affected by programming decisions, particularly in terms of what they can tell us about the consequences of different courses of action. It is also strengthened by availing ourselves of resources and tools developed by those who have worked toward a deeper understanding of specific aspects of programming. Two such tools are *Non-Tenure-Track Faculty in Our Department: A Guide for Departments and Academic Programs to Better Understand Faculty Working Conditions and the Necessity of Change* (Pullias Center, 2012b) and the companion publication *Non-Tenure-Track Faculty on Our Campus: A Guide for Campus Task Forces to Better Understand Faculty Working Conditions and the Necessity of Change* (Pullias Center, 2012c), both produced by and available from USC's Pullias Center for Higher Education (see http://resources.thechangingfaculty.org).

At both the program and the institutional levels, decisions and compromises must be made in balancing goals, resources, and responsibilities for a variety of constituencies. Ethical compromises depend on principled decisions founded on an evidence-based awareness of the consequences of trade-offs or compromises. Although the alignment of these consequences with the values and goals of programs and institutions is important, the integration of ethical perspectives suggests an additional opportunity. Policies and practices may not only reflect a program's or an institution's identity, but they may also be used to express new possibilities, going beyond who we are now to who we choose to become.

Note

1. To date, most studies of adjunct and other contingent faculty (as differentiated from anecdotal reports or advice) have examined this group broadly, that is, without distinguishing between resident and online instructors. Our review for this chapter draws on both the specific and general bodies of literature, with a primary focus on U.S. practice.

References

American Association of University Professors (AAUP). (2010). *Tenure and teaching-intensive appointments*. Retrieved from http://www.aaup.org/report/tenure-and-teaching-intensive-appointments

Association of American Colleges and Universities (AAC&U). (2007). *College learning for the new global century.* Washington, DC: Author.

Betts, K., & Sikorski, B. (2008). Financial bottom line: Estimating the cost of faculty/adjunct turnover and attrition for online programs. *Online Journal of Distance Learning Administration, 11*(1). Retrieved from http://www.westga. edu/~distance/ojdla/spring111/betts111.html

Brockett, R., & Hiemstra, R. (1998). Philosophical and ethical considerations. In P. Cookson (Ed.), *Program planning and teaching for the continuing education of adults: A North American perspective* (pp. 115–134). Malabar, FL: Krieger.

Brookfield, S. (1986). *Understanding and facilitating adult learning.* San Francisco: Jossey-Bass.

Brookfield, S. (1995). *Becoming a critically reflective teacher.* San Francisco: Jossey-Bass.

Campaign for the Future of Higher Education (CFHE). (2012). *About.* Retrieved from http://futureofhighered.org/About

Carr-Chellman, A. (2005). The new frontier: Web-based education in U.S. culture. In A. A. Carr-Chellman (Ed.), *Global perspectives on e-learning: Rhetoric and reality* (pp. 145–159). Thousand Oaks, CA: Sage.

Cervero, R. M., & Wilson, A. L. (2005). *Working the planning table: Negotiating democratically for adult, continuing, and workplace education.* San Francisco: Jossey-Bass.

Coalition for the Academic Workforce (CAW). (2012). *A portrait of part-time faculty members.* Retrieved from http://www.academicworkforce.org/CAW_portrait_2012 .pdf

Ewert, D. M. (1982). Involving adult learners in program planning. In S. Merriam (Ed.), *Linking philosophy and practice* (pp. 29–38). San Francisco: Jossey-Bass.

Godbey, G. (1992). The ethics of adult educators: A senior perspective. *PAACE Journal of Lifelong Learning, 1,* 57–59.

Goho, J., MacAskill, P., & McGeachie, P. (2003). Using a panel of experts to enrich planning of distance education. *Journal of Distance Education, 18*(1), 1–18.

Hill, C. (Ed.). (n.d.). *Best practices for training and retaining online adjunct faculty: Faculty focus special report.* Retrieved from http://www.immagic.com/eLibrary/ ARCHIVES/GENERAL/GENPRESS/F090223B.pdf

Hussman, D. E., & Miller, M. T. (2001). Improving distance education: Perceptions of program administrators. *Online Journal of Distance Learning Administration, 4*(3). Retrieved from http://www.westga.edu/~distance/ojdla/fall43/husmann43.html

Kezar, A., & Gehrke, S. (2012). *Report of findings from values, practices, and faculty hiring decisions of academic leaders study for CCAS leadership.* Retrieved from http://www.uscrossier.org/pullias/wp-content/uploads/2012/12/DELPHI_ Deans_Study_Report_CCAS.pdf

Liu, X., & Zhang, L. (2007). *What determines employment of part-time faculty in higher education institutions?* Retrieved from DigitalCommons@IRL: http:// digitalcommons.ilr.cornell.edu/workingpapers

Mariasingam, M., & Hanna, D. (2006). Benchmarking quality in online degree programs: Status and prospects. *Online Journal of Distance Learning Administration, 9*(3). Retrieved from http://www.westga.edu/~distance/ojdla/fall93/mariasingam93 .htm

Middle States Commission on Higher Education. (2006). *Characteristics of excellence in higher education: Requirements of affiliation and standards for accreditation.* Philadelphia: Author.

Morris, M. (2008). *Evaluation ethics.* New York: Guilford Press.

National Education Association (NEA). (2012). *Contingent faculty deserve professional pay.* Retrieved from http://www.nea.org/home/12677.htm

Naugle, D. (2002). *Worldview.* Grand Rapids, MI: William B. Eerdmans.

New Faculty Majority (NFM). (2012). *Our mission.* Retrieved from http://newfaculty majority.info/equity/learn-about-the-issues/mission-a-identity/nfm-mission-statement

Nowviski, G. (2012, March 10). Lazy consensus [web log post]. *Nowviski.org.* Retrieved from http://nowviskie.org/index.php?s=lazy+consensus

Petersen, R., & Petersen, W. (1960). *University adult education.* New York: Harper.

Pullias Center for Higher Education. (2012a). *National trends for faculty composition over time.* Retrieved from http://www.uscrossier.org/pullias/wp-content/uploads/2012/05/Delphi-NTTF_National-Trends-for-Faculty-Composition_WebPDF.pdf

Pullias Center for Higher Education. (2012b). *Non-tenure-track faculty in our department: A guide for departments and academic programs to better understand faculty working conditions and the necessity of change.* Retrieved from http://www.uscrossier.org/pullias/wp-content/uploads/2013/07/DELPHI-PROJECT_NTTF-IN-OUR-DEPT_Web.pdf

Pullias Center for Higher Education. (2012c). *Non-tenure-track faculty on our campus: A guide for campus task forces to better understand faculty working conditions and the necessity of change.* Retrieved from http://www.uscrossier.org/pullias/wp-content/uploads/2013/07/DELPHI-PROJECT_NTTF-ON-OUR-CAMPUS_Web.pdf

Pullias Center for Higher Education (2012d). *Review of selected policies and practices and connections to student learning.* Retrieved from http://www.uscrossier.org/pullias/wp-content/uploads/2012/05/Delphi-NTTF_SelectedPolicies_StudentLearningConnections_WebPDF.pdf

Puzziferro, M., & Shelton, K. (2009). Supporting online faculty—Revisiting the Seven Principles (a few years later). *Online Journal of Distance Learning Administration, 12*(3). Retrieved from http://www.westga.edu/~distance/ojdla/fall123/puzziferro123.html

Quality Matters. (2010). *Higher Ed Program Rubric.* Retrieved from http://www.qmprogram.org/rubric

Russell, G. (2009). Ethical concerns with open and distance learning. In U. Demiray & R. Sharma (Eds.), *Ethical practices and implications in distance learning* (pp. 64–78). Hershey, PA: Information Science Reference.

Sclove, R. (2010). *Reinventing technology assessment: A 21st-century model.* Washington, DC: Science and Technology Innovation Program. Retrieved from http://wilsoncenter.org/publication/reinventing-technology-assessment-21st-century-model

Shelton, K. (2011). A review of paradigms for evaluating the quality of online education programs. *Online Journal of Distance Learning Administration, 4*(1). Retrieved from http://www.westga.edu/~distance/ojdla/spring141/shelton141.html

Snitzer, M., & Crosby, L. S. (2003). Recruitment and development of online adjunct instructors. *Online Journal of Distance Learning Administration, 6*(2). Retrieved from http://www.westga.edu/~distance/ojdla/summer62/crosby_schnitzer62.html

Sork, T. J. (2010). Planning and delivering of programs. In C. Kasworm, A. Rose, & J. Ross-Gordon (Eds.), *Handbook of adult and continuing education* (pp. 157–166). Los Angeles: Sage.

Street, S., Maisto, M., Merves, E., & Rhoades, G. (2012). *Who is Professor "Staff" and how can this person teach so many classes?* Retrieved from the Inside Higher Ed website: http://www.insidehighered.com/sites/default/server_files/files/profstaff(2).pdf

Tait, A. (2009). Foreword. In U. Demiray & R. Sharma (Eds.), *Ethical practices and implications in distance learning* (pp. 15–16). Hershey, PA: Information Science Reference.

Thompson, M. M., & Kearns, L. (2011). Which is to be master? Reflections on ethical decision making. In E. Burge, C. Gibson, & T. Gibson (Eds.), *Flexible pedagogy, flexible practice: Notes from the trenches of distance education* (pp. 257–270). Edmonton, AB: Athabasca University Press.

Thompson, M. M., & Wrigglesworth, J. (2013). Students and teachers as ethical actors: Reflections on the literature. In M. Moore (Ed.), *Handbook of distance education* (3rd ed., pp. 403–418). Mahwah, NJ: Lawrence Erlbaum.

Tipple, R. (2010). Effective leadership of online adjunct faculty. *Online Journal of Distance Learning Administration, 13*(1). Retrieved from http://www.westga.edu/~distance/ojdla/spring131/tipple131.html

13

ACADEMIC ADVISING

A Link to a Quality Experience for Students

Heather L. Chakiris

On a scale of one to seven, respondents in the *2011 National Online Learners Priorities Report* (Noel-Levitz, 2011) rated the importance of access to academic services, including academic advising, an average of 6.40. As institutions grapple with the growth in online learning, it is critical to understand the role played by the academic adviser in online learner success and to ensure that a thoughtful, intentional structure is in place to facilitate a close adviser-student partnership.

Overview of Advising

Historically, academic advising was built on a foundation that ranged from the ideals of higher education to the pragmatics of enrollment. According to the National Academic Advising Association (NACADA, 2006), the curriculum of academic advising should include

> the institution's mission, culture and expectations; the meaning, value, and interrelationship of the institution's curriculum and co-curriculum; modes of thinking, learning, and decision-making; the selection of academic programs and courses; the development of life and career goals; campus/community resources, policies, and procedures; and the transferability of skills and knowledge.

This foundation is rooted in the developmental needs of traditional-age high school graduates who, in most cases, are experiencing independence for the first time. How does advising change when it is viewed through the lens of online learning? To answer that question, advisers (and their institutions) first need to have a fundamental understanding of whom they are serving.

Building an Understanding of Audience

Traditional Versus Adult Students

It is perhaps a given to say that traditional-age learners differ from adult learners; however, swiftly changing U.S. demographics are forcing institutions to better grasp these differences and adapt outdated approaches and processes to meet adult learner needs. A 2008 U.S. Census Bureau population study projected that by 2020 the number of 25- to 44-year-olds will have increased 8% from 2010 and the number of 45- to 64-year-olds will have increased 4.2%, whereas 18- to 24-year-olds will have increased only 0.3%. This demographic shift is already being felt by higher education, as the total number of working adult learners increased more than 20% between 1990 and 2007, with an additional 18% increase expected by 2016 (Chronicle Research Services, 2009). *Convenience, flexibility, choice, instructional effectiveness, service excellence*—these are not terms typically touted in institutional strategic plans; however, they will need to be taken more seriously in order for institutions to remain competitive in a changing higher education marketplace.

Online Versus Online Distance Learner

"Online learning" is used frequently as a global description for anyone studying online; however, this descriptor is an overgeneralization that can make or break learner satisfaction and success. A traditional-age learner taking an online course from his or her residence hall on campus still has access to the academic support resources and extracurricular activities that make up the traditional brick-and-mortar student experience and lead to close social connections and shared traditions. These, in turn, cultivate a strong alumni base and potential funnel of needed financial support back into the institution (Geiger, 2005). Conversely, an online distance learner may never visit the institution's campus. Without institutions building intentional opportunities for interaction into their distance learners' experience, the online distance learner is at significantly higher risk for dropout owing to feelings of isolation (Schaeffer & Konetes, 2010). Rovai (2003) argues that to reduce online learner attrition, retention programs should include consistent and clear online program policies and procedures; encourage a heightened sense of the student's self-esteem; promote student identification with the school; create strong interpersonal relations with peers, faculty, and staff; and provide ready access to support services such as academic advising.

This chapter will focus on the important role of the academic adviser in helping to retain online distance learners—and how the adviser-learner partnership at Penn State's online World Campus is working toward redefining the concept of community.

Building the Online Distance Learner Advising Infrastructure

NACADA defines *distance advising* as "being able to offer a minimum set of core services relating to academic advising which assist distance learners in identifying and achieving their maximum educational potential" (Varney, 2009, "Strategies for Success in Distance Advising," para. 3). The Distance Education Advising Commission Standards for Advising Distance Learners (NACADA, 2010) includes 14 expectations for institutions engaged in distance education. Several of those expectations revolve around leadership at administrative and academic-program levels. Others, including the following, focus on building a positive connection between academic advising and distance-learning students:

- Advisers should provide support services as they would for students on campus.
- They should provide a single point of contact for services commonly accessed by distance learners.
- They should respond to the unique needs of distance-learning students, rather than expecting them to fit within the established organizational structure (NACADA, 2010).

Before any advising services are offered, however, institutions must make sure the members of their distance-advising team have the right skill sets.

According to Steele (2005), writing for the NACADA Clearinghouse of Academic Advising Resources, from a foundational standpoint, an effective academic adviser must have the advanced education and training to understand that at its core, advising is a teaching partnership that involves the learner in developing and owning his or her educational plan. (The relevant standard from NACADA [2010] is "offer appropriate professional development activities and support for staff and faculty advisors.") Advisers guide learners, regardless of age, through the transition to postsecondary education and serve as a conduit to a network of institutional support resources available to each learner.

Best Hiring Practices

From drafting the job announcement to making an offer to the final candidate, distance-advising administrators must be intentional about finding advisers who will thrive in working with online distance learners. For many advisers, being immersed in a vibrant college or university campus environment is integral to their professional motivation and satisfaction—it is important to emphasize in the job announcement and throughout the interview process that face-to-face interaction with online distance learners is (at best) limited. Interactions will primarily take place through phone and e-mail; depending on the office environment, there may be little to no student traffic in and out of the advising office. Candidates must understand the differences between distance and traditional advising and decide whether distance advising is right for them.

Because distance advisers rely on distance technologies to facilitate communication with their learners, candidates must have exceptional telephone and written-communication skills. I recommend conducting first-round advising interviews via telephone—even with local candidates—to assess phone and verbal articulation skills. Application materials (cover letters and résumés) should be reviewed with a critical eye—will learners be able to trust the quality of the education they are receiving if their distance adviser, their primary contact at the institution, does not have a solid grasp of spelling or grammar? Be conscious of the impact of the adviser's communication skills on the institution's brand.

Effective use of technology is critical in distance advising, yet a 2004 study by W. R. Habley concluded that "the technology revolution has not yet consistently reached advising systems" (p. 96). Only 50% of surveyed campuses used 2 of 10 technologies needed to facilitate effective interactions (phone and fax). Candidates for distance-advising positions should be proficient in no-cost video-chat technologies such as Skype and Google+ Hangout so that they can proactively offer these additional connection options when scheduling appointments.

Suggestions for assessing whether advising candidates' skills are relevant to working with online distance learners include the following:

- Ask candidates why they are interested in working with learners whom they might never meet in person.
- Ask candidates for strategies that might be used in building close working relationships with online distance learners.
- Ask candidates what social media tools they have previously used to communicate with learners and how they have used those tools.
- Hold interviews via Skype or a web-conferencing tool, such as Blackboard Collaborate.
- Incorporate written exercises into the interview process (e.g., ask candidates to draft an e-mail to a learner).

Establish Performance Standards

Written performance standards—developed by the distance-advising team to allow opportunities for input and buy-in—are critical and should be reviewed annually to ensure they are current with institutional changes and technological enhancements. Supervisors of newly hired academic advisers should review the standards with all new hires and hold regular one-on-one meetings during the new hire's orientation and training period to ensure shared understanding of expectations and to allow opportunity for clarification. Examples of advising performance standards may include the following:

- response time to student e-mails and phone calls
- time frame for completing semester reviews of learners' academic records
- time frame for completing degree audits
- appropriate communication with learners prior to extended absences
- adequate staffing of pooled phone lines or e-mail accounts
- use of appropriate identifying language when answering the phone (Penn State World Campus, 2012a)

Adviser-Learner Ratio

Working with an online distance learner can prove to be more time-consuming than working with traditional-age, residential learners because the distance adviser is a one-stop shop. An online distance learner cannot travel to various campus buildings to get questions answered; in fact, online *adult* distance learners—who make up the majority of online distance learners (Noel-Levitz, 2011)—may be contacting their adviser in the only five minutes of free time the learners have all day. It is important for the distance adviser to spend additional time answering online distance learner questions in one interaction. Thus, the administrators of advising offices serving online distance learners should proactively benchmark an appropriate adviser-learner ratio and hire sufficient staff to meet that target. If staffing resources are limited, technology accelerators should be investigated (where appropriate) to create efficiencies that will free advisers to provide proactive service to their larger rosters of learners.

Flexible Hours of Operation

Given that most online distance learners are adults and that most adult learners are working at least part-time while pursuing their education, distance advisers should have office hours at times that reflect the characteristics of online distance learners at their institution. For example, the median age of Penn State World Campus learners is 30, most work at least part-time, and only 38% reside in Pennsylvania. World Campus distance advisers are available Monday through Thursday from 8:00 a.m. to 9:00 p.m. and Friday from 8:00 a.m. to 5:00 p.m. Telephone and e-mail traffic data are used to determine when changes in advising coverage need to be made.

Building the Distance Adviser-Online Distance Learner Partnership

In addition to strong verbal, written, and technology skills, exceptional distance advisers understand that part of their role is facilitating community building. (The relevant standard from NACADA [2010] is "create opportunities for connection and community with the institution, faculty, staff, and other students.") Starks (2012) stresses that technology is simply a tool; distance advisers must use technology to "strive for genuineness, relinquishing pretense for realness, demonstrate positive regard, and express empathy for students' viewpoints, acknowledging students' autonomy while remaining available for guidance and support" (para. 7). This is particularly the case for online adult distance learners who are managing competing priorities, such as families, homes, careers, civic commitments, or elder-care issues, in addition to pursuing an education online while physically separated from their institution's campus. Starks (2011) also suggests that distance advisers look to distance counseling for techniques for building effective relationships with their learners, including the following:

- *Emotional bracketing*: Including emotional content in brackets to help enrich written words. Example: "Wow! Congratulations on getting an A in your math class [so happy for you]. You should be proud of yourself [feeling very proud, myself]."
- *Descriptive immediacy*: Describing observable body language that the learner cannot see. Example: "As I sit in my chair reading your e-mail, I can sense how exhausted you must feel from balancing so many responsibilities. At the same time, I find myself smiling as I read about how you have found that balance and continue to move toward graduation [thinking to myself he knows what he is doing]."
- *Response sequence*: Responding to a learner's concerns in the sequence of (a) presence (being mindful of the technology barrier), (b) emotion (validating the learner's feelings), (c) thoughts (recognizing that they influence our decision-making and problem-solving abilities), and (d) concerns (helping as needed). Example: "Hi, [learner's name—*presence*]. It sounds like this class has been a frustrating experience for you [*emotion*]. [Learner's name], considering what you told me, I can see why you think you might fail [*thought*]. Let's explore this concern a bit more so that I understand your situation more fully [*concern*]. Who knows, [learner's name], together we might just find a solution."

As one-stop shops, distance advisers must have a breadth of knowledge that exceeds curricula. They must adeptly run interference for their learners—they must have a comprehensive understanding of their institution and know where to get questions answered quickly. For example, Penn State World Campus advisers must have ready access to instructions for securing tickets to athletic events in a learner's geographic area and are expected to answer questions about how to place an online order for Penn State Berkey Creamery ice cream with the same level of commitment that they show learners who ask how to register online for their next course. Distance advising is about being an engaged part of a shared community.

Introductions

Distance advisers should be establishing a connection with online distance learners from day one by welcoming the learner to the institution and providing introductory information such as contact information and instructions for getting started. Penn State World Campus advisers each have a biographical web page comprising a photo, contact information, and bits of trivia about themselves to help their online distance learners get to know them as people first and foremost. They also participate in hosting orientation and "Understanding Your Degree Requirements" webinars, serve as the voices behind monthly World Campus podcasts, advise cocurricular student clubs and honor societies, and coordinate student events as additional strategies for engaging World Campus learners. (See the following standard from NACADA [2010]: "provide an orientation to introduce new students to the distance education environment.")

Advising Syllabus

Ultimately, advising involves both teaching and learning. Whether a student is a traditional-age learner on a residential campus, a part-time adult learner attending a commuter campus, or an online distance learner, the academic adviser's role is to guide the student toward ownership of his or her educational goals and the decisions required along the way. An advising syllabus is an invaluable first step in that process and is one of the first tools a distance adviser should review with new online distance learners.

The Penn State World Campus (2011) Advising Syllabus clearly lays out adviser and learner responsibilities:

- For the adviser
  - Providing accurate, timely information
  - Referring to appropriate resources
  - Advocating and supporting
  - Accommodating learner schedules

- Preparing for advising appointments
- Documenting all interactions
- For the learner
  - Developing familiarity with Penn State policies and procedures
  - Contacting adviser each semester prior to the course-registration period
  - Preparing for advising appointments
  - Owning course selections, academic decisions, and completion of graduation requirements

The syllabus also outlines advising learning outcomes by semester:

- End of first semester
  - Learn/complete onboarding process for new students
  - Become familiar with major requirements
  - Understand how transfer credits have been applied
  - Know how to run and interpret degree audits
  - Integrate into World Campus through online communities (as appropriate)
- End of second semester
  - Recognize general education requirements
  - Become familiar with Penn State and World Campus support resources
  - Understand avenues for pursuing prior learning assessment and alternate credit acquisition
- End of third semester
  - Actively integrate/implement specifications of degree requirements and general education principles
  - Articulate needs and identify appropriate support resources
  - Feel empowered to self-advocate
- By final semester
  - Activate intent to graduate
  - Recognize/evaluate value of Penn State alumni resources

The final components of the syllabus include contact information for the learner's assigned academic adviser and a list of commonly used student resources.

Intervening With At-Risk Learners

It can be argued that studying online at a distance sets up a learner to be at risk. An exceptional distance adviser will take a proactive approach to identify a learner on his or her roster who might be at risk for dropping out—for example, is the learner going through a significant life change (marriage, separation, divorce, loss of partner), a health crisis (self, partner, child, family member), a professional transition (new job, job loss, transfer with reloca-tion)? Does the learner have a full-time job and a family, yet wants to register for a heavy credit load next semester? In situations like these, the distance adviser must proactively address the issue and use available and appropriate resources to help the learner. If there is no other choice than for the learner to drop out, the distance adviser should proactively provide instructions for returning to the degree program; if staffing resources permit, the distance adviser should also reach out to the student prior to the next registration window to check in and offer assistance. Similarly, at institutions that have established systems to trigger an alert when a learner is at academic risk, the distance adviser must proactively reach out to the learner via telephone to offer assistance and (perhaps) a voice of reason.

Building Invaluable Campus Partnerships

It can be said that it takes a village to help an online distance learner succeed. As one-stop shops, distance advisers must build close working relationships with support offices on campus to help get questions answered quickly or to provide referrals when needed. While partnerships with registration offices and tutoring resources may be considered a given for distance advisers, what follows is a sampling of equally valuable partnerships that may not be front of mind—but should be.

Crisis Counseling

At times a distance adviser will be confronted with an online distance learner in significant crisis. Administrators of advising offices serving online distance learners must be proactive in developing a plan of action for these frightening and stressful situations—not only for the well-being of the learner, but also for the adviser. It is difficult enough for an adviser to navigate these waters during a face-to-face appointment; the added variable of being physically separated (whether by 5 miles or 5 thousand miles) can exaggerate the situation tenfold.

Some of the distance-counseling strategies outlined earlier may be use-ful in the first moments of the interaction; however, an academic adviser is not a mental health professional. Advisers (and institutions) who cross that delicate line may face significant liabilities. Administrators of advis-ing offices serving online distance learners would be well served to seek professional guidance in putting a plan of action together—for example, by partnering with an on-campus or community counseling center or investigating external vendors that provide level-one crisis counseling via distance counseling. Crisis counseling from a distance is an emerging field and has not yet been fully developed. Working with the appropriate institutional or community offices will (at minimum) help a distance-advising office establish a process for dealing with online distance learners in crisis effectively and with compassion.

Mediation

When disagreements between learners and faculty members arise, distance advisers must be able to point to a designated mediator to help students and instructors work toward possible resolution. A student/faculty affairs specialist at Penn State World Campus is the designated point person for this function. Problems are tracked and shared with academic colleges and the faculty development team for use when orienting faculty to teaching online.

Technical Support

Partnering with technical support specialists is a creative way for distance advisers to intervene with at-risk online distance learners. For example, if a Penn State World Campus learner is working with a technician at the World Campus technical support HelpDesk and the technician thinks that the learner may be high risk (e.g., the learner mentions having failed an exam or is still struggling with basic computer competencies in his or her second year of study), the technician can reach out to the learner's academic adviser to suggest that the adviser intervene.

Building an Assessment Plan

An earlier section of this chapter outlined the importance of establishing performance standards for distance advisers. Once they are in place, what comes next? NACADA (2010) suggests the next step would be to "engage in continuous evaluation of program quality."

With the advent of free web survey tools and technology accelerators, such as customer relationship management systems and automated phone systems that incorporate out-of-the-box survey capabilities, assessing the satisfaction of online distance learners with their distance adviser is no longer as prohibitive as it once was. Penn State World Campus implements a point-of-contact survey, which is sent to online distance learners after every contact with a World Campus distance adviser; learners with multiple advising contacts are surveyed only once monthly to avoid survey fatigue. The survey measures the following (Penn State World Campus, 2012b):

- ease of contacting adviser
- convenience of advising hours
- adviser friendliness
- perception of adviser knowledge level (policies/procedures, transfer credits, course selection/prerequisites, degree requirements)
- primary methods of communicating with adviser
- response time from adviser
- accuracy of referral to different university office for assistance

The survey results for the period of July 1, 2011, through June 30, 2012, during which 2,045 World Campus online distance learners (13.58% response rate) took the survey, are as follows (Penn State World Campus, 2012b):

- ease of contacting adviser: 89.3% very easy or easy (3.7% not applicable)
- convenience of advising hours: 89.3% very convenient or convenient (6.9% N/A)
- adviser friendliness: 91.7% very friendly or friendly (6.8% N/A)
- knowledge of policies/procedures: 65.2% knowledgeable (31.5% N/A)
- knowledge of transfer credits: 50.8% knowledgeable (45.6% N/A)
- knowledge of course selection/prerequisites: 80.4% knowledgeable (15.2% N/A)
- knowledge of degree requirements: 83.0% knowledgeable (13.7% N/A)
- primary methods of communicating with adviser
  - e-mail: 74.9%
  - phone: 41.2%
  - in person: 1.8%
  - live chat: 1.5%
  - other (e.g., Skype): 1.2%
  - Facebook: 1.0%
- response time from adviser
  - e-mail: 58% same or next day; 12.4% within 3 days; 8.3% more than 3 days (6.4% N/A)
  - phone: 33.8% same or next day; 3.3% within 3 days; 3.3% more than 3 days (25.3% N/A)
  - other (e.g., Skype): 0.9% same or next day; 0.0% within 3 days; 0.3% more than 3 days (44.9% N/A)

○ Facebook: 0.7% same or next day; 0.1% within 3 days; 0.4% more than 3 days (45.4% N/A)
• accuracy of referral to different university office for assistance: 31.5% correct (63.4% N/A)

For the 2012–2013 assessment period, the survey was expanded to measure whether learners' perceived value of their relationship with their World Campus distance adviser affected their continued enrollment.

Depending on an institution's infrastructure, additional methods for tracking distance adviser performance could include regularly reporting the number of learner contacts per adviser, shadowing learner appointments, and developing creative methods for capturing and celebrating positive learner feedback shared more informally by students.

You've Built It—Now, Will Anyone Come?

Rendón's (1994) validation model reinforced the critical role that institutions and validating agents play in actively providing encouragement and affirmation to nontraditional students. Research shows that academic advisers are a key institutional validating agent, positively impacting grades, satisfaction, and intent to persist (Morris & Miller, 2007; Pascarella & Terenzini, 2005). During the educational journey for online distance learners, faculty members will change, as will registration clerks and technical support specialists. The single consistent relationship that online distance learners will have with their institution is with their distance adviser—teacher, navigator, advocate, and cheerleader. The recommendations put forth in this chapter reinforce the importance of that relationship and—more important—the importance of getting it right.

References

Chronicle Research Services. (2009). *The college of 2020: Students*. Retrieved from https://chronicle-store.com/ProductDetails.aspx?ID=78921&WG=350

Geiger, R. (2005). Ten generations of higher education. In P. G. Altbach, R. O. Berdahl, & P. J. Gumport (Eds.), *American higher education in the twenty-first century: Social, political, and economic challenges* (pp. 38–70). Baltimore, MD: Johns Hopkins University Press.

Habley, W. R. (Ed.). (2004). *The status of academic advising: Findings from the ACT sixth national survey* (Monograph Series #10). Manhatten, KS: National Academic Advising Association.

Morris, A., & Miller, M. (2007). Advising practices of undergraduate online students in private higher education. *Online Journal of Distance Learning Administration,*

10. Retrieved at http://www.westga.edu/~distance/ojdla/winter104/Morris104.html

National Academic Advising Association (NACADA). (2006). *Concept of academic advising*. Retrieved from http://www.nacada.ksu.edu/Resources/Clearinghouse/View-Articles/Concept-of-Academic-Advising-a598.aspx

National Academic Advising Association (NACADA). (2010). *NACADA standards for advising distance learners*. Retrieved from http://www.nacada.ksu.edu/portals/0/Commissions/C23/Documents/DistanceStandards_000.pdf

Noel-Levitz. (2011). *National online learners priorities report*. Retrieved from https://www.noellevitz.com/upload/Papers_and_Research/2011/PSOL_report%20 2011.pdf

Pascarella, E. T., & Terenzini, P. T. (2005). *How college affects students: A third decade of research* (2nd ed.). San Francisco: Jossey-Bass.

Penn State World Campus. (2011). *World Campus advising syllabus*. Retrieved from http://student.worldcampus.psu.edu/world-campus-advising-syllabus

Penn State World Campus. (2012a). *Academic advising performance standards*. University Park, PA: Penn State Academic Outreach.

Penn State World Campus. (2012b). *FY11–12 point-of-contact survey report*. University Park, PA: Penn State Academic Outreach.

Rendón, L. I. (1994). Validating culturally diverse students. *Innovative Higher Education, 19*, 23–32.

Rovai, A. P. (2003). In search of higher persistence rates in distance education online programs. *Internet and Higher Education, 6*, 1–16.

Schaeffer, C. E., & Konetes, G. D. (2010). Impact of learner engagement on attrition rates and student success in online learning. *International Journal of Instructional Technology and Distance Learning, 7*(5). Retrieved from http://www.itdl.org/Journal/May_10/article01.htm

Starks, S. R. (2011, November 4). What distance advising can learn from distance counseling [web log post]. *DistanceAdvising.com*. Retrieved from http://distanceadvising.com/2011/11/what-distance-advising-can-learn-from-distance-counseling/#.UCwFmKbNnb0

Starks, S. R. (2012, May 29). Distance advising: A personalized approach [web log post]. *DistanceAdvising.com*. Retrieved from http://distanceadvising.com/2012/05/distance-advising-a-personalized-approach/#.UCwF5qbNnb0

Steele, G. (2005). *Distance advising*. Retrieved from the NACADA Clearinghouse of Academic Advising Resources website: http://www.nacada.ksu.edu/Clearinghouse/AdvisingIssues/adv_distance.htm

U.S. Census Bureau. (2008). *Population projections*. Retrieved from http://www.census.gov/population/www/projections/2008projections.html

Varney, J. (2009). *Strategies for success in distance advising*. Retrieved from the NACADA Clearinghouse of Academic Advising Resources website: http://www.nacada.ksu.edu/Resources/Clearinghouse/View-Articles/Distance-advising-strategies.aspx

14

LEARNING ANALYTICS
A Tool for Quality Assurance

Phil Ice, Melissa Layne, and Wallace Boston

The lineage of quantitative research from classical statistics to learning analytics represents several transformations from classical statistics through artificial intelligence, machine learning, and data mining. We will begin our discussion of learning analytics as a tool for quality assurance with the concept of data mining.

Data Mining

Data mining controls the way data are stored and coded to enhance the efficiency of identifying patterns. The patterns identified ultimately contribute to the implementation of learning and discovery. Popularized in contemporary culture through sabermetrics and other sports-related applications of statistics, data mining is often considered as much art as science. Understanding data structures and manipulating them for purposes of analysis requires knowing not only the underlying science but also the discipline to which the data are being applied; as a result, top-end data miners are some of the most sought-after individuals in the marketplace. Thus, while learning analytics may be considered a technology-dependent enterprise, the human capital component is just as important as or more important than the underlying technology.

Learning Analytics

Taking the concepts of learning and discovery to the next level, learning analytics collects the data, analyzes the data, and investigates emerging patterns—revealing patterns yielding pathways to informed decision making.

Not only has this advancement been advantageous to the commercial sector, but it has also quickly moved to the educational sector. All facets of education benefit from the predictive qualities of learning analytics, and the valuable information revealed by this process further provides real-time data from teaching and learning environments. Never before has the need for learning analytics been more apparent than in the ongoing quest for quality assurance in education. The ability to harvest valuable information facilitates quick decision making and yields quick responses and actions. However, if this valuable information is disregarded or goes unused, the next evolution of learning analytics will generally dissipate across the spectrum, with significant advantage falling to those institutions that have the means and discipline to adapt in a decisive and agile manner.

At the time of this writing, it is nearly impossible to pick up a copy of any of the most popular higher education publications without reading an article about *Big Data*. The term's trendiness is further reinforced with ads and e-mails touting conferences that provide further information and applications for the astute manager. Big Data's arrival coincided with the offering and hype of massive open online courses (MOOCs), which can enroll more than 100,000 students. The assumption is that the Big Data generated from MOOCs will enable instructors and their institutions to learn how to improve online learning outcomes. One example of the use of Big Data and learning analytics is the 2012 work by a consortium of institutions organized to quickly aggregate and analyze an extremely large data set. The Predictive Analytics Reporting (PAR) Framework proof of concept was an initiative in which six postsecondary institutions aggregated student and course data to determine factors contributing to retention, progression, and completion (Ice, Diaz, et al., 2012). In this study, 36 variables informing student retention, progression, and completion were identified and federated into a unified database. Subsequent analysis indicated that progression and retention were institutionally specific and related to a variety of hierarchical variables. This study received additional funding to further explore the trends revealed. However, what is truly notable about the initiative is that unlike in the vast majority of academic research, in this study no initial hypotheses were tested. Rather, a variety of data-mining techniques were used to reveal meaningful patterns. Although diametrically opposed to academic convention, this type of approach allows researchers to examine not only apparent relationships but also nonapparent and latent relationships that would otherwise be overlooked.

Administrators (or their trusted designees) need to be comfortable with the activities and processes necessary to conduct analysis as well as with the interpretation and analysis of outcomes. However, even administrators who are comfortable with several data-analysis techniques and tools frequently have to referee debates between research team members when deciding which software to use for Big Data analysis. Although administrators do not have to be experts, they should expect answers to questions that indicate whether the process used to organize the data, the methodology for reviewing the data, and the analysis and interpretation of results are grounded, supportable, and reproducible. Big Data is not for everyone. It has tremendous potential to benefit studies in large institutions or institutions that conduct courses with large enrollments (similar to MOOCs). Coordinating the decisions necessary to implement these studies will require capable administrators who understand the costs, benefits, analysis, and culture necessary to implement changes.

Quality Assurance: A Precursor of Learning Analytics

The lure of defining, describing, developing, and disseminating multiple new quality assurance strategies has driven many administrators and faculty to the point of disillusionment with incremental progress and very little impact. The history of quality assurance models in higher education is characterized by diverse, yet modest efforts that are devoid of experimentation with the unknown and that thus stifled efforts for growth. For example, over the years quality assurance has taken on multiple unique characteristics. Most notable are quality assurance models that represent (a) traditional peer review, (b) a focus on assessment and outcomes of the student experience, (c) a business approach (Boud & Soloman, 2001), and (d) the need for performance indicators (Banta & Borden, 1994). The traditional peer review (Barnett, 1992) was predicated on the notion that all members of the learning enterprise would be nearly equal in their level of engagement and knowledge. Therefore, when the reviewers were found to be unequal, significant problems arose in terms of the degree to which the process could be assumed to fully measure quality. Subsequently, rethinking of the construct led to a more student-centric model, driven by the sum of experiences undertaken; however, this approach also suffered from being dependent on criteria that could be only loosely defined and lacked hard metrics.

Following the student experience movement, quality assurance segued to viewing the student more as a customer, focusing on a market-driven approach with strong behavioristic overtones. This particular model, coined total quality management (TQM), adopted the following goals: (a) to support social, technical, and management systems; (b) to serve the customer through continuous improvement, management with facts, and respect for people; and (c) to place an emphasis on the strategy, process, project, team, and individual and task management (Finch, 1994; Lewis & Smith, 1994). One unfortunate casualty of TQM was the tendency to discard all business-oriented approaches to solving academic problems, thus slowing the growth and adoption of data-driven decision making by the university.

Quality assurance models of the past have been devoid of three important features: (a) a holistic, yet interlacing framework; (b) the use of available institutional, instructor, and student data to inform and implement quality assurance; and (c) malleability to accommodate emerging instructional delivery systems. Previous models have taken into account only one singular type of student learning—face-to-face.

This narrow perspective has limited the accommodation of current and future technologies. The lack of these features has never been more apparent in recent years than in the explosion of distance education. Expansive yet focused approaches coupled with consideration of evolving technologies have redefined and reconstructed administrative, program, course, and student quality assurance and improvement in powerful ways that have changed the face of education as a whole. Institutions that offer distance education have suffered an abrupt awakening and have realized that to survive this continuous state of flux, they must rely on data and analytics to help them make informed decisions and take appropriate preventive action. No longer can administrators present parsed quality assurance models as evidence of quality, nor can they blindly rely on data and analytics. This brazen perspective represents and respects where distance education has been and where it seems to be headed in terms of quality assurance at the time of this writing. Higher education must accept and embrace the knowledge garnered from the past and present in order to fully understand the ever-evolving scope and future of quality assurance.

One technology in particular, the learning management system (LMS), has allowed higher education institutions to capture student data at a granular level. LMSs enable administrators and faculty to predict and curtail potential problems with data aimed to initiate the development of targeted interventions. However, it should be recognized that virtually all LMSs are unable to readily extract granular data. Based on legacy architecture, LMS databases have complicated or incomplete data structures that require high levels of coding to fully extract transactional data at a level that provides deep insight into student learning patterns. However, at the time of this writing, much work was being done in this area, and significant advancements are expected. Progressive administrators need to continually assess not only what is possible but also what future data sources may become available for inclusion in comprehensive quality management constructs.

Various quality assurance models for higher education have been designed with high expectations and hopes that they will eventually gain universal adoption. With the current focus on student retention, progression, and completion, higher education has failed to recognize or respect the multiple shades of success rendered by previous quality assurance efforts. Decision makers in higher education have tended to grasp for narrow, immediate explanations without respecting or acknowledging past efforts and the value of diversity, spontaneity, and unpredictability. Fear of the unknown has been the norm. Perhaps this comfort in routine is derived from the inability to deal with the uncertainty that emerging technologies have abruptly bestowed upon higher education. Despite these plausible explanations, one thing is certain—higher education stands in the middle of a changing world where uncertainty and continuous adjustments are indeed the norm and are vital to student, course, program, and institutional success.

In the remainder of this chapter, we look at the convergence of Big Data, data mining, and learning analytics, emphasizing the elements of quality assurance that these forces seek to uncover. Notably, elements of earlier attempts to define *quality* in the context of critical issues are being incorporated into emerging frameworks, largely thanks to researchers' ability to make connections in ways that were previously not feasible.

Learning Analytics in Action

The degree to which computer processing speeds have increased over the last decade is nearly incomprehensible. In 2002 the fastest computer chips were capable of processing 515 million instructions per second (MIPS). By 2012 the fastest chips on the market were running 198,730 MIPS. Adding to this formidable power are cloud-based implementations that seamlessly link any number of computers together to provide infinite failover for storing, accessing, and analyzing data. Essentially gone are the days when only a select number of institutions, using supercomputers, could engage in ultra-large-scale analysis. Today, institutions of virtually all sizes have the ability to analyze data sets of any size. However, institutions should remain cognizant that they need not reinvent entire processes; rather, they must only reconceptualize processes in light of the immense computing power that is now afforded them.

The power that data has provided over the years has undoubtedly benefited the entire field of education. Further, we have seen the wealth of asynchronous and real-time data that can be collected and analyzed in online learning environments with the help of an array of commercial learning analytics systems and solutions. Many of these systems and solutions harvest valuable data at institutional, instructor, and student levels, thereby addressing quality assurance with the foundational features previously mentioned.

Access to data across institutional departments provides administrators with an overarching perspective that enables insight into how strategic decisions made at the administrative level eventually affect the student. However, we must question whether academia is prepared for the degree of transparency that is coming. In this section, we will examine the current and emerging analytics landscape, contextualizing it against those steps that institutions need to take to fully leverage the data they have at their disposal. As Vander Ark (2012) points out, retail marketers know more about the history of a box of cereal than the overwhelming majority of institutions know about their students. Similarly, Amazon provides us with suggestions related to an array of items that might appeal to us based on demographics and previous browsing and purchasing history. Both of these examples, and numerous others, have been used in countless conference sessions and keynote addresses, with presenters asking why similar functionality cannot be made available to academia. The fact of the matter is that it can; only the will to execute stands as an impediment.

When viewed from an architectural perspective, academia has access to far greater quantities of data related to students than commercial companies have for their customer base. For example, institutions have a wealth of demographic data related to students' gender, ethnicity, age, educational background, financial aid status, and campus-related activities. In addition, as university functions are increasingly carried out online—including, in some cases, the entire educational experience—institutions have unprecedented access to discrete transaction-level data related to how each student interacts with content, other students, the instructor, and institutional resources, such as the library and tutoring services. Data of this richness would be unprecedented in the commercial sector and, if it were available, would immediately be seized upon for the overwhelming market advantage it would give one entity over its rivals.

However, even universities with the most advanced analytical capabilities have yet to harness more than a fraction of the potential that resides within their data stores. When the term *institutional data* is used, it is not uncommon to think of the student information system or the more general enterprise resource planning tools. Although these systems contain significant amounts of information related to student demographics, course registration, and grades, it is important to remember that they are only one source of information that resides within the university. Typically, institutions also have databases that house information related to the library, financial aid, student services, student life, advising, LMSs, and numerous other fields. In fact, it is not uncommon to find more than a dozen separate databases across an institution.

Further complicating matters, it is not uncommon to find that each of these databases is owned by a different vertical within the organization. Thus, it is also not uncommon to find that the owners of each of these systems rarely, if ever, talk with each other and that the databases are not connected. Here it is important to introduce the concept of a data warehouse. Typically, these are structures that serve as a central repository for all data across the institution. However, their utility goes much further than acting as a simple storage space; data warehouses are also used to correlate disparate information through common identifiers, such as student identification numbers or login credentials. Through this process, stakeholders at all levels are provided with the ability to access information in a fashion that allows for holistic understanding of students as a function of the sum of their demographic attributes and activities that they engage in. The degree to which visibility can be achieved is dependent upon the tools and methodologies that are used to analyze the data.

Key Points and Objectives for Initial Exploration of Data Collection Activities

Although techniques such as Bayesian modeling and neural network analysis are common in the commercial sector, it is important to remember that these entities have had decades to hone their data collection and analysis operations. In contrast, most universities are just starting to develop serious analytical capabilities. Thus, administrators should be cognizant of which types of data hold the most promise and where initial collection efforts should focus. The following are key points and objectives that should be considered when engaging in initial exploration of data collection activities at the institutional and instructor/student levels.

The implementation of learning analytics at the institutional level covers many—if not all—core administrative areas serving employees, instructors, and students. Following are some learning analytic functionalities and key tools beneficial to these core areas.

Recruitment, Admissions, and Enrollment

Learning analytic functionalities beneficial for recruitment, admissions, and enrollment include the following:

- targeting the prospective students who are most likely to enroll
- qualifying student leads before making list purchases
- searching for prospective learners based on any data point

- leveraging real-time (or near real-time) student data to target students who fulfill the institution's admission requirements
- tracking recruitment yield by discovering talent, executing marketing campaigns, tracking results, and making data-driven recommendations
- increasing enrollment yield by allowing accepted students to interact with the postsecondary institutions they are interested in before choosing to enroll
- increasing enrollment yield and retention rates using engagement campaigns to identify at-risk students and prevent dropouts or transfers

Financial Aid

The key analytic tool for financial aid offices is the ability to increase the impact of the institution's aid awards on recruitment while improving access to higher education and generating more net revenue.

Institutional Research and Assessment

Learning analytic functionalities beneficial for institutional research and assessment include the following:

- gathering necessary data to satisfy accreditation and accountability requirements
- providing valuable data to members of student affairs, academic affairs, student housing, and athletic programs

Marketing

Learning analytic functionalities beneficial for marketing include the following:

- learning critical data about the higher education market, prospects, and students, with an emphasis on programs offered by competitors
- studying a wide range of key campus issues with flexible, customized survey instruments
- assessing current academic offerings to see which programs best meet the needs of current and prospective students
- uncovering the most effective strategies for e-recruitment, including developing the university website, creating engaging recruitment e-mails, and making connections with prospective students through social networking

At the instructor and student levels, learning analytics provides data through course dashboards or other reports. These data help the instructor monitor student activity within the course, examine and determine student learning levels, and implement the appropriate content or intervention to support student retention. For students, these dashboards allow students to monitor and personalize their own learning paths.

Student Retention

Learning analytic functionalities beneficial for student retention include the following:

- assessing the likelihood of students' persisting in their program of study
- assessing the likelihood of students' persisting in a given course
- increasing completion rates through earlier focused interventions
- implementing custom assessments for first-year, mid-year, and second-year students
- prioritizing student retention initiatives and interventions
- improving retention rates by increasing student engagement through interactive content, surveys, and assessments
- assessing the likelihood of students' being successful in their given area of study postgraduation

Student Learning and Monitoring

Learning analytic functionalities beneficial for student learning and monitoring include the following:

- delivering higher survey response rates compared to paper-based processes
- improving the student experience through anonymity, through ease of access, and by meeting students where they are—online
- engaging students by giving them information to allow them to self-monitor their performance in courses and to compare their performance with that of their peers via student dashboards
- viewing how many students visited the course
- examining the number of slides students visited and how much time they spent on the course and on specific slides
- learning how students performed on assessments and how they answered each question

- viewing when and how often a student left the course and then returned to refer to something in the course
- seeing which scenario branch a student took
- viewing the slides visited most and least by students
- examining student usage patterns in a period of days/weeks/months
- determining the number of students using the interactive features (buttons) in the course
- monitoring specific trends in the usage of your courses and using that knowledge to develop and deliver better content
- providing instructors with critical data to deliver just-in-time interventions to students

Establishing and Refining Institutional Intelligence Systems

While the previous lists are but a sampling of the functionalities that can be explored, we believe that they serve as a starting point for the establishment and refinement of institutional intelligence systems, systems that are analogous to those used in the commercial sector to provide critical, just-in-time business intelligence. However, at their core these and other types of analytics are dependent upon the effective use of information that is extracted from the institutional data warehouse.

As a starting point, once institutions have centralized access to their data, fundamental analyses around topics such as student retention may prove highly efficacious, in terms of both process orientation and attainment of increased stakeholder buy-in for future initiatives. In one such study, Boston, Ice, and Burgess (2012) explored longitudinal patterns in student retention at the American Public University System (APUS) using multivariate regression analysis. Although the scope of the study was large ($N > 100,000$), the methodology was straightforward, providing a classic example of how advanced technologies (e.g., a comprehensive data warehouse) can be paired with more traditional techniques. This foundation was then used to develop a neural network model within APUS that used 187 predictor variables to assess the likelihood that students would disenroll from courses or the university within the next five days (Boston, Powell, Stephens, & Ice, 2012). A derivative of this implementation will be using the same data points, along with others, to help estimate the most effective paths of progression toward degree attainment at APUS.

With respect to these two projects, it is important to note the role of the advancing computing power available. These studies required the use of IBM/SPSS Modular, the top-end product in the SPSS family, deployed on a stand-alone server. Obviously, a significant expense is involved in making use of this type of technology; however, examination of the cost of a student disenrolling illustrated the return on investment associated with the purchase and use of such technologies. Although most in academia are hesitant to look at a situation in these terms, these studies provided a classic example of the return on investment associated with the acquisition and use of technology. Beyond 2013, other nascent technologies will challenge academia in terms of adoption, but these technologies similarly promise to inexorably alter the learning analytics landscape. The first of these is the application of latent semantic analysis, a process that deprecates whole-language constructs and converts them into numerical values for purposes of analysis. Through this process, large volumes of text or metadata can be converted into quantifiable variables that can be analyzed.

An Example of the Possibilities

From the organizational perspective, the overwhelming amount of information associated with online learning that resides in silo structures presents a challenge in terms of the efficacy of instructional design workflows and the codification of tacit knowledge for accreditation by external agencies. In the LMS environment, content management frequently translates into a single-purpose allocation of content resources, with cataloging and meta-tagging being a haphazard affair. This can lead to potential duplication of content and significant time loss associated with asset retrieval for incorporation into new curricula as well as less effective, poorly constructed, and misaligned learning objectives. Because content is created with the notion that all contributors have knowledge of the underlying taxonomies or common vernacular that information is based upon, it is difficult for organizations to survey their content universe for existing objects that can be incorporated into emerging workflows.

By automating the meta-tagging and gap analysis process, semantic analysis allows not only the smart surveying of existing learning objects in a specific curriculum area but also the possibility of examining more learning objects across unrealized curricula. The ability to determine content interrelationships through the mapping of assets across the content universe enables effective and efficient facilitation of object reusability toward curricular goal and objective fulfillment. This process creates opportunities to locate learning objects to fulfill course-level objectives for alignment across course-level objectives, programmatic outcomes, and industry standards. Improvement of instructional outcomes, through the ingestion of work products from implementation of content distillation and semantic analysis, increases the return on investment and time on task. The opportunity to provide detailed analysis reporting that demonstrates curricular alignment to accrediting bodies and others is effectuated.

In 2010 the Institutional Research and Instructional Design groups at APUS worked with the School of Business to align all content for accreditation from the Accreditation Council for Business Schools and Programs (ACBSP) using the Common Library semantic analysis engine. This process resulted in the categorization of thousands of learning objects into goal and objective structures in a fraction of the time it would have taken to sort the objects manually. Concurrently, the university realized a cost savings of more than 75% (Ice, Burgess, Beals, & Staley, 2012). All content at APUS will be semantically analyzed in the future, providing unprecedented clarity into the learning resources and objects that reside within the institution. Further, this technology has the potential to allow for correlation of student work products to specific goals and objectives, providing an enhanced means of assuring quality vis-à-vis the correlation of learning objectives to content and activities.

Administrators need to be attuned to the use of web analytics in learning. Web analytics tools, such as Google Analytics, Core Metrics, and Omniture, allow for the embedding of discrete pieces of Java code on a web page. This code captures user interactions down to the cursor-movement level, as well as larger interactions such as page paths, click-throughs, and abandonment. This data is then correlated with what is known about the user to optimize the experience at a one-to-one level, including the provisioning of unique content. Although at the time of this writing such systems were being used only in the commercial sector, several initiatives to adapt them to online learning—and thus make good on the promise of an "Amazon-like" experience for students—are under way. However, it is anticipated that such systems will be quite expensive (i.e., greater than $250,000 per institution), affordable only for the wealthiest higher education institutions.

Conclusion

Looking to the horizon in education, it is easy for one to see a convergence of data warehouses, advanced analytics engines, latent semantic analysis, and web analytics. As previously emphasized, these systems have already been integrated into the commercial sector, making educational adoption more a matter of will than a technical challenge. However, understanding the impact that this new world of learning analytics will have on higher education will take time. We do know that this convergence will forever alter the face of higher education and challenge administrators to adapt at a rapid pace or find themselves obsolete.

References

Banta, T. W., & Borden, V. M. H. (1994). Performance indicators for accountability and improvement. *New Directions for Institutional Research, 1994*(82), 95–106. doi:10.1002/ir.37019948209

Barnett, R. (1992). *Improving higher education: Total quality care.* Buckingham, UK: SRHE and Open University Press.

Boston, W., Ice, P., & Burgess, M. (2012). Assessing student retention in online learning environments: A longitudinal study. *Online Journal of Distance Learning Administration, 15*(2). Retrieved from http://www.westga.edu/~distance/ojdla/summer152/boston_ice_burgess152.html

Boston, W., Powell, K., Stephens, J., & Ice, P. (2012, March). *Data driven decision making to ensure online academic quality.* Paper presented at 2012 NCA HLC Annual Conference, Chicago, IL.

Boud, D. J., & Solomon, N. V. (2001). Repositioning universities and work. In D. Boud & N. Solomon (Eds.), *Work-based learning: A newer higher education?* (pp. 18–33). Buckingham, UK: SRHE and Open University Press.

Finch, J. (1994). Quality and its measurement: A business perspective. In D. Green (Ed.), *What is quality in higher education?* (pp. 63–80). Bristol, PA: Taylor & Francis.

Ice, P., Burgess, M., Beals, J., & Staley, J. (2012). Aligning curriculum and evidencing learning effectiveness using semantic mapping of learning assets. *International Journal of Emerging Technologies in Learning, 7*(2), 26–31.

Ice, P., Diaz, S., Swan, K., Burgess, M., Sharkey, M., Sherrill, J., . . . Okimoto, H. (2012). The PAR framework proof of concept: Initial findings from a multi-institutional analysis of federated postsecondary data. *Journal of Asynchronous Learning Networks, 16*(3). Retrieved from http://sloanconsortium.org/sites/default/files/jaln_v16n3_6_The_PAR_Framework_POC_Initial_Findings_from_a_Multi-Institutional_Analysis_of_Federated_Postsecondary_Data.pdf

Lewis, R., & Smith, D. H. (1994). *Total quality in higher education.* Delray Beach, FL: St. Lucie Press.

Vander Ark, T. (2012). Tomorrow's college tackles higher ed's greatest challenges: Grit, funding and tech [web log post]. *Getting Smart.* Retrieved from http://gettingsmart.com/2012/10/tomorrows-college-tackles-higher-eds-greatest-challenges-grit-funding-tech/

15

USING PRINCIPLES OF KNOWLEDGE MANAGEMENT FOR EDUCATIONAL QUALITY ASSURANCE

Sebastián Díaz, Wallace Boston, Melissa Layne, and Phil Ice

There is nothing new under the sun, and this applies in part to the emerging field of knowledge management (KM). Although many strategies for manifesting KM in higher education are relatively new, the principles of KM have been around for as long as people have acknowledged the value of the human mind. In his memoir, titled *Antes del Fin*, the Argentine writer and painter Ernesto Sabato (1998) shared his touching and heartfelt appreciation for the impact and value of human knowledge. He cited a conversation in which his friend Léopold Sédar Senghor, the poet and president of Senegal, reflected on the value of wisdom handed down by aging elders in Dakar, many of whom were illiterate, to the young children in their communities: "La muerte de uno de esos ancianos es lo que para ustedes sería el incendio de una biblioteca de pensadores y poetas [The death of one of these elders represents what for you would be like an accidental fire that destroys a great library containing the works of thinkers and poets]" (as cited in Sabato, 1998).

Although he probably did not use banal terms like *KM* in his poetry, Senghor's emphasis on the importance of elders' wisdom is consistent with, and serves as the basis for, the contemporary KM movement. Furthermore, Senghor's use of the library as a metaphor for the vessel of valuable knowledge and perspectives offered by wise elders provides those of us here in the present with an equally valuable insight into how knowledge manifests in the modern academy. Whereas Senghor was concerned with the total loss of wisdom upon the burning of the library (i.e., the death of wise elders), in this chapter we are less concerned with accidental fires and more concerned with unintentional mothballing.

Is it not just as great a catastrophe to create expansive libraries and then accidentally lock off from access entire rooms containing hundreds of thousands of tomes of valuable knowledge? In other words, does not the underuse (or outright nonuse) of valuable resources within the academy equal their total loss? This chapter challenges the reader to identify repositories of actionable knowledge that may have been unintentionally mothballed and to use this knowledge to guide continuous quality improvement.

Before the emergence of what Peter Drucker (1994) referred to as the Knowledge Society, institutions of higher education served as exemplars of organizations that exchanged knowledge as their primary commodity. Since the mid-1990s, the digital revolution has introduced a variety of new industries and organizations that are assuming a leadership role in creating knowledge. Regardless, academia continues to play a pivotal role in defining how knowledge is produced, analyzed, and disseminated. In fact, approaches to online learning will greatly influence how the day-to-day existence of the emerging knowledge worker is defined.

This chapter begins with a brief description of KM. A subsequent section describes how KM is currently manifested in the typical university. In this section the future of KM and its relationship to quality assurance and academia are discussed. In the final section of this chapter, we review how intellectual capital serves as an effective framework for envisioning future approaches to KM and informs the more efficient use of existing data, improving the quality of teaching and learning in the academic enterprise.

Knowledge Management

A critical question for an administrator to answer is, Does the presence and analysis of institutional data provide an opportunity for the institution or not? To answer that question, the administrator or a trusted colleague must understand the complexities of Big Data and be willing to embrace data-driven decision making (see chapter 14, "Learning Analytics: A Tool for Quality Assurance"). Assuming that this condition is met, the institution must then find a researcher (faculty, staff, or consultant) who is capable of organizing the data, finding patterns in the data, analyzing the patterns, and recommending the implementation of actionable steps based on the insights obtained from the data. It is important not to underestimate how much time and how many resources (human and financial) it may take to complete these steps. Many institutions keep data in multiple, separate databases, and consolidating data in a relevant data set may be costly and take significant time if the existing information technology department is busy or understaffed. If real-time (assuming daily) data analysis is required, the costs can escalate significantly. Last, educating the faculty and staff on the merits of data collection and analysis and the subsequent action can be disruptive if the culture of the institution is not receptive to change.

Wheatley (2006) posited that one of an organization's more important competencies is to create conditions that allow for both the generation of new knowledge and the free sharing of that knowledge. Although sophisticated bodies of knowledge created within the academy can be targeted, the mechanisms for producing and sharing that knowledge within and outside the institution are not as sophisticated. Drucker (1994) advocated for defining the quality of knowledge and the productivity of knowledge, especially given their role in the performance capacity and survival of organizations in the Knowledge Society.

The emerging field of KM provides mechanisms with which the academy can begin to define knowledge quality, especially as it relates to the productivity of an organization. Frappaolo (2006) offers a more philosophical definition of KM, describing it as leveraging collective wisdom to increase responsiveness and innovation. Dalkir (2005) offers a more operational definition, describing KM as "the deliberate and systematic coordination of an organization's people, technology, processes, and organizational structure in order to add value through reuse and innovation" (p. 3).

KM is a term at times used synonymously with *intellectual capital* or *data-driven decision making*. However, it is a much broader construct, involving a variety of activities such as (a) creating new knowledge; (b) acquiring knowledge from outside sources; (c) using knowledge in decision making; (d) embedding knowledge in processes, products, or services; (e) coding information into documents, databases, and software; (f) facilitating knowledge growth; (g) transferring knowledge to other parts of the organization; and (h) measuring the value of knowledge assets or the impact of KM (Gupta, Sharma, & Hsu, 2004). Yet these technical definitions of *KM* need to be balanced with real-world examples in the academy. Most readers will be familiar with these examples without realizing that they are examples of KM.

Knowledge Conversion

A complete discussion of all the principles of KM is well beyond the scope of this chapter. For that reason, the focus here is on one particular principle of KM that is germane to its relationship with continuous quality improvement in the academy. Nonaka and Takeuchi's (1995) work on knowledge conversion highlights the importance of distinguishing tacit and explicit forms of knowledge in an organization. Tacit forms of knowledge are those that are not necessarily codified explicitly, yet they exist regardless in the minds of individuals and the collective know-how, traditions, and cultures of groups. One example of tacit knowledge is the expectation in organizations of appropriate dress and good hygiene. Although it may not be expressly codified (i.e., written down) that it is inappropriate to show up at the office wearing pajamas, most members of the organization are aware of this unspoken rule. Another example of tacit knowledge is the traditions carried on through multiple generations of workers that are not necessarily written down or recorded in any fashion.

Nonaka and Takeuchi's (1995) valuable work focused on the processes used to convert knowledge from one form into another. Explicit–explicit knowledge conversion takes place when the bylaws of an organization are updated by converting one written format to another. Tacit–tacit knowledge conversion occurs when workers individually contemplate how they will embody some unwritten tradition or ethic of the university where they work. Explicit–tacit knowledge conversion occurs when faculty members consider the explicit guidelines for tenure and promotion and then internally process how they will pursue these professional milestones. And finally, tacit–explicit knowledge conversion occurs when knowledge not formerly codified is recorded tangibly in some way. For example, the U.S. National Park Service conducts extensive, videotaped exit interviews of its retiring senior staff members in order to codify the valuable stories and perspectives (i.e., knowledge) these individuals have gained throughout their careers.

This last form of knowledge conversion (tacit–explicit) is particularly germane to online learning. As will be discussed later in this chapter, learning management systems (LMSs) continue to revolutionize the evaluation of quality in teaching and learning because they automatically codify so many aspects of the classroom experience formerly left unrecorded. Even though LMSs have already revolutionized how the quality of teaching and learning is evaluated, their nature as a manifestation of KM systems offers tremendous opportunities for expanding and improving the continuous quality improvement processes in the academy.

Examples of Existing Knowledge Management Systems

It is useful to balance an explanation of KM theory with examples of how these systems manifest in the real world. Many readers are already familiar with websites, such as Amazon.com, that use sophisticated systems of electronic data management to provide better service to online shoppers. Amazon is an excellent example of how KM systems can help improve the online shopping experience. Yet another example of a familiar KM system is Netflix. The streamlined, data-driven, one-to-one modeling process that

Netflix uses to provide customers with entertainment—whether it is DVDs by mail or online streaming—demonstrates how similar systems applied to online learning could help improve the quality of academic programs.

Yet to show more directly how KM systems can improve quality assurance in academia, let us examine two popular existing manifestations of KM systems in the university: library information management systems and LMSs.

Library Information Management Systems

Some readers may be too young to remember the old card catalog systems used in libraries to help patrons find books among the endless stacks. A comparison of these card catalog systems with the newer digital library information management systems helps to illuminate how KM systems affect the manner in which data, information, and knowledge are collected, analyzed, and disseminated. Just a few decades ago, to find a book, a library patron would have to access a seemingly endless number of wooden drawers containing thousands of index cards. Each of these cards would contain information for a specific book or holding of the library.

Now the average university library uses relatively complex relational databases to create filing systems for books. Although the differences between the electronic system and the paper-based card catalog system are familiar, the implications of these differences may not yet be understood. Of particular interest here are the implications that digitized repositories have for how quality is recognized.

As an example of one difference with profound implications consider that since patrons access the database electronically as opposed to manually thumbing through index cards, they no longer need to physically visit the library to conduct searches. Importantly, this difference affects not only how library searches are conducted but also how teaching and learning are facilitated. By removing the need for geographic proximity between the customer (whether patron or student) and the institution (whether library or university), it becomes possible to conceptualize quality in a totally different way. Although beyond the scope of this particular chapter, it is important to recognize that bypassing the need for physical proximity between the customer and the institution has called into question the immense economies of scale in the world of higher education.

Another difference with subtle implications is that whereas before users accessed card catalogs more or less anonymously, now an individual needs to log in to the library system to access the digitized repository. At many universities, students and faculty members are required to log in with their unique usernames and passwords. This login requirement allows the institution to link any data it has for the individual to his or her use of the system.

This particular use requirement profoundly affects how the quality of the services that are provided is eventually measured, regardless of whether those services are lending books or providing instruction. And as is the case with so many innovations related to information exchange in the digital age, one small change in process challenges a long history of how work was previously conducted. Consider for a moment how online learning has resulted in often contentious debates about what constitutes quality in postsecondary education. In the end, this seemingly innocuous innovation related to physical proximity of teacher and student could call into question society's return on investment for traditional, face-to-face postsecondary education. A similar simple innovative change may call into question the return on investment for conventional online learning in the future.

Whereas the paper-based card catalog system was indifferent to who flipped the cards, new electronic systems are hyperaware of the unique identity of the user and, in aggregate, understand usage via demographic segmentation. The simple requirement for identification allows systems analysts to now monitor library usage patterns among individuals and the demographic and behavioral subgroups they form.

Another aspect of the digitized database with significant implications is that patrons are able to receive information immediately regarding the availability of books and other materials. This is analogous to finding a little sticker on an index card in the paper-based system; the sticker meant that particular item had already been checked out. However, what fundamentally distinguishes the electronic card catalog system from the paper-based system is the former's ability to take electronic data and information and produce new actionable knowledge for the user. For example, while books on a certain topic are being examined electronically, the system will show the reader titles on similar topics that have been checked out by other patrons. In some exploratory work, similar techniques are being used to show previous users' aggregate rankings of content usefulness and quality, opening the door to crowdsourced curation. This provision of new actionable knowledge is what distinguishes a KM system from what is otherwise merely a digitized electronic repository. KM systems, by definition, not only serve as repositories of data, but also churn that data to create new knowledge.

The previous examples show how the KM system provides actionable knowledge to the user. If this concept is expanded to online learning, we discover seemingly infinite numbers of possible feedback loops to provide our students. Earlier in this chapter, unfortunate mothballing of valuable knowledge was mentioned. If academia deems the use of library resources valuable, does it not behoove us to explore the data related to library usage patterns in order to evaluate our students, our faculty, and their respective academic programs?

In higher education, many are metaphorically sitting on gold mines of evaluative data that are not being used. The secret to organizational inspiration is to build information networks that allow hunches to persist, disperse, and recombine (Johnson, 2010, p. 127). Admittedly, it is no small feat to create the organizational systems needed to access, analyze, and disseminate valuable data. Regardless, over time the academy will increasingly be expected to use KM systems, especially with respect to evaluating quality. We thus must consider both how KM systems will revolutionize approaches to teaching and learning over the long term and how they will change our approaches to quality assurance. One innovation in particular has revolutionized how the quality of academic curricula is evaluated, and that is the LMS currently used in both online and face-to-face learning.

Learning Management Systems

LMSs were originally developed solely for the purpose of facilitating learning online. They were designed primarily to allow faculty and students to replicate, in an online forum, the teaching and learning activities that were normally facilitated in a face-to-face classroom environment. Therefore, what was originally developed as an adaptive technology unintentionally revolutionized how teaching and learning are evaluated for students, faculty members, and broader educational programs. However, the breadth and scope of how KM systems such as the LMS will change approaches to evaluating the quality of teaching and learning in the academy is gaining appreciation.

Earlier we alluded to the notion of knowledge conversion, specifically those instances in which tacit knowledge is converted into explicit knowledge. The LMS has played a key role in demystifying the teaching and learning process through a variety of seemingly simplistic computational tasks that have profound, often unintended implications. The first of those tasks is the continuous cataloging of the user's identity. Any data that is cataloged or warehoused to the LMS can be recorded by students as the unit of record. For obvious reasons, the ability to differentiate usage data by individual student creates a myriad of opportunities and possibilities for data analyses that ultimately inform the quality of the learning experience.

Another mechanism or task inherent in the LMS is codification of many different behaviors exhibited by the individual student. The LMS records data regarding how frequently and when the student accesses the website. Admittedly, there are challenges inherent in how these data are interpreted depending on how actively engaged students remain while the LMS screen is active on their computers. Regardless, the automated recording of usage data becomes invaluable to pedagogical experts who want to evaluate how particular approaches to online teaching and learning affect quality.

Much like an e-mail system, the LMS also records in a tangible format all electronic communications between the student and teacher as well as among students. This seemingly nonutilitarian task has a profound implication for how quality is measured in the classroom. Peer feedback is an important component of adult learning. In a traditional face-to-face classroom, the teacher can ask students to provide one another feedback on a particular assignment they completed through, for example, group discussion. Yet even if the teacher takes the time to walk through the classroom and listen to the feedback being provided, there is no tangible or explicit codification of what was said. By contrast, LMSs used in instruction facilitated online tangibly record the explicit narrative feedback students provide one another on their assignments. In fact, if the LMS allows students to provide one another audio feedback, digitized spoken feedback can be recorded permanently within the LMS as well.

Some may argue that in some instances the personalized face-to-face feedback students receive in a traditional classroom is of much higher quality than that received through an online LMS. There exist a myriad of possible arguments on both sides of this issue. For those concerned with quality, however, what is important here is that the LMS actually creates a tangible, electronic record of these interactions, thus allowing researchers to more easily analyze the data on a large scale.

At many universities professors are even using LMSs for conventional face-to-face classrooms. One of the big incentives for instructors using these LMSs is the systems' ability to more conveniently and accurately document student interactions, student participation, and student performance as manifested in the posting of completed assignments online. What started as an adaptive technology has now come to redefine not just online learning but also conventional face-to-face learning.

LMSs are revolutionizing not only teaching and learning but also how research on pedagogy is conducted. Regardless of whether the approach is quantitative or qualitative, researchers investigating pedagogical phenomena and conventional face-to-face classrooms struggle primarily with access to data. Historically, therefore, pedagogical research most often focused on relatively small sample sizes that ultimately had to be generalized to a much larger population. By contrast, LMSs within any given university are rapidly creating phenomenally large repositories of data that better allow us to conduct pedagogical research, which can then inform high-stakes decisions (Boston et al., 2009). Ultimately, this new approach to research will revolutionize not only how the quality of teaching and learning is informed but also our expectations of sample size, primarily in quantitative statistical research.

When the possibilities for how the LMS repository's data can be used are considered, it is easy to envision a future in which the LMS becomes an adaptive system that tailors the style of instruction to the needs of the individual student. Although the potential benefits of this model to quality of instruction are quite apparent, another foundational shift is much more subtle. As LMSs that are adaptive to the needs of individual students continually develop, the responsibility for differentiation of instruction will shift from the instructor to other experts who traditionally were not considered faculty members.

Increasingly in online formats, the quality of instruction depends not only on the instructor's ability to differentiate the needs of individual students but also on the instructional designers who create the online content. The computer experts who author the complex systems used as part of adaptive LMSs also play increasingly important roles in the quality of instruction. Throughout this chapter, we have alluded to the changing economies of scale that are created by KM in online learning. Eventually, we may find that the change we are least prepared for is a comprehensive redefinition of what constitutes the teaching role. In the future some of the most important stakeholders in the teaching process may be invisible to the student. This very well may be the beginning of the end for the traditional faculty member.

However, most LMSs have been built in an incremental fashion, and the systems' back ends are thus not fully optimized for data collection. As such, efforts by existing LMS providers and new entrants in the market are focusing on entire system rebuilds to optimize data collection and analysis. Interestingly, this increased competition may spur not only the development of new LMS platforms but also a shift away from the LMS itself, to systems capable of providing higher levels of personalized learning.

Changes We Anticipate

Invariably, the increased use of KM systems such as the LMS will present educators with changes that are, at the very least, challenging. The following are a few changes in how continuous quality improvement is measured within the academy that we anticipate:

- The concept of quality will increase in dimension and scope. For not-for-profit institutions in particular, return-on-investment principles based on cost analysis will revolutionize practice. And regardless of an institution's profit-related status, new sources of data that were never anticipated will be used to inform the quality of programs. Coincidentally, some of these sources of data will be found outside of our institutions and beyond our direct control.

- Federated data systems will allow for increased evaluation of quality both intra- and interinstitutionally. Seemingly disparate departments within large universities will suddenly find themselves being compared with one another. Furthermore, seemingly disparate institutions will find themselves being compared with one another through public venues or electronic commons. Stakeholders who advocate for quality assurance processes within their institutions should brace themselves in anticipation of a collective discomfort among their colleagues as increasing transparency becomes possible through the use of KM systems.

- The digitization of data and information throughout electronic commons will allow for more direct observations from stakeholders outside our institutions. Obviously, this may result in our having less internal control over the data that informs the quality of our institutions. While an internal evaluator can certainly survey members of the university community for their perceptions on the organizational culture, an outsider can just as easily scrape the Internet for narrative descriptions of working conditions at that same institution. Increasingly, there may be a need to balance internal perspectives of quality with less tightly controlled perspectives that originate outside the institution.

- Institutional researchers and other quality assurance experts will increasingly rely on multimedia forms of evidence to help evaluate the quality of students, teachers, and academic programs. Computational advances will allow us to use, in addition to numeric measures, large repositories of narrative data, as well as complex visual and other qualitative data.

- Institutional researchers and other quality assurance experts will increasingly need to rely upon (and therefore collaborate effectively with) colleagues with diverse sets of expertise related to computation. There will thus be a need to redefine the roles of quality assurance experts and the training programs that prepare them for these careers. Although admittedly the term *team player* is often overused when describing desirable traits in personnel, this shift in role and training may require that quality assurance experts better balance their analytical skills with the ability to play nicely with others.

- The increased use of larger federated repositories of data will continue to stimulate innovations in quantitative data analyses, especially those made possible by the availability of previously unimaginable sample sizes. These Big Data approaches will advance the field of predictive analytics in a remarkable way.

- KM systems will create opportunities for expanded use of qualitative data in quality assurance analysis. Some of the most important influences on probabilistic ideas have involved qualitative perspectives (Gigerenzer et al., 1989). Semantic analyses of codified narratives within KM systems will particularly affect how students, faculty members, and academic programs are evaluated. Furthermore, quality assurance will rely more on analyses of retrospective data sets generated automatically via information architecture.
- Human interaction facilitated computationally in the online learning world will increasingly serve as a model for electronic interaction by knowledge workers (Díaz, 2012). Therefore, approaches to evaluating the quality of online learning will serve as models for evaluating workers who ply their trades in a similar environment that relies heavily on electronic interaction.
- A rather large and unfounded assumption of KM is that knowledge is eventually made accessible to all knowledge workers in the organization (Dalkir, 2005). Further work on how knowledge, as a valuable and sought-after resource, will be distributed to workers based on their roles, ranks, and particular requirements is necessary, as is exploration of how competition for this knowledge, within and between organizations, will influence organizational politics.
- The work of quality assurance experts will itself be judged primarily on the basis of to what extent the data and information collected, analyzed, and disseminated is actionable and helps stakeholders to improve the quality of their own work.
- A significant shift in paradigm is being experienced with respect to the availability of primary resources, that is, data. Whereas one of the main challenges in the past for quality assurance experts was finding or acquiring sufficient data, the challenge in the future will be quite the opposite. KM systems will produce unbelievable amounts of data. The challenge, therefore, will be to sift through those data and make tough choices about what is most meaningful. Decision making in the analytics-related disciplines will demand more sophisticated objective and subjective methods for determining the quality of data, information, and knowledge.

Intellectual Capital: Proactively Preparing for the Future of Knowledge Management

KM provides the broader philosophical orientation as well as tangible procedures for capturing and capitalizing on the valuable knowledge that is regularly generated in the postsecondary education enterprise. The preceding examples help to show how innovations in online learning are creating, by their very design, KM systems that ultimately will affect how the quality of our students, teachers, administrators, and larger educational programs will be evaluated.

Ideally, however, online educators will not relegate themselves reactively to accidental or unintentional KM systems. Innovations in computational information systems will, by their very design, create KM systems, but academicians need to proactively design such systems to improve the scope and efficacy of our attempts at informing continuous quality improvement. A helpful framework for developing such systems is Thomas Stewart's (1997) concept of *intellectual capital*, which can help us expand our understanding of what constitutes valuable knowledge and how that knowledge can be used to inform quality.

Stewart (1997) defines *intellectual capital* as "the sum of everything everybody in a company knows that gives it a competitive edge" (p. ix). He further describes intellectual capital as comprising human, structural, and customer capital. Human capital is "the capabilities of the individuals required to provide solutions to customers" (p. 76). The second component, structural capital, refers to the structures and processes inherent in the organization that ultimately add value to the enterprise. Stewart refers to it as "capital that doesn't go home at night" (p. 108). Stewart's third component, customer capital, "is the value of an organization's relationships with the people with whom it does business" (p. 77). We will discuss each of these three components of intellectual capital as they relate to how we can more broadly conceptualize KM systems so that they add value to our postsecondary enterprises.

Human Capital

As the design, facilitation, and evaluation of online and blended learning are evaluated, there may be a need to revise traditional job descriptions for faculty and administrators for this new context; the two roles may even begin to merge in some respects. Quality online and blended learning requires a significant amount of input from not just the individual serving as instructor of record but also from instructional designers, software authors, and even computational engineers. The point here is not that everyone will be a teacher. Instead, faculty members will likely have to rely increasingly upon colleagues outside the classroom to effectively facilitate course work.

Redefining roles in the academic environment creates multiple challenges. The first challenge is that the faculty role will need to be reexamined. New approaches for incentivizing these positions and new standards for promotion and tenure may be necessary. This is no small change, especially considering how faculty-centric many institutions are currently. We do not mean to disparage the traditional professor or schoolteacher. When considering advances in either the K–12 or postsecondary environment, the greatest hurdle is often implementing innovation within the constraints of the traditional faculty role. Many of our colleagues in medical schools experienced these constraints when the curricula changed to problem-based learning, which demanded that professors serve as small-group facilitators as opposed to lecturers. As KM systems become better equipped to inform the quality of teaching and learning, we must consider carefully the complex human resources (i.e., capital) issues that arise when redefining how work is done.

Structural Capital

The second, closely related challenge is to ensure that KM systems are proactively implemented to help inform quality assurance. This requires a reengineering of not only the human capital involved but also the university or school. Major components of existing economic structures will be dismantled, and new ones will be constructed from the fallout.

As one of many examples of the new economic structures that need to be built, consider the implications for online learning. As the traditional institutions of higher education shift increasingly to online delivery of courses, what will happen to the physical infrastructure (i.e., the bricks and mortar) around which organizational processes are built? Economically, what will happen to university towns when half the students and faculty move elsewhere to work from a distance? What will happen to the businesses and organizations whose livelihood depended heavily on the physical presence of faculty and students?

It is not the responsibility of quality experts to determine how these changes will play out. However, it is our responsibility to acknowledge that as physical resources and structural mechanisms are realigned, sizable economies will be disrupted in the process. This disruption will draw resistance to initiatives. In fact, the possibility of these changes motivates much of the resistance to innovation in education. Resistance may manifest at the individual faculty member level, the institutional level, the professional level (e.g., in faculty unions), and even the congressional level. More so than ever before, innovations in K–12 and postsecondary pedagogy are high stakes and can potentially disrupt existing economies to the tune of billions of dollars.

Thus, proactive investments must be made in structural capital that provides actionable knowledge. This type of investment demonstrates to stakeholders a commitment to continuous quality improvement. In fact, if current trends continue, over time online programs that rely on LMSs will eventually be perceived as being more credible than face-to-face programs that fail to capture evaluative data (Díaz, 2011).

Creating this structural capital in part requires continued exploration to determine which aspects of the conventional faculty member's role add value to the enterprise of teaching and learning and which fail to add value (or, alternatively, detract from its value). Such an exploration demands the type of industrial engineering advocated by Frederick Winslow Taylor. Admittedly, the mention of Taylor's work as a framework for evaluating academic work is likely to elicit disgust given that much of Taylor's work focused on productivity of manual labor. Yet Peter Drucker (1999) calls for a parallel examination into the productivity of the knowledge worker. And he is quite candid in saying that although the development of this type of quality assurance will be difficult at best, this work is necessary.

As the academic enterprise changes because of innovations such as online learning, new structural mechanisms will be needed to collect data that inform new roles for personnel. Admittedly, this work will first require a significant investment in clearly redefining the functions of given personnel. Yet it will also require new structures throughout the academy. In particular, the structure of quality assurance processes, and the data and information architectures that inform these processes, will require new models. As KM systems are built for our revolutionized forms of teaching and learning, it behooves us to embrace Stewart's (1997) concept of structural capital. How our own quality assurance processes and infrastructure ultimately add value to the academy should be carefully considered.

Customer Capital

Customer capital demands a focus on relationships. In the context of the academy, creating this focus is a sizable challenge. The challenge is significant even when considering only those relationships necessary for the quality assurance functions of our institutions. As mentioned earlier, the future of online learning will necessitate an expanded view of quality assurance's role and impact throughout the academic institution. Quality assurance will become everyone's business within the university.

As KM systems are built for future online programs, many relationships outside the institution will begin to affect and drive the quality of those programs. Our colleagues cite our work from afar, they review our applications for promotion and tenure, and they serve as coauthors and coinvestigators. Yet the importance of relationships extends beyond our faculty and researchers.

In the future, even the relationships among students will affect our approaches to quality assurance and the respective design of our KM systems.

Part of our responsibility is to prepare our students for future work in the Knowledge Society. Work in a wired world manifests quite differently than it did in the mid-20th century; the rise of telecommuting is just one example of recent change in the workplace. Yet one principle remains the same: The Rolodex of yesterday has become the electronic network of tomorrow.

Using innovative approaches to social network analysis, future quality assurance experts in the academy will be expected to evaluate the quality of relationships that faculty, administrators, and students develop. In education, the word *relationships* will probably be replaced with *network analysis*, a term that sounds more professional, more measurable. Yet, ultimately, what educators will be doing is assessing relationships and making subsequent determinations of how those relationships affect the quality of our enterprise.

A simplistic example of this focus on relationships is citation analysis, in which quality is informed by research publications and by assessing how often others use these publications in the field. Our future KM systems will build upon this example and help assess how our relationships related to teaching, research, and innovation ultimately contribute to quality. What may be found is that future KM systems codify our work as employees within the academy every bit as much as LMSs currently codify students' work in face-to-face and online classrooms.

Conclusion

Quality assurance experts can use the principle of KM to better understand how data and information are collected to produce actionable knowledge and thus guide the expansion of the scope and impact of quality assurance efforts in online education. As the amount of data and information collected continues to increase exponentially, quality assurance experts must recognize that their roles within the academy will change as much as have the roles of faculty members. Quality assurance experts will play a pivotal role in the design and implementation of future KM systems in the academy. The significant challenges presented by these changes are balanced by opportunities to effectively improve quality.

References

Boston, W., Diaz, S. R., Gibson, A. M., Ice, P., Richardson, J., & Swan, K. (2009). An exploration of the relationship between indicators of the Community of Inquiry framework and retention in online programs. *Journal of Asynchronous Learning Networks, 13*(3), 67–83.

Dalkir, K. (2005). *Knowledge management in theory and practice.* Amsterdam: Elsevier Butterworth-Heinemann.

Díaz, S. (2011). Knowledge management as an approach to evaluating advanced graduate programs. In D. Callejo-Pérez, S. Fain, & J. J. Slater (Eds.), *Higher education and human capital: Re/thinking the doctorate in America* (pp. 75–88). Rotterdam, Netherlands: Sense.

Díaz, S. (2012). Expanding the COI: Finding hidden wholeness in online learning and online working. In Z. Akyol & R. Garrison (Eds.), *Educational communities of inquiry: Theoretical framework, research and practice* (pp. 429–445). Hershey, PA: IGI Global.

Drucker, P. F. (1994). The age of social transformation. *Atlantic Monthly, 274*(5), 53–80.

Drucker, P. F. (1999). Knowledge-worker productivity: The biggest challenge. *California Management Review, 61*(2), 79–84.

Frappaolo, C. (2006). *Knowledge management.* Southern Gate Chichester, UK: Capstone.

Gigerenzer, G., Swijtink, Z., Porter, T., Daston, L., Beatty, J., & Kruger, L. (1989). *The empire of chance: How probability changed science and everyday life.* Cambridge, UK: Cambridge University Press.

Gupta, J., Sharma, S., & Hsu, J. (2004). An overview of knowledge management. In J. Gupta & S. Sharma (Eds.), *Creating knowledge based organizations* (pp. 1–28). Hershey, PA: Idea Group.

Johnson, S. (2010). *Where good ideas come from: The natural history of innovation.* New York: Riverhead Books.

Nonaka, I., & Takeuchi, H. (1995). *The knowledge creating company: How Japanese companies create the dynamics of innovation.* New York: Oxford University Press.

Sabato, E. (1998). *Antes del Fin* (2nd ed.). Monterrey, Mexico: Editorial Seix Barral.

Stewart, T. A. (1997). *Intellectual capital: The new wealth of organizations.* New York: Doubleday/Currency.

Wheatley, M. J. (2006). *Leadership and the new science* (3rd ed.). San Francisco: Berrett-Koehler.

16

AN ADAPTIVE MODEL FOR CALCULATING CONTACT HOURS IN DISTANCE-EDUCATION COURSES

Karan Powell, Jennifer Stephens-Helm, Melissa Layne, and Phil Ice

Although there are many aspects to consider regarding the varied trajectories that technological and pedagogical change might take, the U.S. Department of Education's (2010) adoption of new regulations regarding an institution's eligibility to award academic credit put an end to ambiguity and lack of clarity regarding institutional eligibility and programmatic integrity authorized under Title IV of the Higher Education Act of 1965. Specifically, the regulations set forth the following: (a) a federal definition of the credit hour applicable to eligible institutions, and (b) requirements for accrediting agencies, as a condition of their recognition, to review an institution's policies and procedures for determining credit hours and the application of those policies and procedures in practice, using the federal definition.

The American Public University System would like to acknowledge the efforts of a warmly remembered member of the APUS team for conceptualization of the APUS Contact Hour Calculator. Randy Nelson served APUS as an administrator to the dean of public safety and health for several years before passing away in 2011. His innovative contributions will undoubtedly expand knowledge in the field of distance education, thus providing even more opportunities for students to excel academically and professionally. The APUS family extends appreciation for this work, and would like to respectfully dedicate this chapter to Randy Nelson.

Note. Portions of this chapter were published previously in the *Administrative Issues Journal* (Powell, Stephens-Helm, Layne, & Ice, 2012). They are adapted and reproduced here with permission of the *AIJ*.

Therefore, in response to these regulations, we wish to focus specifically on the number of hours a student is involved in course learning that is reasonable and that further complies with contact-hour requirements. This initiative stemmed from a comprehensive institution-wide course review process aimed at systematically identifying the strengths and areas for enhancement or improvement for each course offered at the American Public University System (APUS). While conducting the course reviews, we further identified the need for a contact-hour calculator that considers (and is adaptive to) various online learning components and platforms. As a result, a model was developed to ensure adherence to the contact-hour regulations as well as course quality and rigor.

Review of the Literature

Unfortunately, the literature is sparse regarding the emerging topic of contact hours in online learning courses. This paucity of knowledge was determined following an exhaustive literature search using the following databases: Academic Search Complete, EBSCOhost, EBSCO eBook Collection, Education Resources Information Center (ERIC), Institute of Electrical and Electronics Engineers (IEEE) Computer Society Digital Library, Pro Quest Dissertations and Theses Database, and Wilson OmniFile. We also checked one search engine, Google Scholar. Various combinations of keywords and phrases synonymous with the overarching topic were entered into all the databases and the search engine. These keywords and phrases included *contact hours, seat time, academic credit hour, converting, conversion, model, framework, institutional assessing, institutional assessment, institutional policy, institutional infrastructure, calculating, calculation, learning management systems, distance education, distance learning, online learning,* and *online courses.* Of the 30 resulting resources, only 17 resources had a high level of rigor and relevance for inclusion.

Contact-Hour Calculations: Existing Models

Despite the general understanding among those in the field of educational technology that pedagogy precedes technology, calculating contact hours for postsecondary online programs continues to be a topic of much debate. From an overarching perspective, three camps exist in this debate: (a) those who maintain that traditional "seat-time" policies should continue to be recognized in both traditional and online institutions; (b) those in favor of redefining and reconstructing a model accounting for the differences in teaching, learning, and assessment in online environments; and (c) those who believe that there should be flexibility in defining and developing contact-hour models (for both traditional and online institutions), but who assert that established *contact hour* definitions must focus on pedagogy. Underlying each perspective, however, is the shared understanding that the definition of *contact hour* must be determined as a basis for measuring eligibility for federal funding. Accrediting bodies rely heavily on this standard to ensure that students in either traditional or online institutions equally receive required levels of academic quality.

Many institutions that offer both face-to-face and online programs tend to side with the flexibility perspective model as it allows for various modes of instructional delivery, yet adheres to a focus on pedagogy. For example, Corvin, Heyman, and Kakish (2010) suggest a model that places emphasis upon didactic, laboratory, and clinical instruction in the calculation of contact hours. Other models have contributed to the establishment of a framework for calculating online contact hours but have focused on isolated factors determining academic quality, thus excluding other important and integral components. The clock-time model (Plato, SkillsTutor, McGraw Hill Contemporary GED Interactive) places the instructor in more of a motivational role. This particular type of instruction tracks the amount of elapsed time the student is connected to the online program; therefore, contact hours are viewed as instructional hours, and the instructor's role is simply to support the student. The teacher judgment model (GED Connection and Workplace Essential Skills) focuses on three instructional components: videos, workbooks, and online activities. One caveat of this type of program is the inability to monitor student activity. The learner mastery model (Crossroads Café, English for All, GED Illinois) is based on learner mastery of instructional materials, whereby the student is awarded contact hours based upon passing a test on the assigned materials.

Following its regulations for improving programmatic integrity and to further address the inconsistencies in existing models, contact hours, and standards for quality assurance in online learning, the U.S. Department of Education developed the implementation model (Simpson, 2011) to serve as a guide for institutions needing additional direction in calculating contact hours. The model outlines *credit hour* definition by (a) establishing procedures for monitoring regional accreditors' policies and procedures and reporting to appropriate departments any changes in the accreditors' policies, (b) developing policies and procedures to annually assess existing programs for compliance and communicate recommendations for curriculum modifications as warranted to the appropriate administrators, (c) establishing an evaluation policy and procedure, (d) establishing a communication protocol for alerting programs in need of modifications, and (e) establishing a tracking system to ensure that program modifications are implemented. The implementation model was framed upon the definition of a credit hour as "a unit of measure that gives value to the level of instruction, academic rigor, and time requirements for a course taken at an educational institution" (Simpson, 2011, p. 7). This broad definition allows for flexibility in contact-hour calculation for various types of institutions in the following ways:

- The institutions themselves must determine through peer review in the accreditation process whether their credit hour policies and practices consistently meet conventional academic expectations.
- A credit hour is expected to be a reasonable approximation of a reasonable amount of student work in a Carnegie unit in accordance with commonly accepted practice in higher education.
- The credit hour definition is a minimum standard that does not restrict an institution from setting a higher standard that requires more student work per credit hour.
- The definition does not dictate particular amounts of classroom time versus out-of-class student work.
- The institution may take into consideration alternative delivery methods, measurements of student work, academic calendars, disciplines, and degree levels.
- To the extent an institution believes that complying with the federal definition of a credit hour would not be appropriate for academic and other institutional needs, it may adopt a separate measure for these purposes.

The benefit of this definition of *credit hour* is that it lessens the focus on seat time as the only metric for measuring student learning and respects the variance in instructional delivery methods, programs, courses, and student work while maintaining a consistent measure for accrediting agencies and federal programs.

The APUS Online Learning Contact Hour Calculator: A New Model

The Purpose and Process

The development of the APUS Online Learning Contact Hour Calculator stemmed from an evaluation of all university courses to ascertain structural issues, compliance with university guidelines, level of rigor, instructor interaction, and other course issues. As such, the calculator will benefit faculty and program directors by allowing them to effectively and systematically assess total course contact hours. As part of the review, APUS leaders investigated contact hours as part of the course evaluation plan. This investigation led to the refinement of APUS standards for contact, which could be seen as equal to those established and espoused by other universities—whether online or on ground.

The APUS Online Learning Contact Hour Calculator considers many factors related to in-class and outside-class projects, as well as course reading requirements, in order to calculate contact-hour totals. As part of the APUS mission, the calculator model will be revised and updated as more research in contact-hour equivalents is conducted and specific course requirements are added.

The process for completing the course review requires the faculty member to do the following:

- Complete an evaluation of each course in every program using academic guidelines and templates provided.
- Provide a report and action plan for remediation and development of weak program courses.
- Remediate all core and required classes coded as red and as many yellow classes as possible.
- Provide detailed plans for remediation and development of remaining classes within a specified time frame.

A template was developed for evaluating adherence to best practices and includes the essential components of a high-quality online course. The main components reviewed in this assessment were (a) the syllabus, (b) the course objectives, (c) the course materials, (d) interactivity, (e) technology, (f) the assignments, (g) contact hours and student time, and (h) follow-up and next steps.

Defining Contact Hours

APUS uses a variation on the traditional Carnegie unit for measuring the amount of time online students are engaged in specific or assigned course learning. This can be expressed as an "in-class" function or an "outside-class" function. As is usual in Carnegie calculations of contact hours, one clock hour is equivalent to 50 minutes of Carnegie contact units. In traditional brick-and-mortar higher education, contact hours can be viewed as the time that a student spends physically in the classroom listening to a lecture, participating in discussion, taking an exam, or doing whatever is required for time in class. As an extension of this, students are advised that they are to spend two to three hours studying per week for each hour spent in the classroom; this provides a basis for discussion of outside-class hours. Both "in-class" and "outside-class" time contribute to the total number of contact hours for each course.

Contact and Outside-Class Guidelines

APUS defines one unit of class credit as consisting of three to four hours of instructive learning per week for a 16-week class or six to eight hours of instructive learning per week for an eight-week course. For the typical three-credit course, a student is expected to be engaged in classroom learning experiences of 150 minutes per each of the 16 weeks. This is 2,400 total minutes, the equivalent of 48 contact hours using the Carnegie unit of measurement. Students are expected to spend these hours in their online course participating in discussion boards, taking examinations, viewing instructor content via PowerPoint slides, reading information from linked websites, reviewing instructor lecture notes, listening to audio lessons, participating in science labs, watching lectures via video, or otherwise engaging in the APUS class.

Outside-class hours at APUS equate to approximately two to three hours per every singular in-class contact hour for any given course. Learning strategies or assignments that fulfill the outside-class hours at APUS include reading the course text, completing formal writing/research assignments, answering questions on text readings, conducting research, studying for examinations, and other out-of-classroom course requirements. As indicated in Table 16.1, APUS also further established reading expectations for each academic classification level of study, and these are included in the contact-hour calculation spreadsheet.

The spreadsheet also includes number of discussion boards and requirements for posting (both the initial substantive post in response to the discussion and subsequent responses and interactions with peers and faculty in the class), number of tests (including quizzes, midterms, and finals), other research and written papers, projects, class level (100, 200, 300, 400, or graduate study), study time for tests and exams, research time for projects, and other learning strategies and assignments typically found in our classes. Quantitative measurements of time were apportioned to each factor based on predetermined assumptions. These assumptions and measurements are outlined in Table 16.2.

TABLE 16.1
APUS Reading Expectations by Academic Classification

Classification level	*Reading expectation equivalents*
Lower-level undergraduate	400–600 pages or equivalent in online pages
Upper-level undergraduate	600–800 pages or equivalent in online pages
Graduate	800–1,000 pages or equivalent in online pages

Note. From Powell, Stephens-Helm, Layne, & Ice (2012, p. 86). Reproduced with permission.

TABLE 16.2
Outside-Class Time Factors and Associated Time Measurements

Time factors	Quantitative measurement
Composition speed for discussion board postings	25 words written per minute
Time provided for composing discussion board posting	20 minutes allotted per discussion board
Reading peers' discussion board postings	180 words per minute (the assumption is made that students read all their peers' postings for the duration of the course)
Reading instructor's feedback	10 minutes allotted per graded assignment
Quizzes	60 minutes allotted for taking a quiz and 60 minutes of preparation time
Weekly lecture notes	50 minutes allotted per issuance of weekly lecture notes (e.g., 8-week course = 8 weekly lecture notes; 16-week course = 16 weekly lecture notes)
Links to external websites	20 minutes per external URL
Midterm examination	3 hours are allotted for taking the examination 10 hours for studying/preparation
Final examination	3 hours are allotted for taking the examination 10 hours for studying/preparation (20 hours for studying/preparation when a midterm exam is not administered)
General reading assumption	250 words per double-spaced, typed page
Reading course materials	200 words read per minute, or 180 words read per minute for electronic materials
Upper-level undergraduate courses	8 hours granted to students taking this level of study
Miscellaneous assignments	120 minutes granted per miscellaneous assignment

Time factors	*Quantitative measurement*
Composing a formal writing assignment	120 minutes granted for preparation time 20 words written per minute 30 minutes granted for each page of writing
Conducting research for a formal writing assignment	120 minutes granted per page of writing
Science labs	120 minutes lower level 130 minutes upper level 150 minutes graduate
Math problems	120–130 minutes developmental 120–130 minutes general education 120–130 minutes program support (Math 302 >130 minutes) >150 minutes graduate

Note. From Powell, Stephens-Helm, Layne, & Ice (2012, p. 87). Adapted with permission.

TABLE 16.3
APUS Contact Hour Requirements by Academic Classification

Academic classification	*Level of study*	*Academic hour requirements*
Lower-level undergraduate	100–200 level	120 combined outside-class and contact hours
Upper-level undergraduate	300–400 level	130 combined outside-class and contact hours
Graduate	500+	150 combined outside-class and contact hours

Note. From Powell, Stephens-Helm, Layne, & Ice (2012, p. 88). Reproduced with permission.

At both the undergraduate and graduate levels of study, there are minimum requirements and basic expectations at APUS regarding contact hours. The three different levels of study, based on course number, are outlined in Table 16.3 with their suggested minimum total contact hours.

Using the APUS Online Learning Contact Hour Calculator: A Sample Review

From an initial pilot study using the APUS Online Learning Contact Hour Calculator, we concluded that seven weeks of discussion boards plus a final examination and a formal research paper submission will typically cover the minimum in-class contact-hour requirement.[1] However, if a discussion board seems more like an assignment than a discussion, students may not become suitably engaged in the course. Additionally, the amount of time it takes to prepare for an exam or discussion board posting or to research a paper should bring a course within the expected range for total contact hours. Table 16.4 shows the course information requirements common to all contact hour course calculations.

Table 16.5 shows an example of the first section of the spreadsheet, which contains the specific requirements for in-classroom contact hours, including (a) the number of hours, (b) the Carnegie contact hours, and (c) an explanation aiding the faculty member in determining the appropriate information to calculate.

The second section of the spreadsheet (Table 16.6) is the contact-hour calculation spreadsheet for outside-class time. As mentioned, contact hours for outside-class time are based on several factors including (a) length of course, (b) number of discussion boards, (c) number of words for initial posting, (d) number of words required for responses, (e) minimum number of responses, (f) reading instructor's feedback, (g) quizzes, (h) lecture notes, (i) links to external websites, (j) midterm exam, and (k) final exam. Displayed in Table 16.6 are example contact-hour calculation summaries for assignments and course information, including the final determination of whether contact-hour requirements were met.

TABLE 16.4
APUS Course Information Example

Course information	Calculated contact hours	Course material information
Course title: PBHE528	Total contact hours: 145.46	Number of pages read: 200
Length of course (in weeks): 16	Class level: graduate	Number of words: 50,000

Note. From Powell, Stephens-Helm, Layne, & Ice (2012, p. 88). Reproduced with permission.

TABLE 16.5
APUS In-Classroom Contact Time Calculation Spreadsheet Example, Part 1

Course Information	Calculated Contact Hours								
*Course: CMRJ205	Total Contact Hours: 141.28								
*Length of course in weeks: 8	Class Level: Lower-Level Undergraduate								
Complete the Starred Areas (*)									
Difference for Contact Hours: 21.28[a]									
In-Classroom Time[a]									
*Number of Students:	14								
Requirement	How Many of Each[b]		Carnegie Contact Hours[c]	
Number of discussion boards	*7			
Number of words required for initial posting	*500			
Initial posting by student	*7	*280	5.6	3.96%
Reading discussion board postings		*19.44	35.39	25.05%
Number of words required for responses	*250	*420		
Minimum required number of responses	*2	*14	8.4	5.95%
Reading instructor's feedback	*10	*10	2	1.42%
Quizzes	*4	*60	4.8	3.40%
Weekly lecture notes	*8	*50	8	5.66%
Links to external websites		*20		
Midterm exam		*180		
Final exam	*1	*180	3.6	2.55%
Total Contact Hours			67.79	
*# of Contact Hours Per Week: 8				

Note. An asterisk (*) denotes areas the instructor must complete. From Powell, Stephens-Helm, Layne, & Ice (2012, p. 90). Reproduced with permission.

a. This row presents a self-calculating summary of results based on user-entered values in the lower fields of the spreadsheet.

b. Left-column fields indicate the quantity of each activity. Right-column fields indicate estimated total number of minutes for the activity. Blank fields are not applicable.

c. Left-column fields self-calculate the total number of Carnegie contact hours for the activity.

TABLE 16.6
APUS Outside-Class Contact Time Calculation Spreadsheet Example, Part 2

Number of students: 14			
Requirement	How many of each		Carnegie contact hours
Are all course materials electronic?	*1	*180	
Number of pages read in course materials	*500	*694.44	13.89
Formal writing assignment quantity	*2		
Writing calculation			6.8
Researching calculation			19.2
Writing preparation time			4.8
Number of misc. assignments		*0	
Student studying/preparation time			
Midterm preparation		*0	
Final exam preparation		*0	
Final exam preparation (without midterm)		*1,200	24
Quiz preparation		*240	3.8
Total contact hours			**72.49**
# of contact hours per week: 9			

Note. An asterisk (*) denotes areas the instructor must complete. From Powell, Stephens-Helm, Layne, & Ice (2012, p. 91). Reproduced with permission.

Judgments regarding each course are standardized, and these standards serve as criteria for new course development. If enhancements or deficiencies are identified in the course review process, the faculty member is designated to make the agreed-upon changes within a specific time frame, and the course is subsequently reviewed to ensure that it conforms to the APUS academic quality standards. We found it interesting that results of the initial review revealed that the majority of classes met the standards for APUS contact time. Some online courses were discovered to have 300 contact hours or more, and others were found to be short of hours. Courses short or overly ambitious in number of hours were immediately reviewed for student learning and compliance and were redesigned or remediated.

Considerations for Using the Contact Hour Calculator

When calculating contact hours, the approach should not be one size fits all. For example, learning strategies and expectations for a math or science course will be different from those for an English course. The Contact Hour Calculator allows each faculty member to define and identify specified learning strategies for the course. Collaboration between administrators and faculty to determine the standards for measures is critical and should be established according to each course's unique characteristics.

The path to preparing students for service and leadership, however, must keep student learning and success as a top priority. Although contact hours assist in gauging the appropriateness, rigor, and engagement level of a course, the desired course outcome is student learning and academic achievement. Student success, retention, and persistence in learning are direct outcomes of an engaging learning environment. Contact time is only one measure of engagement—the quantity of engagement. To assure quality, APUS also reviews the depth and breadth of interactions (among the student, the faculty member, the program director, and learning specialists) on a regular basis.

Further, the alignment of institutional mission, vision, and core values with infrastructure, technological, and pedagogical frameworks must also be carefully considered to assure a high level of quality in online courses. The following statement by Roschelle, Pea, Hoadley, Gordin, and Means (2000) captures this sentiment: "One of the biggest barriers to introducing effective technology applications in classrooms is the mismatch between the contents of assessments and the kinds of higher-order learning supported most effectively by technology" (p. 91). Although the authors are referring to the traditional classroom setting, this statement becomes even more meaningful in an online learning environment where technologies define the classroom rather than just enhance it.

Summary

With burgeoning numbers of students taking online courses and in response to governmental regulations, higher education administrators must reexamine and reevaluate how contact hours are assessed and calculated for online programs. We found no evidence in the literature of a contact-hour model or technique to calculate contact hours in a distance-education course. Therefore, the development of the APUS Online Learning Contact Hour Calculator will undoubtedly aid administrators in providing guidelines in this regard—but even more important, the calculator will be instrumental in helping students achieve academic and career success.

Note

1. Meeting or exceeding minimal contact-hour standards set forth by the Carnegie Foundation is one means to demonstrate a commitment toward meeting established standards for student contact and student learning. But many in higher education believe that meeting contact hours does not ensure student learning. Although we are focusing on contact hours in this chapter and in this initiative, APUS also emphasizes learning outcomes assessment for each course and program. Assessment measures include student learning assessment reports, which identify and monitor direct measures of learning for course- and program-specific learning. Learning outcomes are a topic for another article. The focus here is contact hours—but not to the neglect of learning outcomes and related assessments.

References

Corvin, D., Heyman, E., & Kakish, B. (2010). *Calculating credit hours in online and blended learning.* Presented at the Eighth Annual National Conference on Allied Health Education, New Orleans.

Powell, K., Stephens-Helm, J., Layne, M., & Ice, P. (2012, October). Quantifying online learning contact hours. *Administrative Issues Journal: Education, Practice, and Research, 2*(2), 80–93.

Roschelle, J. M., Pea, R. D., Hoadley, C. M., Gordin, D. N., & Means, B. M. (2000). Changing how and what children learn in school with computer-based technology. *Children and Computer Technology, 10,* 76–101.

Simpson, J. (2011). *A college implementation model for the U.S. Department of Education Program Integrity Regulations.* Jacksonville: Florida State College.

U.S. Department of Education. (2010). Program integrity issues. *Federal Register 75.* Retrieved from http://edocket.access.gpo.gov/2010/pdf/2010-14107.pdf

17

THE ROLE AND REALITIES OF ACCREDITATION

A Practical Guide for Programs and Institutions Preparing for an Accreditation Visit

Susan Biro, Christine Mullins, and Jean Runyon

Flexible learning options in higher education have created a need to define what constitutes quality in learning environments. Accreditation serves as the validation process by which institutions are evaluated by certified, external review teams that compare the institution's educational practices with established standards to assure a high level of educational quality for internal and external stakeholders. This nationally accepted practice for course and institutional review offers institutions opportunities for self-reflection and peer review to validate successes, document opportunities for improvement, and foster renewed discussions among key stakeholders about core mandates for accessibility, quality improvement, success, and student completion. The accreditation process, coupled with a culture of evidence, provides overall quality assurance and contributes to the achievement of national mandates and, ultimately, student success.

In this chapter we provide an overview of the national focus on accreditation of higher education and the expectations of accreditation bodies. We then discuss how online distance-education programs can prepare for a successful accreditation visit and conclude by examining federal and state efforts to address quality in distance-education programs.

National Focus

The rate of student completion in higher education has become a national imperative. Higher education institutions have an obligation to meet the challenge of preparing world citizens to become members of an educated workforce that can compete in the global economy. To meet this challenge, colleges and universities must renew their commitment to providing students, most often adult learners, with access to high-quality, postsecondary degrees and certifications and must ensure that more students are able to successfully achieve their academic, professional, and personal enrichment goals.

Accreditation in the United States

Accreditation, a process of external quality review created and used by U.S. higher education to scrutinize colleges, universities, and programs for level of quality and areas of improvement, is more than 100 years old (Eaton, 2012). The accreditation structure that exists today is decentralized and complex, effectively mirroring American higher education, an enterprise that in 2012 enrolled more than 26 million credit students (U.S. Department of Education, n.d.; Eaton, 2012).

Unlike most industrialized countries with a complex, decentralized higher education system, the United States has never had a ministry of higher education with direct oversight of the quality of postsecondary institutions (Lezberg, 2007; Middaugh, 2010; O'Brien, 2013). Academic institutions are licensed by one of the 50 states, each of which sets individual rules relative to the institution's ability to operate legally. Individual states' rules describe minimal inputs necessary for the operation of an institution of higher education, rather than identify criteria relevant to its effectiveness. As a result, private accreditation associations have, since the 1880s, provided the mechanism to assure employers, governments, students, and the public that degree-granting institutions are offering acceptable levels of education (Lezberg, 2007).

O'Brien (2013) lists three types of accrediting associations in the United States:

1. Programmatic or specialized associations that accredit programs of study; . . .
2. National associations that accredit faith-based or career-focused institutions; . . . and
3. Regional associations that accredit degree-granting colleges and universities. (p. 482)

Six regional accrediting associations for higher education are the most widely accepted and respected in the United States today: (a) the Middle States Association of Colleges and Schools, (b) the New England Association of Schools and Colleges, (c) the North Central Association of Colleges and Schools, (d) the Southern Association of Schools and Colleges, (e) the Northwest Commission on Colleges and Universities, and (f) the Western Association of Schools and Colleges (Council for Higher Education Accreditation, 2012)[1]. According to Eaton (2012), the four roles of accreditation that are the foundation of today's process are assuring quality, providing access to federal and state funds, engendering private-sector confidence, and easing transfer. The regional accrediting bodies are membership organizations comprising colleges and universities that engage in a voluntary process of peer review to ensure compliance with the accreditation standards articulated by each region (Middaugh, 2010).

In March 2001 the eight regional accrediting commissions made their first formal, concerted effort to address quality in distance education when they developed and adopted the *Best Practices for Electronically Offered Degree and Certificate Programs* (Southern Association of Colleges and Schools, 2001). The regional commissions realized that an increasing number of higher education institutions were using technology to disseminate learning opportunities and that a systematic review of online course development, teaching practices, and institutional processes was warranted to ensure that institutions were implementing basic and effective standards of quality when it came to their distance-learning efforts to guarantee the application of "well-established essentials of institutional quality to distance learning" (Southern Association of Colleges and Schools, 2001, "Introduction").

On one hand, distance-education administrators knew that they would have to work harder to demonstrate and document their institutions' compliance with these best practice principles. On the other hand, most were grateful to have a common, nationally based set of quality standards they could consult and implement. These benchmarks made it easier for institutions to justify the need to establish institution-wide practices—such as offering comprehensive student services that distance-learning and face-to-face students could access equally—to the college president and other higher-level administrators and to help persuade them to change their current, well-established processes to accommodate a new type of learner. Distance educators recognized that access to these services was not an optional extra—to succeed, learners need to be able to access all the institution's services, just like face-to-face students. These critical services include the college bookstore, career advising, enrollment, disability services, the library, orientation, registration, and tutoring.

Technically, off-campus course delivery was always included as part of an institution's regional accreditation because accreditation is never partial (Lezberg, 2007). However, Lezberg (2007) and O'Brien (2013) noted that in the 1950s criteria and various groups, beginning with the Distance Education and Training Council, established standards relative to the acceptability of distance education (Distance Education and Training Council, 2012). The American Council on Education and consortia such as the Western Interstate Commission for Higher Education also joined these efforts to provide guidelines in the area of distance and web-based education.

As institutions undertook efforts to expand their menu of distance-education offerings, they realized that the assurance of external quality control in these offerings was critical to the same stakeholders who were concerned with their other accreditation efforts—that is, state and federal governments, employers, students and families, and the general public. As a result, throughout the last decade, institutions have sought and begun to implement guidance from their regional accrediting associations about controlling quality in their distance offerings (Lezberg, 2007). The regional accreditors recognized that the mode in which students learn does not change an institution's need to obtain regional accreditation to establish credibility. Accordingly, the eligibility of an institution to offer students federally funded financial aid and receive federally funded government grants hinges on whether it has received this credential. Many institutions will only recognize or accept the credits students have earned at other regionally accredited institutions.

Distance-education administrators have experienced an increasingly pressing need to address course quality and design, faculty training and preparation, course assessment, and improvements in student readiness and retention. They have adapted to how students use technology and have used technology to apply quality standards and improve their courses. Since work is completed online, technology allows administrators to use learning analytics and computer systems that offer early warning, triggering mechanisms that enable administrators to track student persistence and achievement. This means they can intervene to help struggling students—who have not logged into the learning management system (LMS) or completed necessary course assignments by a certain date—before they drop out. The gap in completion or retention rates between distance-education and face-to-face students, which has historically been lower for distance education, has significantly narrowed. In 2011 half of the Instructional Technology Council (ITC) survey respondents indicated that they had achieved equivalency (Lokken, 2012).

Technology also allows instructors to use quality controls that can help prevent or detect cheating and plagiarism. For example, most LMSs allow instructors to automatically change the order of questions in multiple-choice quizzes, record or limit the amount of time students have to complete a quiz or exam, and check written work with antiplagiarism software or search the Internet to identify suspected plagiarism (WCET, UT Telecampus, & ITC, 2009).

The 2011 ITC survey showed that most campuses recognized the need to introduce or expand their virtual student support services. However, respondents indicated a marked decrease in their online support offerings during the past year, in contrast to the consistent increase shown during previous years of the survey. This shortfall could be attributable to budget cuts that reduced the number of administrative staff or to lack of funds available to pay outside vendors to provide these services. The ITC survey respondents might also be less confident about the level of service their college provides. Accreditors may have drawn attention to the importance of these student support services and raised the bar for what is deemed "adequate."

Expectations of Accreditation Bodies for Distance Education

In fall 2011 the Council of Regional Accrediting Commissions (C-RAC) released the *Interregional Guidelines for the Evaluation of Distance Education* (Middle States Commission on Higher Education [MSCHE], 2011b). All the regional higher education accrediting organizations in the United States adopted and endorsed these guidelines, intended for use by accreditation evaluation teams. The interregional guidelines replaced the *C-RAC Statement of Best Practices for Electronically Offered Degree and Certificate Programs* (MSCHE, 2002), and are intended for use in conjunction with the relevant standards and policies of each accreditation body.

The 2011 guidelines identify "nine hallmarks of quality" that serve as a framework for institutions involved in distance education (MSCHE, 2011b). They also provide a road map that colleges and universities can use to determine how distance education aligns with an institution's mission, vision, and strategic plan. Additionally, they offer an assessment framework for institutions that already provide online learning options to their students. Institutions preparing for an accreditation visit must document and provide evidence that regional accreditation standards have been met. Institutions should also provide evidence of the extent to which the nine hallmarks outlined by C-RAC are met.

Online learning initiatives must be consistent with an institution's mission and fully supported by its infrastructure, academic programs, technology, systems of governance, student support services, planning, and budget processes. Institutions must have developed processes to meet quality expectations for critical components of an exemplary online program, including course design, faculty preparation, teaching performance, course and program assessments, student readiness, and retention. In terms of rigor and content, accreditation standards require that distance-education courses be equivalent, or better than, those taught in a traditional face-to-face classroom environment. The learning outcomes must be the same, regardless of instructional delivery method.

Initiatives at the local, state, and national levels have resulted in an increased awareness of the online learning environment and further serve as evidence of quality that should be shared with internal and external stakeholders, as well as with accreditation teams. Institutions may consider adopting and implementing established programs and standards to demonstrate an evidence-based quality assurance package, to showcase their commitment to academic excellence, and to support efforts to document excellence to their respective accreditation agencies.

For example, in 2001 the Michigan Community College Association's Michigan Community College Virtual Learning Collaborative (MCCVLC) identified elements of quality assurance their colleges should address when developing online courses, resulting in the MCCVLC Online Course Development Guidelines and Rubric. MCCVLC created the guidelines based on reviews of other guidelines and documents from the American Council on Education, the Higher Education Program and Policy Council of the American Federation of Teachers, the North Central Association Higher Learning Commission, the American Association of Higher Education, and the Michigan Virtual University. The guidelines focus on several key areas, including outcomes, course design and development, interaction, assessment, and technologies. They propose that a college that adopts and implements these guidelines demonstrates a commitment to quality assurance in online learning.

The Quality Matters (QM) standards of quality in design of online courses and online elements of blended courses provide guidance in addressing one of the critical components of a quality assurance plan. QM, which is the outgrowth of a 2003–2006 federally funded grant, has received national recognition for its peer-based approach and continuous improvement in online education and student learning. QM is a faculty-centered, peer-review process that is designed to certify the quality of online and blended courses. QM subscribers include community and technical colleges, colleges and universities, K–12 schools and systems, and other academic institutions. These subscribers have adopted the QM tool set and processes to provide evidence of a commitment to quality assurance through the recognition of quality in online education.

MCCVLC's Online Course Development Guidelines and Rubric and QM are just two examples of initiatives colleges and universities have implemented to demonstrate a commitment to quality. They can be used as components in an overall accreditation or reaccreditation tool kit that can be shared with evaluators. Colleges that offer significant distance-education programs can act as communities of practice by sharing similar efforts they have made to ensure quality course development, teaching, student services, and pathways to degree completion on their campuses.

Preparing for an Accreditation Visit

A regional accreditation body evaluates an entire educational organization in terms of its mission and against established accreditation benchmarks and standards. Preparing for an accreditation visit provides an opportunity for administrative staff to reflect on and demonstrate a culture that values assessment, data-informed decision making, and a commitment to continuous quality improvement. In a perfect world, preparing for an accreditation visit would begin during the discussion and development of any new initiatives at an institution. Laying the foundation for a quality program is paramount and should be grounded in principles of best practices with a focus on assessment. However, formal preparations should begin at least 12 to 18 months prior to the scheduled on-site accreditation visit.

Engage the College Community

Every member of the college or university community should be actively engaged in reflections and discussions about an institution's strengths and weaknesses in preparation for an accreditation visit. This reflection, coupled with sound evidence, provides opportunities to objectively examine the current state of affairs and to create a framework for future directions. In their self-assessment tool, *Community College Inventory: Focus on Student Persistence, Learning, and Attainment*, McClenney and McClenney (2010) described a culture of evidence as one in which "institutional and individual reflection and action are typically prompted and supported by data about student learning and institutional performance" (p. 4). Guidelines for quality online education and benchmarks should be identified—and evidence should be cultivated long before an accreditation visit.

Plan Strategically: Identify Quality Guidelines and Benchmarks

Cohesive strategic plans allow all areas of campus governance the opportunity to be part of this process, which further instills a sense of ownership in how distance-education offerings are identified, developed, implemented, supported, and evaluated (Laws, Howell, & Lindsay, 2003; Shapiro, Morales, & Biro, 2009). In promoting distance education, administrators would do well to also establish support by cultivating relationships with academic leaders, faculty, information technology staff, and student services departments, so that all members of the college community appreciate their stake in successful distance offerings (Berge & Schrum, 1998; Laws et al., 2003).

An institution's strategic plan, driven necessarily by mission, should articulate support for distance-education initiatives and create and define the culture for these efforts. One outcome of such strategic planning is the framework it can offer administrators in planning for effective delivery and in gathering and analyzing data specific to these programs, which can then lay the foundation for a successful accreditation visit (Berge & Schrum, 1998). In fact, Berge and Schrum (1998) pointed out that preparing for an accreditation visit should begin during administrative discussion and development of new initiatives. Laying the foundation for a quality program is paramount and should be grounded in principles of best practices, with a focus on assessment of the program that is both summative and formative. When preparing for an accreditation visit, institutions must identify and examine expectations of regional and national accreditation associations. The Higher Learning Commission (2010) provides general information about the criteria for accreditation, frequently asked questions, and resources.

The process for identifying guidelines for quality online education begins with a review of regional accreditation guidelines, ideally carried out by a variety of individuals at the institution who represent the diversity of the college and who commit to examining current practices, identifying needs, and developing new strategies or practices as needed. These individuals would likely include distance-education administrators, as well as representatives from the institutional research (IR) or assessment department. An institution's distance-education team should begin preparing for an accreditation visit by becoming actively involved in the self-study report that forms the basis of an evaluation team's visit. Throughout this self-study process, it is critical that distance-education administrators have the opportunity to work with the campus's IR department to identify and collect data relative to distance offerings, such as enrollment trends, course offerings, course and instructor evaluations, student withdrawals and completions, and earned grades.

Conduct a Gap Analysis

We recommend that distance-education administrators conduct a gap analysis—an examination of the differences between the accreditation standards and their ultimate delivery—to assess where an institution is in relation to the expectations of their accreditation agency. A spreadsheet can be created and used to assess activities and performances—with regard to the guidelines and benchmarks the accreditation agencies specify—and be used to develop action plans to address any identified gaps in preparation for the accreditation visit. The college should conduct the gap analysis early in the preparation and planning process so that there is time to correct any flaws or implement strategies to address a lack of services.

Another helpful tool is the Sloan Consortium's Quality Scorecard for the Administration of Online Programs, which measures and quantifies 70 quality indicators within online education programs. The scorecard examines performance in several key categories, including institutional support, technology support, course development and instructional design, teaching and learning, and evaluation and assessment. This benchmark tool creates a systematic approach for examining a program and can be used to foster a dialogue among key stakeholders about the program and standards for quality.

Gather Evidence

Institutions must systematically and regularly collect, compile, aggregate, summarize, analyze, and use data to make informed decisions throughout an accreditation cycle. Institutions that continually use performance data for program review or improvement find that preparing for an accreditation visit occurs on an ongoing basis. By following internal guidelines relative to the completion of regularly scheduled academic program reviews, administrators, staff, and faculty work collaboratively to evaluate current online learning programs and identify goals. Additionally, performing a program review allows stakeholders to identify areas for improvement, establish timelines to complete tasks, and assign appropriate oversight. In this regard, completing an institutionally mandated academic program review can be one of the best ways to prepare for an accreditation visit.

Measurement in education is intended to provide evidence and to communicate information to constituents about operations, strategic planning, services, support, and learner achievement and success. Data collection must be deliberate and coupled with analysis and response. The quantity and quality of the information collected contributes to effective decision-making processes that ensure program and institutional effectiveness. Institutions must use the results of evaluations to enhance the attainment of institutional goals, to ensure student success and achievement, and to provide future directions for distance-education programs.

Distance-education courses and programs must be coherent, cohesive, and comparable in academic rigor to programs offered in traditional instructional formats. An accreditation visit provides an opportunity to demonstrate quality and effectiveness through the use of data; those preparing for a visit should consult with their regional accreditation agency to ascertain the type of data required in support of an accreditation or reaccreditation process.

Prepare the Self-Study Report

Preparing for a successful on-site accreditation visit begins with a review of institutional resources made available by the accrediting agency. For example, MSCHE provides an extensive list of publications to guide institutions through this process, beginning with the self-study and continuing all the way through hosting a successful team visit (www.msche.org/publications.asp).

MSCHE (2012) explains the accreditation cycle and offers a step-by-step approach for organizing staff and resources, identifying faculty and staff to serve on the steering committee and in work groups, developing research questions, managing the process, and preparing for what to expect once institutions have completed the self-study report and are preparing for the on-site evaluation team visit. As self-study work groups are created, it is important that a distance-learning administrator advocate for having someone with historical knowledge of distance offerings assigned a role in working with, or advising, the work group charged with distance education. In this way, a fresh perspective about distance programs can be encouraged and historical accuracy can be ensured in the final report.

MSCHE also offers guidance more specific to distance learning on accepted standards through two additional publications: *Characteristics of Excellence in Higher Education: Requirements of Affiliation and Standards for Accreditation* (2011a) and *Distance Education Programs: Interregional Guidelines for the Evaluation of Distance Education (Online Learning)* (2011b), noted previously.

Showcase Best Practices

Institutions can demonstrate their commitment to continuous improvement and quality assurance for online learning programs in several ways. One of those ways is to showcase application of best practices. A good beginning includes a formal academic program review, which is tied to the college's mission and goals, and offers opportunities to highlight best practices for institutional success. Administrators can use elements of formal program reviews, final recommendations, and ongoing practices within a larger self-study report to an accrediting agency, as well as during an on-site visit from an evaluation team. Moreover, identifying institutional or departmental best practices in the design, delivery, and support of distance-learning offerings can enhance conversations and collaborations across the institution during times of accreditation preparations and the work that invariably follows such a visit and final report.

For example, in 2009 educators at Carroll Community College completed a distance-learning program review, which allowed the institution to chart the historical development of distance offerings and, more important, to develop recommendations that were then incorporated into annual distance-learning academic goals. These goals contained established timelines for completion and assigned oversight responsibilities among distance-learning staff. Establishing standards for online course design was one of the recommendations that grew out of Carroll Community College's formal program review of distance learning. To that end, the distance-learning office created a standard course template for on-site, online, and hybrid offerings in the LMS. This template is built following the 21 essential standards of the QM Rubric and reflects the use of specific LMS features at Carroll Community College.

Federal and State Efforts to Assure Quality for Distance Education

Higher education institutions must demonstrate compliance with the benchmarks and standards that the recognized, regional accrediting associations have adopted; they must have "criteria reflecting the qualities of a sound educational program and have developed procedures for evaluating institutions or programs to determine whether or not they are operating at basic levels of quality" (U.S. Department of Education, 2012, para. 2). In addition, colleges and universities must also provide evidence of compliance with state and federal mandates.

With the growing popularity and expansion of distance-education programs, it seems that everyone has a stake in making sure students receive a high-quality educational experience. Many players want to offer a top-down approach for quality assurance. The Obama administration is no different from previous administrations that have attempted to influence and mandate quality assurance initiatives through their administrative arm, the U.S. Department of Education. In 2009 President Obama asked community colleges to play a critical role in meeting his goal for helping the United States once again lead the world in college-degree offerings—he asked colleges to increase the number of students who earn certificate and associate degrees, or who continue on to graduate from four-year colleges and universities, by an additional 5 million graduates by 2020.

Community college presidents responded to this call to action the following year, when members of the American Association of Community Colleges pledged to take steps to reexamine their administrative procedures and courses and implement strategies that encourage student success. Recommendations included enhancing instructional programs by identifying and disseminating best practices, redesigning curriculum and instruction to reflect contemporary pedagogical practices, enhancing faculty engagement, offering professional development for faculty and staff, improving student engagement, enhancing student services, strengthening technology and research infrastructure, strengthening internal and external communication, and building a culture of completion. (See full list of recommendations in Johnson McPhail, 2011; see also Lee & Rawls, 2010.)

Distance-education administrators are responding to this so-called completion agenda because of the spotlight on the rapid growth of online distance-education programs, often as the only area of growth for the college (Allen & Seaman, 2011). With a renewed focus on excellence, many administrators are working feverishly to meet this challenge as it relates to current, and planned, distance-education programs. In addition to raising the bar for course quality and implementing systematic training opportunities for instructors, they have installed learning analytics and other systems to track students. They hope to spark a campuswide recognition that offering a comprehensive package of student services is instrumental to helping students attain their educational goals and raise overall college completion rates—whether students learn online or in a face-to-face environment.

Not surprisingly, congressional, federal, and state government interest in distance education has intensified as student demand and enrollment in distance education has increased. In particular, there has been an increased focus on the value of for-profit institutions and whether their high tuition rates have robbed the coffers of the student financial aid fund—without giving students (or U.S. taxpayers) value for their money. The U.S. Department of Education has called for colleges and universities to give students opportunities for gainful employment in return for their time and money. This demand perhaps puts added pressure on the regional accreditation agencies to ensure that our higher education institutions offer students excellent educational opportunities that result in their ability to attain jobs, improve their lives, and enhance the U.S. economy (U.S. Senate Committee on Health, Education, Labor, & Pensions, 2012).

Many distance-education programs fear that new, burdensome, and expensive federal and state government regulations—imposed to rein in fraud perpetrated by rogue for-profit institutions and diploma mills—will force them to devote precious staff time and resources to make them more "accountable," even though they have already gone through an extensive and rigorous accreditation process to document their commitment to offering high-quality educational opportunities at a distance. Three recent government initiatives that address quality in distance education—state authorization, student authentication, and prevention of financial aid fraud rings—are described in more detail in the following sections.

State Authorization

In October 2010 the Department of Education proposed a regulation to accompany Congress's reauthorization of the Higher Education Act in 2008. This regulation would have required colleges and universities to obtain state authorization from any state in which the college was teaching out-of-state distance-learning students. If these neighboring or distant states did not provide the necessary authorization, institutions would be unable to offer federally funded financial aid to the out-of-state distance-learning students who requested it. In July 2011 the U.S. District Court struck down this proposed regulation, stating the department did not follow proper procedures to issue the rule. The U.S. Court of Appeals upheld the verdict in June 2012.

Regardless of the court's decision, the department's proposed regulation in October 2010 alerted states to their legal authority to require out-of-state higher education institutions to seek permission to teach their residents online; many were not aware of or did not previously enforce this right. The proposed regulation also prompted many state governments to learn about the variety and scope of out-of-state distance-education programs.

Many distance-education institutions, especially those that teach a national audience, are beginning to obtain authorization from the states in which they teach out-of-state students, but the process can be expensive and time-consuming. Many are taking a wait-and-see approach. State Higher Education Executive Officers (SHEEO) has created several regularly updated directories to help institutions navigate this process. These include a state-by-state summary of regulations and fees and a state-by-state contact list of state regulators to contact in order to obtain approval (SHEEO, 2012).

As of 2012, state regulators, higher education administrators, and representatives from several regional compacts, such as the Western Interstate Commission for Higher Education (WICHE), the Southern Regional Educational Board (SREB), the Midwestern Higher Education Compact (MHEC), and the New England Board of Higher Education (NEBHE), were working to create a state authorization reciprocity agreement in which state governments would recognize the institutions that teach their distance-education students at no additional cost.

The drafters of a comprehensive agreement are still working out the details, which can be quite controversial. By 2013 they hope to have a single, final document that state governments will have the option to support or sign.

Student Authentication

In 2008, when it reauthorized the Higher Education Act (also called the Higher Education Opportunity Act), Congress required institutions offering distance education and correspondence education to

> have processes in place through which the institution establishes that the student who registers in a distance education or correspondence education course or program is the same student who participates in and completes

the course or program and receives the academic credit. (Higher Education Opportunity Act, 2008, Sec. 602.17)[2]

In its rule-making proceeding, the Department of Education clarified that accrediting bodies only need to require

> institutions to verify the identity of a student who participates in class or coursework by using, at the option of the institution, methods such as—a secure login and pass code, proctored examinations, and new or other technologies and practices that are effective—in verifying student identification. (Higher Education Opportunity Act, 2008, Sec. 602.17)

This allows institutions to continue using the process they typically use to authenticate their online students within their course management system—a login and password—rather than impose a more rigorous or costly method.

Financial Aid Fraud Rings

On September 26, 2011, the Office of the Inspector General released a report that alerted the Department of Education and higher education institutions to the presence of an increasing number of financial aid fraud rings that have targeted community colleges and other distance-learning course providers (Hamel, 2011). The members of these rings have applied for, and obtained, student financial aid after enrolling to take courses from higher education institutions that they never intended to complete. On October 20, 2011, the Department of Education sent higher education institutions a "dear colleague" letter that outlined several steps colleges could implement to detect and address the fraud occurring on their campuses by students who are learning in face-to-face as well as distance-education formats (U.S. Department of Education, 2011).

Although most of the best practices suggested by the Department of Education are helpful, the inspector general's initial report includes some troublesome recommendations to address this problem. The most troubling recommendation is the Department of Education's request that Congress exclude distance-learning students from being eligible for receiving living expenses as part of their financial aid package (Hamel, 2011).

The Senate Committee on Appropriations included this language in its 2013 appropriations bill, a step that concerns distance educators because it discriminates against legitimate, financially needy distance-education students who are trying to pursue their educational goals. Most distance-learning students take courses at a distance because they need to—because they are working during normal class hours, live too far from campus, are taking care of their children or other family members at home, or are disabled or because the course they need to graduate is offered at a time that conflicts with another course. They are not any less needy than traditional students—most are working and trying to make ends meet just like any other student. Distance educators are concerned that these types of hastily drafted government and state regulations will impose blanket "solutions" that hurt distance-learning students but do not solve the quality control or financial fraud issues that the Department of Education and college administrators need to address.

Congress is next scheduled to reauthorize the Higher Education Act in 2014, as it has every four to six years since it passed this legislation in 1965. Distance educators need to pay close attention to any attempts Congress makes to impose new burdensome or expensive regulations that could restrict their ability to offer educational opportunities to meet the growing student demand to learn at a distance—all in the name of quality control. The need to ensure a student's identity is paramount, but not at the expense of this wonderful new use of technology to expand educational access.

Conclusion

In the age of accountability, higher education institutions need to continue to provide finer levels of evidence of quality and outcomes. Institutions must align practices with benchmarks and standards established by state and federal mandates, in addition to those established by accreditation agencies. Accreditation visits provide institutions with opportunities to showcase successes and to identify areas for improvement and ultimately have a positive impact on student success.

Notes

1. The Council for Higher Education Accreditation (CHEA) is a nonprofit association that focuses exclusively on higher education accreditation. CHEA is the private-sector organization that, like the U.S. Department of Education, "recognizes" accrediting organizations. See www.chea.org/Directories/regional.asp for a complete list of CHEA-recognized institutions. Institutions must comply with standards endorsed by regional accreditation associations when preparing for an accreditation visit.
2. The Higher Education Opportunity Act (Public Law 110-315) was enacted on August 14, 2008, and reauthorizes the Higher Education Act of 1965, as amended. This web page provides information on the department's implementation of the Higher Education Opportunity Act: www2.ed.gov/policy/highered/leg/hea08/index.html.

References

Allen, I. E., & Seaman, J. (2011). *Going the distance: Online education in the United States, 2011*. Retrieved from the Sloan Consortium website: http://sloanconsortium.org/publications/survey/going_distance_2011

Berge, Z. L., & Schrum, L. (1998). Linking strategic planning with program implementation for distance education. *CAUSE/EFFECT, 21*(3). Retrieved from http://net.educause.edu/ir/library/html/cem/cem98/cem9836.html

Council for Higher Education Accreditation. (2012). *Directories: Regional accrediting organizations 2013–2014*. Retrieved from http://www.chea.org/Directories/regional.asp

Distance Education and Training Council. (2012). *Accreditation handbook*. Retrieved from http://www.detc.org/accreditationhandbook/

Eaton, J. S. (2012, August). *An overview of U.S. accreditation*. Washington, DC: Council for Higher Education Accreditation. Retrieved from http://www.chea.org/pdf/Overview%20of%20US%20Accreditation%202012.pdf

Hamel, W. (2011, September). *Investigative program advisory report: Distance education fraud rings*. Retrieved from Office of the Inspector General website: http://www2.ed.gov/about/offices/list/oig/invtreports/l42l0001.pdf

Higher Education Opportunity Act. (2008). Retrieved from http://www2.ed.gov/policy/highered/leg/hea08/index.html

Higher Learning Commission. (2010). *Understanding accreditation*. Retrieved from http://www.ncahlc.org/Information-for-the-Public/public-information.html

Johnson McPhail, C. (2011). *The completion agenda: A call to action*. Retrieved from the American Association of Community Colleges website: http://www.aacc.nche.edu/Publications/Reports/Documents/CompletionAgenda_report.pdf

Laws, R. D., Howell, S. L., & Lindsay, N. K. (2003). Scalability in distance education: Can we have our cake and eat it too? *Online Journal of Distance Learning Administration, 6*(4). Retrieved from http://www.westga.edu/~distance/ojdla/winter64/laws64.htm

Lee, J. M., & Rawls, A. (2010). *The College Completion Agenda 2010 progress report*. Retrieved from the College Board website: http://completionagenda.collegeboard.org/

Lezberg, A. K. (2007). Accreditation: Quality control in higher distance education. In M. G. Moore (Ed.), *Handbook of distance education* (pp. 403–417). Mahwah, NJ: Lawrence Erlbaum.

Lokken, F. (2012, April). *Trends in eLearning: Tracking the impact of eLearning at community colleges* (2011 Distance Education Survey Result). Retrieved from Instructional Technology Council website: http://www.itcnetwork.org/attachments/article/66/ITCAnnualSurveyMarch2012.pdf

McClenney, K., & McClenney, B. (2010). *Community college inventory: Focus on student persistence, learning, and attainment*. Retrieved from http://www.hewlett.org/uploads/Community_College_Inventory_-Focus_on_Student_Persistence_Learning_and_Attainment.pdf

Michigan Community College Association. (2001). *Online course development guidelines and rubric.* Retrieved from http://www.mccvlc.org/~staff/content.cfm?ID=108

Middaugh, M. F. (2010). *Planning and assessment in higher education: Demonstrating institutional effectiveness.* San Francisco: Jossey-Bass.

Middle States Commission on Higher Education (MSCHE). (2002). *Distance learning programs: Interregional guidelines for electronically offered degree and certificate programs.* Retrieved from ERIC database. (ED468791)

Middle States Commission on Higher Education (MSCHE). (2011a). *Characteristics of excellence in higher education: Requirements of affiliation and standards for accreditation.* Retrieved from http://www.msche.org/publications_view.asp?idPublicationType=1&txtPublicationType=Standards+for+Accreditation+and+Requirements+of+Affiliation

Middle States Commission on Higher Education (MSCHE). (2011b). *Distance education programs: Interregional guidelines for the evaluation of distance education (online learning).* Retrieved from http://www.msche.org/publications/Guidelines-for-the-Evaluation-of-Distance-Education-Programs.pdf

Middle States Commission on Higher Education (MSCHE). (2012). *Self-study: Creating a useful process and report* (2nd ed.). Retrieved from http://www.msche.org/publications_view.asp?idPublicationType=11&txtPublicationType=Manuals+on+Accreditation+Protocols

O'Brien, P. M. (2013). Accreditation: Assuring quality and fostering improvement. In M. G. Moore (Ed.), *Handbook of distance education* (3rd ed., pp. 481–492). New York: Routledge.

Shapiro, P. J., Morales, C. R., & Biro, S. C. (2009). Distance learning growth and change management in traditional institutions. In *Proceedings of the 25th Annual Conference on Distance Teaching and Learning.* Madison: University of Wisconsin–Madison.

Southern Association of Colleges and Schools, Commission on Colleges. (2001). *Best practices for electronically offered degree and certificate programs.* Retrieved from http://www.sacscoc.org/pdf/commadap.pdf

State Higher Education Executive Officers (SHEEO). (2012, July). *Directory of state authorization agencies and lead contacts.* Retrieved from www.sheeo.org/stateauth/stateauth-home.htm

U.S. Department of Education. (n.d.). *Overview of accreditation.* Retrieved from www2.ed.gov/admins/finaid/accred/index.html

U.S. Department of Education. (2011, October 20). *Subject: Fraud in postsecondary distance education programs—Urgent call to action.* Retrieved from http://ifap.ed.gov/dpcletters/GEN1117.html

U.S. Department of Education. (2012, November 30). *Financial aid for postsecondary students, accreditation in the United States.* Retrieved from http://www2.ed.gov/admins/finaid/accred/accreditation_pg2.html

U.S. Senate Committee on Health, Education, Labor, & Pensions. (2012, August). *For profit higher education: The failure to safeguard the federal investment and*

ensure student success. Retrieved from http://www.help.senate.gov/imo/media/
for_profit_report/Contents.pdf

WCET, UT Telecampus, & Instructional Technology Council (ITC). (2009). *Best
practice strategies to promote academic integrity in online education.* Retrieved
from http://www.itcnetwork.org/attachments/article/88/AcademicIntegrityBest
PracticesColor.pdf

PART FOUR

FINAL THOUGHTS

18

SAYING "QUALITY ASSURANCE" WHEN WE MEAN SOMETHING ELSE

Julie Porosky Hamlin

In the short history of online education, demands for proof of quality have been asserted at different junctures, with different levels of stridency. In the earliest days, members of the education community and the public at large wondered if education delivered asynchronously via computer could possibly be as good as education in the classroom. Readers of this book will likely be familiar with Russell's *The No Significant Difference Phenomenon: A Comparative Research Annotated Bibliography on Technology for Distance Education* (2001). New entries continue to be added to Russell's compilation of more than 350 research reports and papers that document no significant difference in student learning outcomes attributable to the format of educational delivery, whether face-to-face or at a distance.

But we have to acknowledge that many online education stakeholders do not do their homework, and skepticism about online education persists. The Babson Survey Research Group's 10th annual survey of online learning, conducted in 2012, found that although 32% of students in higher education—6.7 million—took at least one course online in the fall 2011 semester, only 30% of chief academic officers believe their faculty are convinced of the value of online education (Allen & Seaman, 2013). Yet these officers are increasingly reporting that online learning is critical to their long-term strategy. A majority of them see lower retention rates in online courses as impeding widespread adoption of online education (para. 5). When questioning the fundamental acceptability of education delivered online, is it "quality" we mean or "legitimacy"?

The troubling matter of lower-than-acceptable retention rates in online programs coupled with online students having reached a critical mass made the concern about quality assurance more urgent by the end of the first decade of the 21st century. Another demand-for-proof juncture was reached as private studies and governmental investigations revealed that significant amounts of federal financial aid were flowing to students who were not able to successfully complete online courses and programs, especially at for-profit institutions. The for-profits have been targeted for scrutiny because many have substantial online offerings and because they have machinery for high-volume student recruitment that in most cases is not matched by effective mechanisms for student retention. Military service members form a sizable subset of online education consumers, and it was cause for alarm when the services became aware that approximately three-quarters of taxpayer-supported military tuition assistance was being used by service members taking, and not always completing, online courses at nonprofit and for-profit schools.

A perfect storm was forming at this juncture. The price of a college education had been steadily rising, and now there was evidence, especially in this popular new form of education known as "online," that purchasers may not be getting what they paid for. How could consumers of education be guaranteed they were getting their money's worth?

Documentation of learning was the answer. As the largest third-party funder of education, the federal government had a stake. Initiatives in both the executive and legislative branches put indirect pressure on regional accrediting commissions to require transparent documentation of student learning by member institutions, thereby performing a policing role beyond the original purpose of accreditation. (Accreditors have begun to respond by adopting new policies and plugging loopholes.) Invoking provisions of the Higher Education Act, the Department of Education also became poised to require institutions enrolling students in other states, primarily through online programs, to undergo an authorization process that would be costly to both institutions and states. "Quality assurance" may be the ultimate goal of clamping down on institutions, accreditors, and states, but the more immediate purposes are "accountability" and perhaps "fiscal integrity."

A third demand-for-proof-of-quality juncture has been reached recently. The emergence of online education 2.0 in the form of the massive open online course (MOOC) has riveted the education community and the mainstream media, and not only because of doubts about the quality of an unregulated educational product. MOOCs are news because of their potential to disrupt the foundation upon which the higher education industry rests.

The MOOC challenges not only conventional standards of class size and instructional delivery format but also other elements of the higher education superstructure—most important, how learning is counted, credentialed, and paid for. Competency-based education, mastery learning, and prior learning assessment are all getting a fresh look, both inside and outside academia. As mainstream MOOC watcher Friedman (2013) put it,

> We're moving to a more competency-based world where there will be less interest in how you acquired the competency—in an online course, at a four-year-college or in a company-administered class—and more demand to prove that you mastered the competency. (para. 6)

So perhaps, still, we are not talking about "quality" so much as about an end product, like "proficiency."

Even at this early stage, at some provider institutions MOOCs have begun to mutate so they resemble conventional online courses, but the original, pure, not-for-credit, elite-professor-taught MOOCs are free and open to the world. A straightforward consumer revolt against escalating college tuition rates is not likely to occur, but a sideways revolt may be under way through the embrace of MOOCs, or of what they stand for.

Not all MOOCs are equally successful, though, as reported by a growing number of enrollees in more than one MOOC. Likewise, not all traditional online courses are equally successful. And here is where a conversation that is really about "quality" and "quality assurance" in online education can take place: at the level of individual courses and programs and their components. Several of the authors in this collection have shared ways to look under the hood, from the perspective of both instructional inputs and learning results.

The Quality Matters Program, discussed earlier in the book, represents the willingness of thousands of faculty at now more than 700 colleges and universities in the United States and abroad to put the quality of their individual online courses to the test, using a communally developed set of standards and a peer-review process. Program director Legon (2012) noted, "The movement toward online and hybrid education is strong and unrelenting. It seems destined to change the face of higher education. That means instructors must be willing to adapt, experiment, and innovate" (para. 9). Online education consumers and their sponsors depend on a set of steps, which we term *quality assurance*, being taken. In a field that is maturing as it diversifies, the creators and deliverers of online education will adapt, experiment, and innovate and, in so doing, strengthen the framework for defining and assuring quality.

References

Allen, I. E., & Seaman, J. (2013). *Changing course: Ten years of tracking online education in the United States.* Babson Park, MA: Babson Survey Research Group and Quahog Research Group.

Friedman, T. L. (2013, March 5). The professors' big stage. *New York Times.* Retrieved from http://www.nytimes.com/2013/03/06/opinion/friedman-the-professors-big -stage.html?_r=1&

Legon, R. (2012, September). *Public misperceptions of online education and the advent of MOOCs.* Paper presented at the meeting of the Florida Distance Learning Association, Orlando, FL.

Russell, T. (2001). *The no significant difference phenomenon: A comparative research annotated bibliography on technology for distance education* (5th ed.). Chicago: International Distance Education Certification Center.

19

BUMBLEBEES *CAN* FLY—AND SO CAN WE!

John Sener

Perhaps you've heard the story about how scientists have proven that bumblebees can't fly. Bumblebee flight reputedly violates aerodynamic theory; their wings can't generate the lift required to fly—yet somehow they do it anyway.

It turns out that the idea that science says that bumblebees can't fly is itself a myth—a bit of urban folklore that encourages people to think less highly of scientists. However, the persistence of this myth has also inspired further scientific research to study insect flight from multiple perspectives, yielding new insights about the complexities of powered flight (Adams, 1990; Peterson, 2004).

As diligent practitioners, we should use the persistent myths about online education as a similar source of inspiration to study from multiple perspectives how to improve it and to find new insights about its complexities. That's what this volume does; the work compiled here reflects a beehive of activity representing two decades of research and practice in the field of online education.

Here are some inspirations that I hope readers of this book take away:

Work to assure quality in online distance education is work to assure quality in education, period. Although this volume clearly focuses on online distance education, the first sentence of its preface could also read, "This book is about practices and processes for assuring quality in education"—no reference to online or other delivery mode is needed. Online education has become a leading wedge in pedagogical innovation as a form of quality improvement, as illustrated by the now long-running practice of using online courses to improve classroom courses (Sener, 2012).

This is all the more important to do since, as the preface also notes, quality in traditional U.S. higher education has been based on perceptions—of institutional status, faculty expertise, and discipline-specific criteria—more than on actual research. To my knowledge at least, there is still no comparable discussion of quality assurance and improvement in traditional classroom education—no widespread adoption of a Quality Matters–like rubric for classroom courses, no Quality Pillars or Quality Scorecard to assess the quality of classroom-based programs. Online distance educators have maintained an intentional focus on quality, which was originally born of necessity (i.e., the need to establish legitimacy); as a result, we have become a key focal point for discussions about quality in education. Let's continue our efforts to share our findings about educational quality with other educators, irrespective of delivery mode.

Our focus should be on both quality assurance and quality improvement. As practitioners, we need to make sure it is clear that we are talking about both and that our focus is on moving forward—continuous improvement, ever-better quality, onward and upward. The connection between the two was made fairly obvious in this book, whose preface alone mentions the word *improve, improvement,* or *improving* no fewer than 20 times. At the same time, we need to make sure that the rest of the world understands that this is the focus of our efforts.

The notion persists that the best way to measure the quality of online education is by assessing it relative to traditional, classroom-based programs. From the "What's the Difference?" paper by Phipps and Merisotis (1999) to the recently reported findings of Columbia University's Community College Research Center (*New York Times*, 2013), conventional wisdom treats traditional education as if it were some sort of gold standard and argues that online education's task is to measure up. These studies have invariably concluded that colleges need to proceed slowly before deploying online courses widely—do more research, produce the same percentage of course completers, and so on.

Fortunately, online education practitioners have used this myth in an inspired way: they have ignored the advice to move slowly, but they have also used the findings of this research to improve their programs. The online practitioners' actions reflect a deeper truth: aiming for parity with traditional education is aiming low. Instead, online education researchers have focused on effectiveness, improvement, and even transformation. So when we talk about quality assurance and improvement, let's move beyond sterile comparisons and make sure our audiences know we are aiming much higher than that.

Also, we must continue to make room for the serendipitous. No one involved in online education in the early 1990s would have predicted that it would become a significant source of faculty development and rejuvenation, but that is what indeed happened. The process of having to figure out how to use new technologies to redesign instruction has changed many faculty members from being reflexive to being reflective, reexamining long-held or previously unexamined assumptions about teaching and learning, and acting on the insights they gain through the process of developing and teaching courses online (Sener, 2012, p. 51).

So, for example, what makes massive open online courses (MOOCs) so interesting is how they resemble bumblebees: by design, there is no way that they are capable of flying as viable educational experiences. And yet there they go, starting to buzz all over the place. If we explore beyond the myths, we find many serendipitous nuggets that tell us how MOOCs can fly; for example, they are enabling a new audience of professors to explore new ways of teaching and learning, fulfilling the same faculty development and rejuvenation function that online education has long performed.

And we must keep discussing how to move quality forward. I'd like to see more rapid movement in some areas. For example, if we focus on student learning outcomes, then let's make sure to expand the range of acceptable outcomes beyond the dreary litany of grades, retention, and completion. I'd rather talk about "effective practices" than "best practices," and I'd like to move beyond "student-centered" (which to me is excessively reactive) courses to "learning-centered" (which takes both learning and teaching more squarely into account) courses. But these are relative quibbles in the grand scheme; the more important thing is that we are having these discussions, period. Focusing on quality assurance and quality improvement also makes us more relevant, more responsive, and more vital in meeting the challenges that American education faces. The discussion on quality assurance and improvement is also a vast source of inspiration for us to find new insights, practices, and processes.

References

Adams, C. (1990, May 4). Is it aerodynamically impossible for bumblebees to fly? *The Straight Dope.* Retrieved from http://www.straightdope.com/columns/read/1076/is-it-aerodynamically-impossible-for-bumblebees-to-fly

New York Times. (2013, February 18). The trouble with online college [Editorial]. Retrieved from http://www.nytimes.com/2013/02/19/opinion/the-trouble-with-online-college.html?_r=0

Peterson, I. (2004, September 9). Flight of the bumblebee. *ScienceNews.* Retrieved from http://www.sciencenews.org/view/generic/id/5400/description/Flight_of_the_Bumblebee

Phipps, R., & Merisotis, J. (1999). *What's the difference? A review of contemporary research on the effectiveness of distance learning in higher education.* Retrieved from Institute for Higher Education Policy website: http://www.ihep.org/assets/files/publications/s-z/WhatDifference.pdf

Sener, J. (2012). *The seven futures of American education: Improving learning and teaching in a screen-captured world.* North Charleston, SC: CreateSpace.

Editor

Kay Shattuck was a member of the initial group of Maryland educators who developed what would become the Quality Matters Program. She continues to serve as director of research. She is an adjunct assistant professor of education at The Pennsylvania State University and has been teaching online with the World Campus since 2000.

Series Editor

Michael Grahame Moore, Distinguished Professor Emeritus of Education, The Pennsylvania State University, is known in academic circles for pioneering the scholarly study of distance education, nowadays commonly referred to as e-learning and online learning. Retiring from teaching in 2013, Moore now consults internationally and focuses on his editorial work, especially *The American Journal of Distance Education* and the Stylus Publishing series Online Learning and Distance Education.

Contributors

Deborah Adair is the managing director and chief planning officer of the Quality Matters Program, a widely adopted nonprofit program for quality assurance in online learning serving K–12, colleges and universities, education-related organizations, government entities, and corporations in the United States and internationally. She has more than 20 years' experience in higher education, has held advisory roles for education associations, and has written and been interviewed as an expert in quality assurance for online learning.

Julie Atwood is the director of assessment at American Public University System. She has worked in higher education for more than 20 years, in the areas of adult learning, program evaluation, and assessment.

Susan Biro, director of distance learning at Carroll Community College in Maryland, has worked in higher education since 2000, holding administrative positions at Widener University (Pennsylvania), Fordham University

(New York), and Berkeley College (New York–New Jersey). She has presented and published on distance-learning topics, including faculty support, program management, and student retention.

David Black is an associate professor in the School of Communication and Culture at Royal Roads University in Victoria, British Columbia, Canada. He is the author of a book, *The Politics of Enchantment: Romanticism, Media, and Cultural Studies* (Wilfrid Laurier University Press, 2002), and a number of articles in media theory, history, and pedagogy.

Leonard Bogle joined the Department of Educational Leadership at the University of Illinois–Springfield, where he teaches online and blended graduate classes, in 2005, after serving 34 years in public education. His scholarship focus is the delivery of online instruction that increases student interaction and enhances achievement through the use of a variety of tools.

Wallace Boston is president and chief executive officer of American Public University System (APUS), and has guided APUS through two successful accreditations with the Higher Learning Commission of the North Central Association. During his tenure, APUS has grown to more than 100,000 students majoring in 88 degree programs. He has authored, coauthored, and presented papers on the topic of online student retention in higher education.

Heather L. Chakiris leads the mission-driven Advising and Learner Success Unit of Penn State World Campus and Continuing Education. The unit includes 80 full-time staff members addressing academic advising (undergraduate), academic support resources, administrative support, career counseling, cocurricular student engagement, student communications, and student/faculty technical support.

Scott Day is associate professor and chair of the Department of Educational Leadership at the University of Illinois–Springfield. He teaches online courses on instructional leadership and assessment. The Educational Leadership Program was awarded the Sloan Consortium Outstanding Program of the Year in 2010. The same year he was awarded the Pearson Faculty Award for Outstanding Teaching at the University of Illinois–Springfield.

Sebastián Díaz serves as associate vice president for marketing analytics at American Public University System. Previously, he served as associate professor in the Department of Technology, Learning, and Culture at West Virginia University. His research focuses on developing measurement instruments and evaluation methodologies germane to intellectual capital and knowledge management.

Barbara A. Frey is a senior instructional designer with PittOnline at the University of Pittsburgh. In addition, she teaches with the Online Teaching and Learning Program at Colorado State University's Global Campus. She is also a master reviewer and trainer with Quality Matters.

Julie Porosky Hamlin is executive director of MarylandOnline, a consortium of 20 colleges, and was senior vice president of University of Maryland University College. Hamlin has served on various boards, commissions, and accreditation and other evaluation teams, and teaches in an online PhD program in higher education administration.

Janice Maloney High is an associate professor of English at Alaska's Kenai Peninsula College, where the student body is rich in cultural diversity. High teaches online courses in both communication and literature. Previously, as the news director of a television/radio station, she traveled extensively throughout Asia and the Pacific, covering international and intercultural issues.

Phil Ice is the vice president of research and development at American Public University System. His research focuses on the impact of emerging technologies on online learning. He is a member of Adobe Higher Ed Leaders, the Sloan Consortium, and the New Media Consortium/EDUCAUSE Learning Initiative Horizon Board (2010–2013).

Lorna R. Kearns is director of online programs at the Center for Instructional Development and Distance Education at the University of Pittsburgh, where she oversees development of graduate-level online courses and associated online programs.

Gary W. Kuhne is associate professor of education and the lead faculty for online graduate programs in adult education at the Pennsylvania State University. He is a consultant to business, government agencies, and higher education institutions, and his research interests include distance education, asynchronous learning, needs assessment, program evaluation, leadership, and staff development. Author of numerous books and articles, he was the winner of the 2000 Outstanding Distance Education Teaching Award from the Pennsylvania State University.

Melissa Layne is the director of research methodology at American Public University System and serves as editor in chief for *Internet Learning*. Layne's research focus includes student retention, adaptive learning, multiuser virtual environments, self-paced instructional design, informal learning, and quality assurance in online learning at all levels in academe. She has been published in more than 35 journals and books and also serves on the

New Media Consortium/EDUCAUSE Learning Initiative Horizon Board (2010–2013).

Jennifer A. Linder-VanBerschot is an instructional designer for a large contractor and an adjunct professor for University of Colorado–Denver. Her scholarly interests include the use of technology and social software to promote interaction across cultures and among international learning communities.

Carrie Main is an eLearning Specialist at Virginia Commonwealth University. Previously, she designed and delivered the first online Spanish courses at the University of Northern Colorado. Her research focuses on global e-learning design.

Daniel Matthews is an associate professor at the University of Illinois–Springfield. His research interests include geographic diversity in online education, identifying factors related to success in online education, and improving online education through the use of the Quality Matters and Community of Inquiry frameworks.

Carol A. McQuiggan is manager of the Faculty Center for Teaching and Instructional Technology for Penn State Harrisburg. In this position she directs the design and development of online, hybrid, and residential courses, as well as professional development opportunities for faculty, and she facilitates program assessment. She is interested in the transformational learning opportunities in online teaching.

Janet C. Moore, consultant, was chief knowledge officer for the Sloan Consortium and editor in chief for the *Journal of Asynchronous Learning Networks*. She is the author of *Elements of Quality: The Sloan-C Framework* (Sloan Consortium, 2002) and coeditor with Kaye Shelton of *A Quality Scorecard for the Administration of Online Programs* (Sloan Consortium, 2011).

Cali Morrison, WCET communications manager, is responsible for communication strategies, social media, and management of various project-related tasks. Previously she has served in grant management, assessment, and student affairs roles.

Christine Mullins has served, since 1991, as the executive director for the Instructional Technology Council (ITC) of the American Association of Community Colleges. ITC represents colleges and universities that teach via distance education and is located in Washington, DC.

Susan Patrick is the president and chief executive officer of the International Association for K–12 Online Learning (iNACOL). iNACOL is a nonprofit association that provides policy advocacy, national quality standards, research on best practices, next-generation learning models, professional development, and networking opportunities to groups involved in K–12 online and blended learning.

Karen Paulson is a senior associate at the National Center for Higher Education Management Systems (NCHEMS). Her areas of expertise include assessment, evaluation, accreditation, and the use of data in state policymaking. She has worked at over 60 postsecondary institutions and in over 30 states.

Stella C. S. Porto has extensive experience in the leadership, management, administration, delivery, and development of distance-education programs, as well as in e-learning systems and methodologies, including international initiatives and partnerships. She is director and professor of the University of Maryland University College's Master of Distance Education and e-Learning Program.

Russell Poulin is deputy director of research and analysis at WCET. He has a long history of researching the effective use of technology-mediated instruction, sharing information about successful practices, and advocating for reasonable regulations of distance education.

Allison Powell is the vice president for state and district services of the International Association for K–12 Online Learning (iNACOL). Before joining iNACOL, she helped build the Clark County School District's Virtual High School and an online professional development program.

Karan Powell is executive vice president and provost of American Public University System. She has more than 30 years of experience in learning, leadership development, organization performance enhancement, and transformation in education, nonprofit, business, and government settings.

Lawrence C. Ragan serves as the codirector for the Center for Online Innovation in Learning at The Pennsylvania State University. He directs the center's mission of research, scholarship, technology innovation, and leadership development programming. Ragan is also codirector of the Institute for Emerging Leadership in Online Learning, a Penn State and Sloan Consortium leadership development collaboration.

Jean Runyon is associate vice president of Learning Advancement and the Virtual Campus at Anne Arundel Community College in Maryland. In this position, she provides leadership and vision for the creation, continuous planning, and evaluation of learning outcomes assessment, prior learning assessment, institutional professional development, special sessions, military/ veterans initiatives, weekend college and off-campus programs, and distance-education initiatives.

John Sener is the founder and chief knowledge officer of Sener Knowledge LLC, a consulting practice that cocreates knowledge leading to positive change in education, learning, and society. His career in education and training over the past 30-plus years is a unique mixture of broad practical experience and academic expertise and includes almost 20 years in online distance education and more than 10 years in program assessment and evaluation.

Kaye Shelton is an associate professor of educational leadership at Lamar University. Her research in the field of online education includes *An Administrator's Guide to Online Education* (IAP, 2005) and *A Quality Scorecard for the Administration of Online Education Programs* (Sloan Consortium, 2011).

Jennifer Stephens-Helm is the dean and vice president of institutional research and assessment at American Public University System. She has presented at national and international conferences in the areas of school reform, distance learning, faculty development, institutional research, and assessment.

Karen Swan is the Stukel Distinguished Professor of Educational Leadership and a research associate in the Center for Online Learning, Research, and Service (COLRS) at the University of Illinois–Springfield. She has published extensively on online learning and accordingly was given the Sloan Consortium Award for Outstanding Individual Achievement in 2006.

Melody M. Thompson is associate professor of education at The Pennsylvania State University. Formerly director of the American Center for the Study of Distance Education and director of research and evaluation for Penn State World Campus, she has published extensively about online education and currently serves on the editorial board of several journals.

Li Wang is associate faculty at Ashford University. She has worked in higher education institutions since 1999 and directed course redesign institutes and faculty cohort programs striving for quality in course design, development, and delivery. She is a certified Quality Matters peer reviewer and facilitator.

Matthew Wicks is the chief operating officer for the International Association for K–12 Online Learning (iNACOL). He was cofounder of the Illinois Virtual High School, founding board member of iNACOL, and coauthor of iNACOL's *National Standards of Quality for Online Programs* (iNACOL, 2009).

Principles of Good Practice for Higher
  Education Institutions Serving
  Adults at a Distance, 131–32
program evaluation
  accountability in, 128–31
  by administration, 124–33
  benchmarking for, 126
  of curriculum, 126
  from data analysis, 126
  of e-resources, 126
  by faculty, 124–33
  for K-12 online public education, 56
  of learning effectiveness, 129
  of library, 126
  of outcomes, 127, 131–32
  for quality assurance, 14, 29–30
  in Quality Scorecard for the Admin-
    istration of Online Programs, 46
  of student profiles, 127
program review committees, 125–28
programs. *See also* courses
  decision-making and, 167–68, 169,
    179–80
  ethics and, 165–80
  learning objectives for, 48
  purposes and goals of, 168–71
  stakeholders in, 170
  students and, 170
  trust the expert for, 170–71
progress monitoring
  learning analytics for, 205–6
  quality assurance and, 30
Pullias Center for Higher Education,
  174, 180

QM. *See* Quality Matters
qualitative data analysis, 10, 220
quality assurance
  for accessibility, 134–47
  accreditation and, 5, 25, 64
  assessment and, 12, 34–35
  within black box, 5
  in change, 3–15
  collaboration and, 11, 115–16
  from course design, 81–90

courses, 10–11
for cultural diversity, 149–59
curricula and, 10–11, 31
Department of Education and, 249
for disabilities, 134–47
e-resources for, 28
ethics and, 166–68
exclusivity and, 18–19
existing standards for, 24–26
faculty and, 25, 27–32
faculty development and, 11, 14,
  91–107
faculty support for, 12–14
federal policies for, 249–53
funding requirements for, 6
future steps for, 74–75
institutional commitment to,
  9–10
instruction and, 10–11
interaction in, 27
in iron triangle, 18–37
for K-12 online public education,
  50–62
KM for, 210–24
learning analytics for, 197–209
myths about, 263–65
new technologies for, 25
pedagogy and, 263
planning and oversight for, 30
program evaluation practices for,
  14, 29–30
progress monitoring and, 30
progress toward, 64–76
quality improvement and, 263–65
revised and expanded framework for,
  26–33
selectivity in, 6
stakeholders and, 4–5, 25–26
state policies for, 249–53
students and, 11, 27–32
student support for, 12–13
systems for, 5
transparency and, 66–70
when we mean something else,
  259–61